THE NORTHERN HOME FRONT
DURING THE CIVIL WAR

Recent Titles in
Reflections on the Civil War Era

THE NORTHERN HOME FRONT DURING THE CIVIL WAR

PAUL A. CIMBALA and RANDALL M. MILLER

Reflections on the Civil War Era
John David Smith, Series Editor

An Imprint of ABC-CLIO, LLC

Santa Barbara, California • Denver, Colorado

The Northern Home Front during the Civil War
Library of Congress Cataloging in Publication Control Number: 2016049440

ISBN: 978-0-313-35290-4
EISBN: 978-0-313-35291-1

21 20 19 18 17   1 2 3 4 5

This book is also available as an eBook.

Praeger
An Imprint of ABC-CLIO, LLC

ABC-CLIO, LLC
130 Cremona Drive, P.O. Box 1911
Santa Barbara, California 93116-1911
www.abc-clio.com

This book is printed on acid-free paper ∞

Manufactured in the United States of America

Dedicated to our friend
John David Smith

CONTENTS

Contents

A photo essay follows p. 118.

SERIES FOREWORD

"Like Ol' Man River," the distinguished Civil War historian Peter J. Parish wrote in 1998, "Civil War historiography just keeps rolling along. It changes course occasionally, leaving behind bayous of stagnant argument, while it carves out new lines of inquiry and debate."

Since Confederate General Robert E. Lee's men stacked their guns at Appomattox Court House in April 1865, historians and partisans have been fighting a war of words over the causes, battles, results, and broad meaning of the internecine conflict that cost more than 620,000 American lives. Writers have contributed between 50,000 and 60,000 books and pamphlets on the topic. Viewed in terms of defining American freedom and nationalism, Western expansion and economic development, the Civil War quite literally launched modern America. "The Civil War," Kentucky poet, novelist, and literary critic Robert Penn Warren explained, "is for the American imagination, the great single event of our history. Without too much wrenching, it may, in fact, be said to be American history."

The books in Praeger's *Reflections on the Civil War Era* series examine pivotal aspects of the American Civil War. Topics range from examinations of military campaigns and local conditions, to analyses of institutional, intellectual, and social history. Questions of class, gender, and race run through each volume in the series. Authors, veteran experts in their respective fields, provide concise, informed, and readable syntheses—fresh looks at familiar topics with new source material and original arguments.

"Like all great conflicts," Parish noted in 1999, "the American Civil War reflected the society and the age in which it was fought." Books in *Reflections on the Civil War Era* series interpret the war as a salient event in the hammering out and understanding of American identity before, during, and after the secession crisis of 1860–1861. Readers will find the volumes valuable guides as they chart the troubled waters of mid-19th-century American life.

John David Smith
Charles H. Stone Distinguished Professor of American History
The University of North Carolina at Charlotte

INTRODUCTION

During four years of Civil War, most Northerners conducted their lives as they had before Confederate forces had fired on Fort Sumter in April 1861. Mothers nursed sick children, families earned their livelihoods, and youngsters attended school. Young adults did not give up courting, and men and women did not give up their amusements. Storekeepers tended to their customers and stocked their shelves. Politicians ran for office, listened to the concerns of their constituents, and generally conducted themselves as they had and always will, guided in their actions by a mixture of civic duty and self-interest. Local authorities still had to deal with chicken thieves and other petty criminals. Battles in Virginia, Tennessee, and elsewhere did not keep ministers and priests from worrying about the souls of their congregations and the roofs of their churches. Indeed, in April 1864, Irvine Masters, mayor of Cleveland, Ohio, admitted, as the city continued to prosper, it had "not directly felt the shock of war."[1]

Despite such aspects of normality, the war insinuated itself into all of these activities and thus the lives of even the most unaware people living in the free states of the North. In August 1861, Ralph Waldo Emerson warned that the war will "engulf us all," and "no preoccupation can exclude, & no hermitage hide us."[2] That same month, Nathaniel Hawthorne admitted his isolation to his daughters, noting that he either chose not to read or had no access to newspapers, a state that left him unaware of any Union disasters. Even so, he could not avoid the sounds of war. "Almost every hour," he wrote, "however, I hear the noise of drums, over the water, from Marblehead to Salem, and very often the thunder of cannon, which sometimes continues for an hour together; so that I begin to think the war has overspread the whole country except just this little precinct in the neighborhood of West Beach."[3] Almost a year later in his article in the July 1862 *Atlantic Monthly*, Hawthorne admitted: "There is no remoteness of life and thought, no hermetically sealed seclusion, except, possibly, that of the grave, into which the disturbing influences of this war do not penetrate."[4] Yankee writers, poets, and philosophers had the luxury to engage in exaggeration, but they also accepted their responsibility to speak the truth.

Too often, the devastation in the Confederate states and the impact of emancipation, which fundamentally altered people's lives in the rebellious states, distracted attention from the many intrusions and disruptions the Civil War brought to people in the free Northern states. Most of the region escaped being trampled underfoot by invading armies or ravaged by guerilla raiders. But the war did indeed come to the North. As Massachusetts resident Charles A. Currier recalled, the war was always on the minds of the civilians from morning to night, discussed on the streets, in places of business, and in houses of worship. "[I]t turned our churches into depositories of hospital supplies, and made lint pickers of worshippers," he noted, and while the romantic notions of the earliest days had passed, the conflict now "settled thoughtful men into the conviction, that until it was fought to a conclusion, it must be made the absorbing business of the entire North."[5]

If children continued to attend school, they also added to their daily concerns the welfare of brothers, fathers, and uncles who were in the army and new burdens and responsibilities once deferred to an older age. If families continued their economic routines, they did so in a marketplace influenced by new government policies and the demands of a wartime economy. If women continued to manage households, they also extended their talents and interests outward to support the war effort. If young women and men courted, they often did so separated by the distance from home front to battlefield. And no one could long ignore the steady drumbeat of casualty lists, maimed veterans, and funerals that became part of the routines of their communities. Even as Cleveland's Mayor Masters reported on the progress of his city, he acknowledged the human cost that reminded his constituents of the consequences of the conflict. "Individual families have indeed been reminded by the sad bereavements, or longing absence of loved ones," he commented, "that war, in all its cruel and desolating power is raging in the land."[6] It did not stop there, for the memory of the war also became part of the Northern mentality, as civilians and soldiers alike tried to make sense of what the conflict had wrought, insisting that the nation not forget the sacrifices so many people made to bring victory.

Northerners, willingly or unwillingly, found their lives marked by America's ordeal.[7] They could not escape being a part of the war and in fact were more than passive recipients of its consequences. In July 1861, William Y. Ripley, a Vermont businessman, wrote to his soldier son, explaining that despite what ideas politicians in Washington might have, "This war is a war of the *people*."[8] That sentiment echoed Abraham Lincoln's insistence, on July 4, 1861, that the war was and must be "essentially a People's contest" that demanded steady resolve and commitment from everyone to save the great experiment in democratic self-government and realize the hope for freedom.[9]

Armies alone could not win the war. Thus, it becomes important to understand how the war intersected with the lives of those ordinary people on the home front beyond the policies set forth by Washington, because, in the end, they were the ones who gave shape and substance to the Union's final victory. Any consideration of what the people did for the war, however, must also assess what the war did for and to them. Understanding the ways the Northern people engaged and understood the war, and the war's impact on Northern society, culture, economy, and politics, is the principal concern of this book.

* * *

In completing this volume, we have accumulated a number of debts that we can hardly repay, but wish to acknowledge. First is recognizing the book's genealogy. The seed for this book came from a much longer draft version of a book chapter by Paul A. Cimbala that appeared as "The Northern Home Front during the Civil War," in *Daily Lives of Civilians in Wartime Early America*, Vol. 1: *From the Colonial Era to the Civil War*, edited by David S. Heidler and Jeanne T. Heidler (Westport, CT: Greenwood Press, 2007). Many of the ideas on subjects to investigate and the basic framework for our book derived from that initial chapter. Our book also owes much to the librarians at universities and archives who facilitated research, but special thanks go to the librarians at the Connecticut Historical Society, the Rockland, Maine, Historical Society, the Rockland, Maine, Public Library, Saint Joseph's University, the Historical Society of Pennsylvania, the Library Company of Philadelphia, Haverford College, and the University of Pennsylvania for their knowledge and assistance in identifying resources and providing them. We thank ABC-CLIO/ Greenwood Publishing for permission to use material from *Daily Lives of Civilians in Wartime* noted above. Michael Millman, our editor at Praeger, deserves thanks for facilitating our request and for his patience in dealing with us over the many years we took to complete this book. John David Smith, the editor of the series in which this volume appears, has also stuck with us, encouraging this work as he has done so generously with other projects over the years. He also provided wise editorial counsel to insure our book's accuracy and enhance its value. He is our very good friend and mentor. Our beloved and uncommonly tolerant wives, Elizabeth C. Vozzola and Linda Patterson Miller, both esteemed scholars in their own right, kept us on task by reminding us that health and happiness can come from writing good history. We hope we have done so.

ONE

COMMUNITIES ON
THE VERGE OF WAR

THE LIGHT TOUCH OF GOVERNMENT

Antebellum Republicans and their Whig predecessors might have wished for a more active government, while their Democratic rivals might have feared one, but in practical terms, for most of the antebellum era, Washington had rarely intruded into the people's lives, neither overburdening them with taxation nor providing assistance for them in their personal times of trouble.[1] Businessmen and community boosters understood the need for federal action in matters of tariffs, public land sales, and protection of contracts and for federal financial support for transportation improvements. The average citizen might come into contact with the national government through the postal service and land purchases; in some areas, they might observe the government at work in the presence of lighthouses, courts, customs houses, land title offices, armories, or naval establishments. Perhaps they were aware of other military installations, but the small army, hardly visible to most Americans, had the majority of its forts and barracks on the West Coast and the interior frontier. Nevertheless, few Americans worked for the federal government.[2] Consequently, the men and women who went to war in 1861 were neither connected to nor familiar with the national government of the country they hoped to preserve.

Before the war, politicians funded their work in various ways that encouraged people to expect the light touch of government on their pocket books, especially in a direct way. The federal government generally relied on the sale of land and on import duties to cover its operating expenses. Indeed, in 1861, tariffs made up over 90 percent of the government's income, with land sales making up much of the rest of its revenues. In fact, for over half a century before secession, the federal government had not tapped into an internal revenue source, except for some select excise taxes. It did not even tax liquor anymore.[3]

States were equally adept at limiting direct taxation. New Jersey simply avoided it by relying on money paid to the state by railroad and canal companies.[4] Tax revenues tended to stay close to those who paid, with local governments keeping the majority of the money collected. In Wisconsin, this meant that local governments held on to over 80 percent of the tax revenue collected. Residents there paid taxes on real estate and also at the county level on personal property.[5]

Towns, such as Springfield, Massachusetts, offered limited services that did not require broader revenue sources. They therefore could rely on local government's traditional tax on property, which property owners did their best to keep low.[6] If special needs arose, municipalities often borrowed money. Jacksonville, Illinois, for example, relied on private subscriptions or county and town bonds to pay for transportation improvements.[7] While individuals might prefer such an approach to funding government, they could suffer inconvenience or worse from the consequences. In Connecticut, Hartford's antebellum water system, built in the mid-1850s, delivered an inadequate supply of river water through its undersized pipes to the city's residents. Neither New Haven nor Hartford, the dual state capital cities of Connecticut, had a system of paved streets; wartime taxes for wartime concerns kept it that way for the duration.[8] In Wisconsin, no municipality had a system for delivering fresh, clean water to its residents, who generally depended on private wells. And no town in that Midwestern state, including Milwaukee, had a sewage system. In the late 1840s and early 1850s, such poor sanitation arrangements led to regular cholera epidemics across the state.[9]

The government as stranger did not last long once the sectional crisis turned into war, but it did influence the initial reaction to war's outbreak. Northerners eventually saw the federal government asserting greater control over raising troops when it implemented a military draft. The government raised taxes on many products and, aided with a new Internal Revenue Bureau, put a levy on a man's hard-earned income.[10] During the war, the people felt the government intrude into the economy and their lives in other ways as it sold bonds and printed paper money, exerted power over the judicial process as it suspended the writ of habeas corpus, and used military necessity to justify its attack on the constitutionally sanctioned institution of slavery.

By the end of the war, some Northerners came to expect more of their government, if only in limited ways for a limited time, when they considered how to deal with wounded veterans, war widows, and ex-slaves. The war's long-lasting effects, however, did not include a much more powerful or intrusive federal government beyond the efforts at reconstructing the erstwhile Confederacy. While most Northerners abhorred secession, they also continued to hold on to notions of federalism and states' rights. It was in fact upon the belief in the power of states within this governmental arrangement that had provided the rationalization for the passage of personal liberty laws that undermined the federal fugitive slave legislation of 1850.[11] It also was upon federalism and the power of the state governments that the states began to build the nation's Civil War army.[12]

COMMON INSTITUTIONS, COMMON VALUES

Despite the dynamics of the war, Northerners, used to minimal contact with their national government, remained very much rooted in the personal connections of their localities and their states.[13] The circumstances of war could reinforce those loyalties. Military companies were recruited among neighbors, thus allowing their men to take a local identity with them to war. Regiments carried states' names and flags with them into battle, helping to nurture feelings of loyalty and affection even for home folk who did not have loved ones in their ranks as they closely followed their progress through the war.

Other wartime events also confirmed community loyalties as the nation endured its most serious crisis since the founding. When her husband William left for the war, Iowan Mary Vermilion went to reside with her in-laws in Indiana for some time, but grew homesick. Living with Democrats in a region rife with what she considered disloyal sentiment had an impact on the patriotic woman and she longed to return "to our brave, loyal Iowa."[14] After she fulfilled that wish, she expressed her satisfaction with her home state and made it clear to her husband that she did not "want to live anywhere else." At the close of one spring day in 1863, she wrote to William about the beauty of the area that reinforced her sense of place. "I sat in the west door this evening and watched the sun sink to rest in a bed of gold and purple clouds," she told him. "I looked over the landscape and thought what a goodly prospect it was. What a beautiful country!"[15] Yet, after the war, Northern families did not hesitate to leave similar settings to seek out new opportunities and transfer their loyalties to new communities.

Loyalty to or affection for a community was less and more than loyalty to a particular place, and both were eminently transferable by choice. Northerners might have already been members of several communities before the war began, suggesting that what a community might provide for them was at least as important as any particular community. They moved about, especially from east to west, either out of necessity or by inclination to find a place and a life that suited them. A decade before the Civil War, only 25 percent of the population of the frontier territory of Minnesota, which entered the Union in 1858, claimed it as their state of nativity.[16] Most residents there shared the experiences of the Caleff family, whose daughter Lizzie Caleff Bowler would long remember her rugged youthful experience of "leaving behind the eastern home with all of its comforts" to settle in Minnesota, where her family "built a new home on the raw prairie."[17] Minnesota experienced a town-building boom during the latter part of the 1850s as settlers came together in new communities, but when pressed by the economic hardships caused by the Panic of 1857, many new residents pulled up stakes and looked elsewhere for their prosperity.[18] The opportunity provided by land free of slavery gave these seekers an equal chance to become prosperous, even if it meant hard work, disappointment, and renewed effort, and upon these multiple successes, American democracy would endure.[19]

Thus it was for many antebellum Northerners. Ulysses S. Grant launched his Civil War career from Illinois. He had attempted to make his way in Missouri after leaving the antebellum army before he finally took up employment at the family store in Galena.[20] William Vermilion, another future Civil War officer, had a facility for moving to where he thought he could best make a life. He came to his antebellum Iowa community, where he farmed and practiced medicine, after having lived in Indiana and Illinois.[21] As a young man, Madison Bowler, also a future Union officer, traveled from Maine to Minnesota. He ended up teaching in a school in the new town of Nininger City, where he met Lizzie Caleff, his future wife, who happened to be a student in his classroom.[22] Thus it was for many Americans, sojourners who sought opportunity where they could in the years before the war. The Caleffs and the Vermilions along with most Midwesterners would not have been surprised to find that they had neighbors originally from Vermont, Connecticut, or New Hampshire, as it had been a common practice before the war for Easterners to sell their property and seek opportunities in the newer states and territories farther west.[23]

What was important for both peripatetic Northerners who settled in new communities and those with deep-seated roots in old ones was that individuals could find in those communities across the region the institutions that brought stability and a sense of belonging. If schools, churches, and other indications of Northern civilization were not yet present on the frontier's edge, the settlers recreated them.[24] Normally, the federal government, after convincing or forcing Native Americans to cede their territories, would survey the land and give some land to the state or to railroad and canal companies, which could then sell the property to settlers. Otherwise, the government would auction or sell off the remaining land, all of which would have titles properly registered. Before the war, Wisconsin, which became a state in 1848, was never lacking in federal land for sale and settlement, in part because disappointment or events such as the California gold rush convinced people to move on and in part because there was so much of it.[25]

The orderly progression of surveyors to settlers and title registration often had to catch up with the individuals hungry for property who ran ahead of the process. Iowa drew settlers eager for fresh lands even before a territorial government was organized. The earliest of the settlers lived through the harsh winter of 1833–1834 but came together to help one another build shelter and then celebrate the community effort. Despite the absence of officials to regulate and register their land claims, they continued to stake out farms and to form community associations to protect their claims, ready to resist any late arrivals and speculators who intruded on their legally illegitimate holdings. In doing so, they had little need for the federal government.[26]

This pattern was similar to what people had done back east, especially where New England settlers spread out and built new communities in villages and towns, nurtured relationships along common ethnic and religious ties, and guaranteed the continuation of their values in the schools they supported. During the early 19th century, in the Nanticoke Valley region of New York, homesteads grew into full-fledged communities. Churches drew people together through religious and other social events. Town government provided order, and growing businesses aided by the antebellum transportation revolution developed commercial connections beyond the region. In the Nanticoke Valley in the half-century before the Civil War, the people created the community connections that most of them desired.[27]

Just as important, if not more so, the institutions nurtured by old and new communities were critical in shaping a commonly held set of values, ideas shared by a majority of Northerners by the time the war came. Beyond the family, Northerners cherished schools, churches, political parties, town meetings, civic celebrations, voluntary organizations, and other associations not only because they helped to anchor them in a community, but also because they recognized them as the "free institutions" that provided the foundation for their liberties. As young people matured and participated in these institutions, they learned the importance of individualism, self-control, personal sacrifice, discipline, hard work, democracy, moral righteousness, and the manifest destiny of their nation.

Even without formal education in newly settled lands, self-taught individuals such as Abraham Lincoln, whose experiences were far from being unusual, absorbed these ideals. German revolutionary and immigrant Dietrich Gerstein reported as much from his "Hinterwald" or backwoods Michigan farm in early 1860. "Thanks to the press and the most rational and liberal institutions in our counties and towns," he wrote to his brother, "the republican way of life has taken hold of the people, and no comparison you care to make with France, Rome or a Greek republic fits the United States."[28] The people might not have thought much about the mechanics of the national government with its various bureaus and departments, but they did understand that the essence of their nation, their free institutions, would flourish only in an environment that recognized the importance of law and order provided by the Constitution. Thus, the potential for success in their lives was intimately connected to access to land free of slaves and the survival of what they considered to be the best government in the world. When a regressive oligarchy of duplicitous, traitorous slaveholders threatened that government, they rallied to defend it and the constitution that protected their way of life.[29]

Even many individuals on the fringes of Northern society, while not agreeing with those beliefs of free soil and free men, would accept the idea that secession was a challenge to their own liberty. Those settlers who had moved from slave states into the lower counties of the states made from the Old Northwest Territories were not likely to be sympathetic to the more reform-minded New England Protestants who had settled in the northern counties of their shared states. "Butternuts"—loyal to the Democratic Party, suspicious of Yankees and their ways, less likely to cherish education or practice more reformist types of Protestantism—feared emancipation might then spark a migration of freed blacks into the counties in which these former Southerners had settled and their families now lived.[30] During the 1850s, in southern Indiana, the intrusion of railroads and the growth of towns did not shake the population's conservative outlook. Those emigrants from Southern lands neither liked slavery as an institution nor blacks as individuals. Far from seeing the institution as absolutely wrong, they had no problem with watching it expand into western territories, just as long as slaves or free blacks did not become their neighbors. Yet when secession came, they voiced their loyalty to the Union, seeing danger to liberty and to the Democratic Party in the rash actions of Southerners while at the same time placing a good bit of the blame for the crisis on radical Republicans.[31]

AFRICAN AMERICANS AND NORTHERN RACISM

The Northern states were growing much more rapidly than their slave state rivals, something that caused concern for white Southerners wary of the increased political power that went in tandem with those population numbers and a reality that would make it much more physically possible for the Union states to maintain an extensive and intensive war effort. In 1860, there were over 31 million Americans, with about 4 million of them being enslaved African Americans living in the slave states. Of that total number, just over 19 million residents of the free states and territories were of white European descent, while only about 226,000 free blacks lived among them. A few states in the Northeast exceeded the 1.2 percent average of the larger free region, while Midwestern states with the exception of Ohio had even smaller percentages of African Americans living within their borders. Furthermore, black Northerners tended to congregate in urban areas, making the rest of the region even more predominantly white.[32] Most white Northerners, therefore, went to war hardly knowing what free blacks let alone slaves experienced, but that reality did not stop them from developing personal prejudices and public policies that made black Northerners into disadvantaged residents of an ostensibly free region. Despite their small presence and because of these experiences, African Americans expected to see the war bring about positive changes in their lives.

Black Northerners established noticeable communities in urban areas. Philadelphia was home to the largest number of African Americans, totaling over 22,000 in 1860, followed by New York City with over 12,000 that year. Cities such as Brooklyn, Cincinnati, and Boston had smaller black populations, but still significant enough to allow African Americans to establish communal institutions.[33] Many of the better-off Northern blacks made themselves known to their white neighbors by their involvement in reform movements, especially abolitionism.[34] Even more African Americans, however, lived quiet lives as urban workers in the Northeast and farmers or laborers in the Midwest who were primarily concerned with providing for themselves and their families. Some black mariners gained middle-class status during the antebellum era, were able to purchase property, and wore the mantle of respectability.[35] By the time of the war, a small black professional class existed in Boston, but some laborers, such as porters, also enjoyed a privileged place in the black community because of their steady employment.[36]

Smaller Northern cities such as Newark and Jersey City, New Jersey, were home to middle-class blacks, but could boast only a few property holders among them. Landowning black farmers in New Jersey enjoyed a degree of prosperity, but farther west in Ohio, rural blacks were most likely to work the soil as laborers or tenants on someone else's land.[37] In fact, most Northern African Americans lived the hard lives of laborers primarily concerned with providing the basic needs for themselves and their families.[38] Too many of them shared the circumstances of the black population of Trenton, New Jersey, where in 1844 the teacher Mary Ann Shadd, an African American from a free family, criticized them for failing to make her school a priority while they expended their resources on food, clothing, and shelter.[39]

Regardless of their economic situations, Northern blacks endured racial discrimination—both by custom and by law—that made their freedom something less than that claimed by their white neighbors. Most African Americans lived in states that kept them from exercising the franchise, and not long before the war Michigan, Iowa, and Wisconsin defeated efforts to change that situation within their borders.[40] Some Northern states, such as Ohio, prohibited blacks from offering testimony in court cases involving whites, and all of the Northern states, except Massachusetts, barred blacks from jury service.[41] Restrictions on the movement of African Americans into Indiana, Illinois, and Iowa made it clear that they were not welcome even in the ostensibly free states.[42]

Widespread discrimination frequently kept working African Americans from improving their stations in life. Furthermore, changing demographics imposed limitations. In antebellum New York City, the ever-increasing number of Irish immigrants led to the replacement of black domestic servants with Irish women, while Irish men dominated the carting trade to the exclusion of blacks until a small number of African Americans began entering the occupation in the mid-1850s.[43] In 1860, African American abolitionist, teacher, and physician John Rock believed even in Boston prejudice hurt black economic security. "Colored men in business here receive more respect and less patronage than in any other place I know," he declaimed.[44] "I am free to confess that I have strong attachments here, in this my native country," he also admitted, but frustrated by the circumstances of African American life, he proclaimed "American liberty" to be "a name without a meaning—a shadow without substance."[45]

If state restrictions and local prejudices were not enough, the federal government with the passage of the Fugitive Slave Law of 1850 reinforced the fact that being an African American resident of a free state did not make one a free person if a slave catcher could imply a tie to past slavery. Also the Supreme Court's Dred Scott decision of 1857, which said that blacks were not eligible for citizenship and its commensurate rights, made it clear that the federal government would not support the notion of racial equality.[46] In 1860, some Republican Party politicians insisted that wanting to keep slavery out of the territories did not mean that they wanted free blacks as their neighbors. Despite such sentiment, black Northerners such as William Anderson, a Connecticut abolitionist, could still muster the resolution to argue, "It is of no use for the Republican Party to smother the uprising of liberty by declaring that they want free territory for white men."[47]

Thus, on the eve of a conflict prompted by slavery and its spread, the Northern states were not particularly hospitable places for black Americans. No wonder there were tens of thousands of African Americans who sought true liberty north of the Canadian border where black refugee settlements flourished before the war.[48] There were also African American advocates of emigration to less familiar regions of the world, but areas where there might be a chance to establish black communities free from the control of white men. Throughout the 1850s, black physician Martin Delany was a leading proponent of emigration to South America and then later to Africa. He once informed the abolitionist Frederick Douglass that African Americans had to be independent of white men and their ways if they ever were to elevate themselves. "I am weary of our miserable condition," he wrote, "and [am] heartily sick of whimpering, whining and sniveling at the feet of white men, begging for their refuse and offals [*sic*] existing by mere sufferance."[49]

Other Northern blacks, however, made it clear that they were Americans and wanted their white neighbors to see them as such. In October 1853, at a convention held in Chicago, African Americans in attendance demanded equal treatment because "We are Americans by birth, and we assure you that we are Americans in feeling." And these sentiments remained, the authors continued, "in spite of all the wrongs which we have long and silently endured in this country." These men demanded "no special privileges or peculiar favors" but simply wished for equal treatment before the law.[50]

IMMIGRANTS AND NATIVISM

Immigrants added fresh ethnic diversity to the Northern states, contributing to the growth of industry, the expansion of the population, and an increase in the number of voters. In the decade before secession, almost 2.6 million immigrants entered the United States, with most of them settling in the Northern states and with the overwhelming majority of them being German and Irish.[51] Attracted by better wages and living conditions than those offered in Europe, they came in great numbers in the years before the war and gravitated to new homes where the economy did not require them to compete with slavery.[52] St. Paul, Minnesota, attracted Irish immigrants from across the Atlantic as did the Eastern cities, where they then found unskilled work in town; Irish and Scots Canadians fortunate enough to possess clerical skills or some education found employment in shops and offices there.[53] Milwaukee, Wisconsin, benefited greatly from the large German population that made the city its home; by the outbreak of the war, Germans not only dominated the laboring classes there, but also occupied numerous positions among the professional and merchant classes.[54] Textile factories in the Mid-Atlantic states provided work for Irish and English immigrants, but even New England mills, noted for their early use of female employees, began to turn to such workers before the war. During the 1850s, for example, immigrant workers settled in Lowell, Massachusetts, where they built canals, hired on as day labor, and by 1860 came to dominate the labor force in the textile mills.[55] Given such demographics, it should not have been surprising that when Union recruits from the textile town of Rockville, Connecticut, said their farewells, soldier Benjamin Hirst later recalled, it was "in almost every language spoken in Europe."[56]

Reform organizations, especially temperance groups, aimed their attention at immigrants and especially the almost universally Catholic Irish, whom they considered at the root of so much of America's troubles.[57] Anti-immigration Americans, fearful of the impact new arrivals would have on their communities, subjected immigrants to various expressions of prejudice, including violence and scurrilous literature often filled with fear of some sort of Vatican conquest.[58] Irish immigrants were poor, and nativists blamed them for their poverty. Suspicious Protestants also identified the Irish and German Catholics as the source of all of urban America's ills, especially because of how the immigrants concentrated in Northeastern and Midwestern cities. In 1834 a Boston mob attacked a convent, while in 1844 Philadelphia Protestants burned two Irish Catholic churches, razed their homes, and murdered many of their neighbors.[59] Consequently, the new ethnic Americans tended to shy away from the Republican Party because of its evangelical Protestant reformer connections and association with the moribund nativist American Party.[60]

German immigrants were more diverse, with the liberals among them leaning to humanitarian reform and the Republican Party, and others, especially Catholics and Lutherans, having more in common with poorer Irish immigrants and the ideals of the Democratic Party.[61] The Protestant liberals among them had no difficulty assigning the basest attributes to Catholic immigrants, arguing along the same lines as the nativists. "[E]ven the Catholics who want nothing to do with the Bible are wild for slavery," wrote German immigrant and former revolutionary Dietrich Gerstein in February 1860, "especially that dumbest and most beastly of all nations, the Irish." The Vatican was, according to Gerstein, encouraging Catholic immigration to the United States because "the republic is a thorn in Rome's flesh, and if they send all the religious riffraff in the whole world over here, then when the next revolution comes . . . there will be a good chance of subjugating the North as well." However, Gerstein, probably aware of how nativist Know-Nothings migrated into the new Republican Party, had faith that the Republicans would be "on the alert because they know what to expect from the spread of Catholicism."[62]

Immigrants, along with the Protestant natives who voted Republican, accepted the core idea of that party's free-labor ideology that hard work and self-discipline could make better lives for themselves, a concept that flourished in the intellectual and economic environment of the free states. German immigrant Emile Dupré had been a businessman without resources, unable to strike out on his own back home, but in November 1860, he was in New York happily working long hours because "I know what goal I am working toward." Furthermore, he told his mother, "It is the first job where I earn more than I actually need and which would allow me to get married."[63] German immigrant Otto Albrecht, who was living in Philadelphia at the time of the November 1860 presidential election, also saw good prospects in America, especially in the person of the newly elected president, Abraham Lincoln. "This man shows how far you can get here: his father was a farmer and he himself used to build fences around the fields," he reported. However, the president-elect went on to study and practice law, revealed his talent and good character, and became involved in politics "and now he's arrived at the position of the greatest honor here or anywhere else in the whole world."[64]

These individuals proved their commitment to their new homes with their hard work, whether it was in a factory or on a farm. Irish railroad workers took on jobs as dangerous as the men who worked on India's early rail lines.[65] Factory workers spent on average 11 hours a day on their feet, regulated by the requirements of their machines and not by their own rhythms.[66] Farm laborers found their days consumed from sun up to sun down with breaking sod, digging wells, planting, and harvesting during the growing cycle, while they spent the rest of the year engaged in other kinds of hard labor, such as logging.[67] At the outset of the war, 18-year-old English immigrant William R. Oake did this sort of work for a farmer near his family's Iowa home making a fair $12 a month before he joined the army.[68] There was always the chance that the hard factory work of the men in the Rockville, Connecticut, mills, along with the wages of other family members including their children might earn them enough to buy land or enter into business. They expected the factory floor to provide temporary employment before they took advantage of free labor's promise of economic independence.[69]

THE PEOPLE AND THEIR WORK

In 1861, the communities in which Northerners lived were still primarily rural and agricultural, but the region as a whole was evolving into something new, modern, and more dynamic than that of their Southern opponents. In 1820, only 10 percent of the population of the free states was living in towns of 2,500 or more, but in 1860 that number had climbed to 26 percent. At the beginning of the century, 68 percent of people in the free states were involved in agricultural labor; in 1860 that number had declined to 40 percent. In New Jersey, for example, farm workers began to migrate to urban areas where they found better paying jobs in factories. In the process, internal migrants helped to boost the populations of cities in the state, whose farms continued to provide produce for Trenton, Jersey City, and other urban areas, including nearby New York City and Philadelphia. The greater use of technology on the farm and in the factory as well as the development of an efficient railroad transportation network and a capitalist financial system all contributed to these changes.[70]

With the coming of war, some Confederates took comfort in their belief that the soft life supposedly lived by Yankee clerks and shopkeepers who would make up the invading Northern armies would cause them to cower before the rugged young men raised on the countryside of the rural South. This assessment of their enemy's capabilities was based on an erroneous demographic assumption. Urban populations certainly had grown by the time of the Civil War, and during the 1850s, smaller towns in places such as the frontier state of Minnesota were attracting their fair share of residents. But the North remained primarily a rural region and in some places demanded more frontier determination than the settled areas of Virginia and Georgia.

Michael H. Fitch discovered as much when he recruited in northwestern Wisconsin. He traveled through a "sparsely settled" region, which made "raising a volunteer company for service, an arduous task." Undiscouraged, Fitch rode "across the prairie and through the woods for several days" visiting towns and farms, traveling on roads in "wretched condition" turned into muddy tracks when it rained. Along the way, he discovered that "Every rugged backwoodsman, whether American, German or

Norwegian, was full of patriotism." By the time Fitch had completed his task, he had a company made up of small-town boys, farmers, and "lumbermen and loggers." "There were no better soldiers in the army than many of these backwoods farmer boys," he later judged.[71] Far from being stiff-collared clerks, many of the initial officers and recruits of the First Michigan Engineers had worked with their hands before the war, cleared forests for farms, and tilled the land.[72]

Factory workers did not share in these frontier experiences, but they endured difficult work lives of a different sort. In 1861, the Rockville mill workers in the 14th Connecticut Volunteer Infantry and factory workers in other comparable regiments probably had developed an understanding of collective effort and discipline of army life thanks to their long hours at work, exchanging obedience to the orders of managers and foremen for the orders of commissioned and noncommissioned company officers.[73] Consequently, life in many areas of the Northern states had its unanticipated benefits for future soldiers. The hard outdoor toil of the frontier logger or the farm hand and the routines of the factory worker might very well have made the men who had engaged in such activities better suited to the rough, regimented, disciplined life of the army than their Southern counterparts would have allowed.

TWO

THE SECESSION CRISIS

Sectional tension had waxed and waned from the inception of the Union as Northern and Southern societies and economies matured in their own distinct ways.[1] Southern complaints about Northern insensitivity to their section's particular needs on occasion rose above the normal clamor of American politics with threats of disunion, especially when Southerners perceived a threat to their "peculiar institution" of slavery. But it was the issue of the expansion of slavery into the territories that led to the destruction of the Whig Party, strained the unity in the Democratic Party until it fractured, and gave birth to the Republican Party in the mid-1850s. From the time of the war with Mexico in 1846, slavery, which Democrats and Whigs had sought to keep out of national debate, now agitated almost all aspects of national public discourse and policy-making and changed the way both Southerners and Northerners approached politics and each other. The Republican Party, which grew out of elements of various moribund or disintegrating political organizations in reaction to the Kansas-Nebraska Act of 1854, appealed to Northerners who wanted to keep slavery out of the new territories and resented the slaveholder's constant intrusion into Northerners' civil liberties, especially the forced compliance with an invigorated and expansive federal fugitive slave act in 1850.

The desire to keep the territories free of slavery was at the heart of this new political association. The party's antislavery agenda united individuals of various political stripes who were committed to a nation that promised white men the opportunity to advance by their own hard work and the open land to become independent farmers unhindered by the competition of an oligarchy based on the exploitation of slave labor and the concentration of social and political power in an elite. That success in achieving the goal of containing slavery would lead to the ultimate extinction of that institution was not a secret, as slaveholders well understood.[2]

The Republican Party also gave white Southerners a political focus for their fear and hatred. As far as Southerners were concerned, the rise of a party that appealed primarily to Northern voters was a threat to slavery, the foundation upon which their way of life, their domestic stability, and their understanding of racial purity rested. Republican protestations that they had no plans or constitutional right to tamper with slavery in states where it already existed could not, and did not, change this perception. And acts such as John Brown's attempt to foment a slave rebellion with his raid on Harpers Ferry, Virginia, in 1859, only served to confirm Southern fears about a supposedly fanatical abolitionism driving Northern passions aimed at the destruction of their way of life.

THE LOOMING CRISIS

From the presidential campaign of 1860 and through the secession winter of 1860–1861, Northerners experienced what activist Mary Livermore later called, "a time of extreme and unconcealed anxiety."[3] They could not help but pay attention to the extraordinary events beyond their own electoral districts and states, and they did not wait for community leaders or politicians to direct their attention to the crisis.[4] The people's foremost sources of information were their newspapers. The secession crisis came at a time when American publishers were turning out a record number of newspapers for a growing market with high literacy rates. Residents of the larger cities such as New York, Philadelphia, Boston, Chicago, and San Francisco could choose from among several dailies and other journals, while those in smaller towns usually had access to at least one local paper published on a weekly schedule.[5]

The need to remain connected to worlds left behind contributed to the spread of newspapers across the continent through newly settled regions. Boosters believed that the newspaper was essential for encouraging the growth of their new communities, an attitude that furthered the spread of antebellum print culture.[6] In 1849, for example, Minnesota territory had its first newspaper. By the late 1850s, St. Paul, Minnesota, was home to over 10,000 residents and seven newspapers, and in 1861 the new state counted 125 newspapers.[7] In Indiana, during the decade before secession, the number of newspapers grew from about 100 to almost 500.[8] On the eve of the secession crisis, Wisconsin supported over 100 weekly newspapers.[9] Thus, during the crisis of 1860–1861, newspapers across the North provided detailed information about the various phases of the crisis, all with their own partisan slant. Wilhelm Francksen, a German immigrant who served in the Union army, would later try to explain this phenomenon to his family. "Nearly everyone reads a newspaper here, but only the papers from their own party," he wrote home to Germany, "which all the facts are colored or changed according to the party line and that contain nothing but lies and poison aimed at the other parties."[10]

Readers of these journals gathered at public spaces and in private homes to exchange news, debate, and speculate about what would happen next. During the 1860 campaign, residents of the village of Courtland, New York, congregated at a local dry goods store to discuss events and listen to people read aloud the New York papers and no doubt continued to do so into the future.[11] In the Great Barrington, Massachusetts, area, farmers read newspapers aloud and discussed the pressing issues of the day when they met regularly at a distillery where their animals consumed the by-products of whiskey making.[12] Conversations at upper-class social gatherings in New York, Philadelphia, and other cities could not avoid the subject of disunion.[13]

In April 1861, as the crisis came to a head, the people of Nantucket Island, Massachusetts, met daily in a square on their main street looking seaward for a signal from a steamship out of Hyannis to keep them up to date.[14] No doubt they took the opportunity to discuss their fears and express their opinions to those standing with them as they shuffled about waiting for news. Elsewhere, expecting trouble any moment, people checked for incoming telegraph messages that might be posted in public places. Great Barrington, Massachusetts, residents who normally relied on weekly newspapers studied posts on bulletin boards placed by telegraph operators, editors, and people with access to out-of-town papers.[15] Chicagoan Mary Livermore tried to do her daughterly duty caring for an ill parent in Boston, but also "vibrated between my father's sick room and the bulletin board" as she sought out news about the unfolding situation in South Carolina.[16]

Those people who generally tended to their own business found it difficult to ignore what was going on around them. Attending Sunday services, for example, could mean sitting through sermons in which preachers addressed the state of the Union. At Thanksgiving, Cleveland, Ohio, churchgoers listened to their preachers present sermons about the preservation of the Union.[17] Ministers across the North not only declaimed upon the crisis from their Sunday pulpits, but also wrote about it in their sectarian journals.[18]

A FIRM STAND FOR UNION

Knowing what was going on in South Carolina and elsewhere in the Deep South did not mean agreeing on how the nation should handle the disgruntled region.

Philadelphia preacher Henry A. Boardman spoke for many when he argued in a Thanksgiving Day sermon that national unity was "too sacred a trust to be sacrificed except upon the most imperative grounds" and urged Americans to explore "every practicable means for preserving it" rather than allowing its disintegration.[19] Other clergy believed that they should offer concessions before matters worsened to prove the North's benevolent intentions toward the South. Prior to South Carolina's secession, the editor of the Philadelphia *Presbyterian* was specific in his suggestion for easing the fears of slaveholders, arguing that personal liberty laws, which protected runaway slaves, should be repealed; such laws, he judged, were just another form of extraconstitutional nullification.[20]

In early December, Philadelphian Sidney George Fisher went even further by suggesting that the country could head off all but South Carolina's secession if its lawmakers passed an act allowing a state to leave the Union.[21] More frantically, Northern businessmen appealed for conciliation, lest secession disrupt the national economy and bring on a new market collapse. Recalling the Panic of 1857, they sought unity above all else. In December, for example, a group of businessmen in New York City gathered at the office of a commission merchant to reaffirm the right of slavery and called upon citizens to support political compromise favorable to Southern interests.[22]

Other Northerners, however, believed that preemptive concessions were unnecessary either because Southerners would not take radical action against the Constitution they professed to respect or because such actions would fail to appease slaveholders who wanted nothing less than a national guarantee of protection for slavery. Republicans, confident in their ability to govern the entire nation, failed to grasp the danger in secessionist threats.[23] Vermonter Marshall Harvey Twitchell years later recalled that he did not believe that Abraham Lincoln's coming to power would lead to "anything serious."[24] Loud fire-eaters might attract some attention, but, as one New York City editorialist proclaimed in November, "The secession strength in the South is overrated."[25] Still other Northerners were not so certain of the slaveholders' lack of will. Reassuring words about the future did not calm these pessimistic souls. Minnesotan William G. Le Duc heard William Seward tell a crowd, "there was no danger of any serious trouble with the South." Le Duc, who had spent some time in the South, concluded, "such erroneous opinion expressed by one so prominent in public life could only lessen the chance of averting war."[26]

Even Northerners who accepted that the slaveholders would take states out of the Union were convinced that any concessions would be futile. They considered it would now be best to stand firm and not abandon principle for a period of illusory harmony. Abolitionists were naturally disposed to oppose compromise.[27] After all, as black abolitionist Thomas Hamilton concluded shortly after South Carolina left the Union on December 20, the slave states in spirit had left the Union years earlier, bullying Northern states to bend to their will on any number of issues. "The Republican party may, by bowing down to the required depth, stave off for a month, or a year, or two years, the formal withdrawal of these cotton States," Hamilton argued, "but the event is as certain as the sunshine and the rain, and depends on laws as inevitable as the laws of nature."[28] Republican politicians in Washington and in state capitals across the land came to accept this view.

As if to confirm suspicions about the insatiable demands of Southerners, on December 17, Senator John Crittenden of Kentucky shaped a compromise from the various and numerous proposals before Congress that would allow for the expansion of slavery, at least below the old Missouri Compromise line, along with other provisions guaranteeing slavery's safety where it already existed. Politicians also expanded it to include not only the disfranchisement of the small number of Northern blacks who could vote but also the removal of free African Americans residing in Northern and Southern states to Africa. Northern blacks and their friends were outraged by the notion that politicians would sacrifice on the altar of national unity the minimal rights and expectations for a free nation that blacks enjoyed, but, in the end, the compromise plan failed to capture the support of Congress.[29]

Black abolitionist Thomas Hamilton admitted, "secession must soon triumph" because, among other things, Southerners now "regard as a hopeless task the effort to convince the North that slavery is a blessed and divine institution."[30] That, indeed, was the rub. The compromise propositions considered before and after South Carolina seceded on December 20 required the victorious Republican Party to abandon its core belief concerning stopping the expansion of slavery. Such a compromise was at odds with the very platform that had won Republican candidates their elections across the North. The best that the party could offer secessionists were reassurances about leaving slavery alone where it presently existed, which was not much as far as slaveholders were concerned. As Wisconsin Republicans resolved at a convention in December before the secession of South Carolina occurred, "we can make no compromise which will appease the South without yielding the whole ground which brought the Republican party into existence."[31]

Compromise threatened not only the new party's existence, but also the nation's democratic ways. Abraham Lincoln had carried the day in all the free states but for New Jersey, where he had won four of the state's seven electoral votes. Giving in to the secessionists would undermine the election's outcome and corrupt the democratic process. Furthermore, Union-loving Northerners believed that secession was, as Lincoln said in his March 4, 1861, inaugural address, "the essence of anarchy"; its rejection of majority rule could only leave a nation with "anarchy, or despotism in some form."[32] Thus, unchecked secession would be a challenge not only to the nation's domestic tranquility and prosperity, but also to its liberty and to its role as the world's beacon of republican government.[33]

Some men continued to look for compromises, but radical Republican James Ashley, a Congressman from Ohio, accepted that secession provided his party with an opportunity. He believed the newly elected president's war powers gave Lincoln the means to free slaves in the traitorous states. If war came, for Ashley it would be one that would bring to an end that hated institution.[34] Beyond the parlors of radicals, abolitionists, and African Americans, however, Northerners voiced little concern about the South's slaves as victims or even as people deserving respect. It was, after all, the threatened expansion of slavery and the arrogance of slaveholders that had driven Northerners into the Republican Party, and the desire to preserve the old constitution that kept many of them in line behind Lincoln. Although slaves did not matter for much among most Northerners, whatever their party affiliation, they certainly mattered to Southerners. On December 24, 1860, the South Carolina secessionists, desirous of explaining their actions, issued "A Declaration of Causes" that made it plain that Northern actions against slavery had forced the state out of the Union.[35] Indeed, Maine soldier Oliver Otis Howard made little headway when he tried to explain to a Southern lady that Republicans were not abolitionists but only wished to stop the extension of slavery into the territories. According to Howard, she corrected him by explaining, "it is all the same thing!" "Why stop the extension of slavery?" Howard recalled her arguing, "It shows that they are against us. It is all very plain." She promised bloodshed.[36]

Many residents of the Deep South states shared the concern that the Republicans were "against" them and their interests and that only secession might save them. They soon followed South Carolina's example, beginning on January 9, 1861, when Mississippians voted to secede. Five other Deep South states left in turn. The lull in the disintegration of the Union in the aftermath of Texas's secession on February 1, 1861, gave Northerners a few months to continue to debate the best approach to handling such an extraordinary situation.

Northerners may have fumed about the traitorous audacity of those first Confederate states, but, even so, they remained divided on the proper course of action for dealing with secessionists. Some people believed it was not prudent or even desirable to embark on an immediate campaign to reverse secession. In January 1861, leading men in Keokuk, Iowa, met several times to discuss the proper course of action after secessionists began to act, but they could not agree on a strategy.[37] Northern Democrats especially were trapped in a bind of disavowing disunion, but not knowing how to arrest it without seemingly giving in to fire-eaters and selling out the North. They worried that they might be blamed for the crisis if war followed disunion, which intensified their calls for compromise and their condemnation of Republicans as the real causes of all the troubles.[38] While Democrats urged caution and compromise at any price, Republican jurist Samuel Freeman Miller argued that it would be an embarrassment to give in to the demands of traitors at a time when the nation should be willing to enforce its laws and protect its government.[39] Elsewhere, a Columbus, Ohio, editorialist shared Miller's views when he pronounced that "beyond certain limits forbearance ceases to be a virtue. . . . The time is now upon us to test whether we have a government or not."[40]

Some Northerners, however, were not so keen on forcing the slave states to remain in the Union. They concluded that it would be best to let the slave states go their own way, an action that would in the end free the nation from the intractable problems related to slavery and profit the remaining states. Future president Rutherford B. Hayes, for example, confided in his diary that a new and free northern nation would thrive without the seceded states.[41] A New Yorker even wished that all of the other slave states would follow their brethren into the Confederacy, for if they did not, the nation would still endure the unhappiness of disunion without the benefit of ridding itself of slavery.[42]

There remained individuals across the North who continued to call for a cautious response in hopes that the crisis would resolve itself with some sort of national reconstruction. Some Northerners, as Oliver Otis Howard recalled, assumed that time eventually would restore calm, "that these first symptoms of rebellion were merely dark days of passion—the sheer embodiments of windy fury which time under the sun rays of good sense would dissipate."[43] In January, William Henry Seward, a leading Republican, continued to tell visitors, according to the wife of one of them, "There is no danger of civil war. It will all be over in six weeks."[44]

Many Northerners probably took comfort in knowing that after Texas's secession in February 1861, important slave states such as Virginia had resisted the impulse for disunion.[45] But as New Yorker Jane Stuart Woolsey learned, such comfort might be short-lived. In early February 1861, a Virginian warned her not to be optimistic about the secession crisis burning itself out. The guest informed her that Virginians' understanding of the meaning of Union was different from that of New Yorkers'. The quiet from that state only meant delay, and Virginia would eventually take its place in the new Confederacy.[46]

Doing nothing, however, was not a good option for many Northerners. In the southern regions of the Old Northwest, Democrats continued to advocate compromise. On December 22, immediately after South Carolina's secession, for example, the people of Patoka, a community with a significant number of German Catholics located in Democratic Dubois County in the southern tier of Indiana, urged acceptance of the Crittenden Compromise, specifically called for the repeal of personal liberty laws, and reaffirmed their belief in white superiority.[47] The Democrats at the January 1861 meetings in Keokuk pleaded that no concession was too great if it saved the Union.[48] Nothing good would come of coercion, compromisers believed, and most Democrats, while they did not sympathize with Southern desires to break up the republic, argued that talk was the only weapon at the disposal of their government for ending the crisis. The rash fire-eaters who had caused the trouble would soon have to yield to the majority of Southerners who still loved the old flag.[49]

Within this debate, there were some Democrats who went so far as to admit that states could indeed leave the Union if their people wished to do so.[50] Indeed, the more radical among these Democrats in Midwestern states, especially in the lower counties that had been settled by migrants from Southern states, even contemplated their own secession.[51] Many of these lower-county Midwesterners believed that Republicans had drawn them into a needless crisis because of what they wrongly assumed were the party's abolitionist views.[52] In January 1861, Ohioan Hugh Anderson assured a grandson residing in Alabama that his sympathies were with the South, and that he understood the "Lincolnites" to be the unreasonable fanatics. Hugh's son Parker made it clear that if war came, he would not support the "*red mouthed abolitionist disunionists nigger elevators, nigger lovers of men* who make laws making my children only *equal to be raised up educated at the same school and associated with*, a race perhaps two removes from a babboon [*sic*]." But he also assured his family's Alabama relative not to worry, because even if war came Lincoln would have a difficult time raising an army in Ohio. He averred that thousands of anti-Lincoln men would resist, and the new president's supporters were "generally quaker abolitionists [who are] not the material for an army" anyway.[53]

Racism and constitutional ideals prevented some Northerners from supporting an aggressive response to secession. So, too, did economic interest. Northerners had hardly recovered from an earlier financial crisis, the Panic of 1857, and now they faced a period of political discord and economic uncertainty that threatened the tranquility and trust essential for cross-sectional trade. In December, after South Carolina's secession, the *Philadelphia Press* reminded its readers of the Northern states' lucrative trade connections with the South that "is of as great value annually to the free States as that of the Union is to all Europe, Asia, and South America." That business, alone, the editorialist argued, is sufficient "a motive to conciliation."[54] Businessmen and workingmen alike argued for compromise; they understood that breaking their economic ties with the South would undermine their livelihoods even as they had begun to expect an end to the troubles ushered in by the financial difficulties that had begun with the Panic of 1857. Limited credit, property devaluation, declining prices, factory closings, bankruptcies, and extensive unemployment had undone the prosperity of mid-decade.[55] Now secession promised to do the same.

In Dubuque, Iowa, the Republican victory and the secession of South Carolina halted an economic recovery.[56] In New Jersey, Newark and other cities with Southern business connections also paid an economic price for sectional instability.[57] During the antebellum era, Wisconsin banks had found favorable investments in the bonds of several Southern states; the secession crisis devalued those investments, which undermined confidence in those institutions.[58] At least one Northern businessman received defiant letters from his Southern clients informing him that they would be paying their debts with Confederate money or violence.[59] As Lincoln's inauguration approached, Wall Street experienced "Feverish anxiety."[60] And Midwestern businessmen and newspaper editors worried openly that secession might close the Mississippi River to traffic or disrupt transportation on that vital waterway.[61]

SECESSION AND WAR'S APPROACH

Shortly after South Carolina's secession vote, on December 26, 1860, the U.S. Army contingent in Charleston harbor moved from its vulnerable position at Fort Moultrie to the more defensible Fort Sumter. The federal government attempted to supply and to reinforce those soldiers when it sent the merchant vessel *Star of the West* southward, only to have the ship turned back from the harbor on January 9 when Southerners opened fire from shore batteries. This hostile act outraged many Northerners who would come to see this volley as the opening salvo of the war. Citizens cried treason, demanded action of their representatives, and mustered into volunteer military companies, offering their services to their governors to defend the flag. South Carolina had started a fight that they could not ignore unless they wished to accept dishonor for themselves and their nation. The lame-duck President James Buchanan, however, avoided taking action and a period of quiet ensued, even as some politicians unsuccessfully continued to explore avenues of compromise.[62]

Lincoln's inauguration on March 4 gave Northerners an opportunity to celebrate American democracy despite the crisis.[63] It also reminded Americans throughout the land that the Republican Party, an organization committed to the nonexpansion of slavery, would be guiding national policy for the next four years. While divisions remained among Northerners on how to handle secession, many people continued to urge the Republican Party not to abandon its principles. The party, eager to prove that it had the will and the power to honor the campaign pledges that embodied its ideals, obliged them throughout the months of crisis. If the party bent to Southern demands and compromised away its principles, the politicians reasoned, it would prove itself to be illegitimate and weak to supporters and enemies alike.[64] The more strident antisecessionists declared that the time for compromise had passed. Black abolitionist Frederick Douglass, echoing Thomas Hamilton's earlier words, argued that "The contest must now be decided, and decided forever, which of the two, Freedom or Slavery, shall give law to this Republic." There was nothing else to do but "Let the conflict come."[65]

Northern loyalists agreed that it was important to protect federal property in the South, lest federal authority appear to be impotent in the face of challenges. Once again, attention focused on Charleston harbor and Fort Sumter. With the firing on that fort on April 12 and the surrender of its garrison on the following day, the

Confederacy took matters out of the hands of Northerners. On April 15, President Lincoln declared that people in seceded states were engaging in an insurrection "too powerful to be suppressed by the ordinary course of judicial proceedings." He also called out the militia of the loyal states to the number of 75,000 men to do what the courts could not. "I appeal to all loyal citizens," the president continued, "to favor, facilitate and aid this effort to maintain the honor, the integrity, and the existence of our National Union, and the perpetuity of popular government."[66] Not long thereafter, on May 3, the president called for volunteers to enlist for three years or until no longer needed.

Lincoln's call to arms and his stated intention of regaining control of federal property that had fallen into rebel hands were deciding factors in convincing Virginia, North Carolina, Tennessee, and Arkansas to leave the Union. It also united loyal citizens in their desire to resist the destruction of their country in what many expected to be a quick fight that would resolve the issue by the end of the summer, a prediction that a few wary citizens failed to accept with the same unqualified enthusiasm. Friends told Theodore Upson, an Indiana farm boy, "that it would all be over soon; that those fellows down South are big bluffers and would rather talk than fight." Upson, however, questioned their optimism. He had Southern family relations, knew their pugnacious spirit, and concluded, "I am not so sure about that."[67]

THREE

FORT SUMTER AND THE
PATRIOTIC RESPONSE

NEWS OF FORT SUMTER FROM
PRESS AND PULPIT

The concerns of the spring of 1861 disrupted the rhythms of everyday life across the Northern states. As tensions increased before Confederates fired on Fort Sumter, Northerners became consumers of any and all news relating to the situation in Charleston harbor. As they had during the secession crisis, people assembled near telegraph and newspaper offices hoping to pick up the national news or just milled around the streets expecting to hear something of importance. Wilbur Fiske, a young Vermonter, and his friends were awaiting news at the post office in their small town where they heard of the violent events in Charleston from an emotional elderly postmaster.[1] In New Haven, crowds filled the streets to buy freshly printed newspapers, while out-of-town couriers rushed back to their smaller Connecticut communities burdened with copies of the big city's paper.[2] On the agricultural frontier, the news of Fort Sumter's fall came in the old-fashioned manner familiar to patriots of a much earlier time. In one rural Michigan region, farmers were at work in the fields, sharing the community's one threshing machine, when a man on horseback reared up to announce Lincoln's call for troops in reaction to the disaster.[3]

If someone had by some strange chance missed the reports concerning events in Charleston harbor, he or she would probably have heard about Fort Sumter's fate at a

Sunday service. Across Connecticut, ministers preached war and, at a more practical level, New Britain preachers announced a war meeting scheduled for that evening.[4] In neighboring Massachusetts, Boston churches "thundered with denunciations of the rebellion."[5] Mary Livermore recalled the messages from that city's pulpits being "such as were never heard before . . . not even from radical preachers."[6]

One would expect such sermons in New England, but even conservative preachers now changed their minds when confronted with this explicit example of Southern treachery.[7] Sometimes, ministers realized they had to catch up with the patriotic sentiment of congregations that would not stand for anything but support for putting down the rebellion. Before the town of Courtland, New York, held a community meeting on April 20, one local preacher had spoken out against using violence against the wayward Southern states; after the rousing gathering, things changed and Courtland ministers preached against treason.[8] Indeed, for the most part, mainstream Northern Protestant clergymen spoke as one on the issue of Union, sometimes judging the new enemy with little regard for Christian charity. A few days after Sumter, in the state senate chamber at Madison, Wisconsin, the Methodist chaplain prayed "these men who have thus turned traitors against their country ought to be hung in this world and damned in the world to come."[9] Across the North, such ministers added a political dimension to their preaching and a moral dimension to the national crusade about which they would continue to remind their congregations throughout the war.[10] Also, as the sectional crisis progressed, Northerners, whether they believed in an antislavery crusade or a war for the Union, could add to their motives for resisting secession their Christian duty to wage battle against a people who were doing the work of Satan, the original secessionist.[11]

REACTION TO FORT SUMTER'S FALL

When they absorbed the news, Northerners reacted to the events with shock, worry, anger, and resolve. As Mary Livermore recalled, the telegraphic transmission concerning "the lowering of the stars and stripes, and the surrender of the beleaguered garrison" brought "news [that] fell on the land like a thunderbolt."[12] Some sober heads understood what was awaiting their men. The uncle of Elbridge Copp, a New Hampshire boy eager to go off and fight the rebels, believed that it would be "a terrible war."[13] Such concerns, if not common or loudly expressed, certainly reached across the nation. Theodore Upson and his father, Jonathan, who had family in the South, were husking corn on their Indiana farm when a friend informed them of the firing on Fort Sumter. The elder Upson "got white and couldn't say a word." He stopped work for the day, returned to the family house, and after discussing the event with his wife, according to the son, "looked ten years older." Theodore's grandmother added to the emotional scene as she cried over the fate of her Southern relations. "Now they will suffer!" the younger Upson recalled her saying, "God knows how they will suffer! . . . Oh to think that I should have lived to see the day when Brother should rise against Brother."[14] Such considerations, however, generally gave way to excitement fueled by patriotism and a belief that the loyal states would quickly deal with the traitors.

Northerners might have wondered why they had taken their country for granted in the years preceding a crisis that challenged its very existence. Mary Livermore recalled, "Never before had the national flag signified anything to me." Now, as she witnessed it flying all across Boston, "all that it symbolized as representative government and emblematic of national majesty became clear to my mental vision."[15] New Yorker Jane Stuart Woolsey would have understood such emotion. "It seems as if we never were alive till now; never had a country till now," she admitted some weeks after Sumter fell. "How could we ever have laughed at Fourth-of-Julys?"[16] Even William Lloyd Garrison, the editor of the *Liberator* and the abolitionist who had condemned the Constitution as a bulwark for slavery, now found beauty in a flag that slaveholders scorned.[17]

Northerners now gathered in town halls and town squares, at schoolhouses and opera houses to hear patriotic speeches, condemnations of southern traitors, and plans of action. "All normal habits of life were suspended," Mary Livermore noted, "and business and pleasure were alike forgotten."[18] In the town of Manitowoc, Wisconsin, people stopped working, congregated on the streets, and attended courthouse meetings.[19]

So it was, with the excitement drawing people away from their usual routines across the land. Vermonter Ann Stevens wrote to her brother on April 21 that "There is scarcely anything else thought or talked about here, men gather in the streets and a crowd is ever in the bar room talking hotly concerning the state of affairs."[20] Bells rang out in Concord, Massachusetts, calling people to the commons to listen to a reading of the president's proclamation.[21] In Belleville, Illinois, in the southwestern part of the state, old and new Americans listened to speeches in English and German before vowing to preserve the Constitution and enforce the laws of the land.[22] Later in June in Greenville, Wisconsin, residents gathered for a flag raising at which the local Catholic priest played a prominent role; they also heard speeches in German and Gaelic.[23]

Distracted by the momentous events of the day, University of Vermont students found it "hard . . . to study or do anything but get excited."[24] So it would be at other institutions where young men were ready to commit themselves to the preservation of the Union. John Langdon Sibley, Harvard University's librarian, noted how his institution was disrupted by the emotional reaction to the fall of Fort Sumter. The students, similar to their Vermont counterparts, could not tend to their books, and many of them dropped everything to answer Lincoln's call for volunteers. Governor

John Andrew also helped to deplete enrollment when he commanded those Massachusetts militia members in the student body to report to their companies.[25]

People expressed their patriotic sentiments by adorning themselves, their tables, and their animals with the national colors.[26] Liberty poles sprung up in many towns, and national flags became part of the landscape, flying from public and private buildings across the North, along city streets and rural byways, and even from the church steeples, just one more example of much of the Northern clergy's unapologetic commitment to the Union.[27] All across New Jersey flags appeared, and while the people of New York City, a place that had important commercial connections with the South, lagged a little behind their neighbors across the Hudson River, they soon followed suit.[28] New Yorker Jane Stuart Woolsey probably contributed to the increasing public pressure on business to show their support for the Union with flag flying. On April 18, she "amused herself in shopping . . . by saying to everyone: 'You have no flag out yet! Are you getting one ready?'"[29]

Newspapers across the North helped sustain this patriotism, giving readers a sense of purpose as they urged readers to rise to the challenges thrown before them by the secessionists. Not only would the fight against the secessionists lead to an end to the attempt to destroy republican government, it would revive the spirit of the North, stop disruptive party squabbling, purge Washington of corruption, and restore a sense of honor that had been lost in the scramble for material gain. The country, so wrote an editorialist in the *New York Herald* in late April, "will come out of the fire like gold purified of its dross."[30] Fighting secession would revive public virtue from the businessman to the lowliest of urban dwellers. Battling to keep the nation whole would even absolve the North of its sinful cooperation with Southerners in the past to maintain the institution of slavery. "Blood it is then," the Madison *Wisconsin Daily Patriot*, a Democratic Party paper, proclaimed on April 30, "and let it flow till the past is atoned, and a long future secured to peace, prosperity, happiness, and honor."[31]

Northerners repeated in their letters these themes as well as those that Lincoln had struck in his March 1861 inaugural address when he argued for the perpetuity of the Union and the validity of constitutional processes.[32] Joseph L. Perkins, a medical student at the University of Vermont, understood that secession challenged national liberty. Perkins acknowledged that the nation had a constitution and a duly elected president. "Shall we support him in doing his duty—in executing the laws or desert him?" he asked his brother. "We the light of the world toward which all nations are gazing," he continued, "shall we allow it to be extinguished becaus[e] demons prefer darkness?" For Perkins, the answer was not debatable; they must do everything within their power to save the country. "My life is at my country's disposal and if possible should be given ten thousand times ere I'd be ruled by tyrants and *much less traitors*." After all, he told his brother, "What would be the pleasure of homes without Liberty?"[33]

The cause for the Union was, consequently, not just a constitutional necessity and a patriotic duty; as many Northern ministers made clear, it was a sacred obligation that the loyal citizens must fulfill. William Parmenter, an Oberlin College student, explained to his mother why he volunteered to fight the rebels in these terms, also indicating that despite the Republican Party's professed limited political and constitutional aims, there were some Northerners who from the start were willing to fight a war to end slavery. "This is not a mere sentiment of patriotism, either," he wrote. "Christian people throughout the North have been praying for this time, and God has answered their prayers. The conflict is now between Liberty and Slavery, Christianity and Barbarism, God and the Prince of Darkness. There never was a time when Christians were so united in one common cause, and there never was a cause which received so many prayers from praying people. No man is worthy of the name Christian, who shrinks from any duty which the Lord places before him."[34] No wonder William T. Shepherd believed that Christians should feel comfortable becoming soldiers in such a cause; they would be joining the army with "the approbation of a Heavenly Father."[35]

After the firing on Fort Sumter, patriotism united people who had been divided only a day earlier. Now most Northerners hoped that their section could move beyond old-fashioned political partisanship. There was good reason for them to assume that a united people would stand up to the secessionists in the aftermath of Fort Sumter. Public displays of patriotism and unity spontaneously appeared throughout the Northern states. Ulysses S. Grant noted of his town of Galena, Illinois, "for a time there were no party distinctions; all were Union men, determined to avenge the insult to the national flag."[36] Back East the reaction was comparable. Horace Binney, a Philadelphia lawyer, explained that the news of Fort Sumter "started us all to our feet, as one man; all political division ceased among us from that very moment. . . . There is among us but one thought, one object, one end, one symbol,—the Stars and Stripes."[37]

It was one thing to leave the Union, and something quite different to fire on the national flag. The compromisers might once have discounted talk of a slave power conspiracy designed to undermine the liberties of white Northerners, but they now gave it credence. The mendacious slaveholding oligarchy had long contemplated secession, they concluded as they came to understand present events in light of the past sectional controversies.[38] The editor of the *Pittsburgh Post*, a paper that had supported Democrat Stephen Douglas during the 1860 election, made it clear to his readers that now was the time to maintain "the integrity of a great government." "Political partizanship [*sic*] must now cease to govern men on this issue," he declared. Hearing out the complaints of America's slaveholders was proper "*in* the Union." But once the South "becomes an enemy of the American system of governance . . . and fires upon the flag, which she, as well as we, are bound to protect, our influence goes for that flag, no matter whether a Republican or a Democrat holds it, and we will sustain any administration, no matter how distasteful its policy may be to us personally."[39]

Just below this noisy consensus, however, was a strain of dissent that would become more apparent as war talk turned into war making. In New Jersey, for example, Democrats gave notice that party differences had not disappeared; they supported war measures but fought with Republicans over how far the state should go in appropriating the funds needed to conduct the war. Suspicious of the Republicans and of the Lincoln administration, they were not yet ready to abdicate all rights to dissent. Yet in the end, most of them voted for Governor Charles S. Olden's request for two million dollars to deal with the emergency.[40] For the time being, there was no party when it came to supporting the larger effort to put down the rebellion.

During the spring of 1861, despite some indications to the contrary, there appeared to be more harmony than discord. The war's direction would soon give the parties ample reason to conduct their partisan business. In the meantime, enthusiasm for the cause of the Union could not help but lead to attempts to silence the remaining bold dissenters or to generate some violence against individuals who had previously expressed sympathetic views of the secessionists. In Philadelphia, immediately after the fall of Sumter, rowdy patriots attacked "well-known persons, who had openly expressed secession opinions" and threatened others of like mind. The mayor and police rescued from a mob a newspaper where "the editor had been foolish enough to hang out a [South Carolina] Palmetto flag." The crowd "then visited all the newspaper offices & insisted on their showing the American flag." Sidney Fisher reported that it was essential for Philadelphians who had expressed sympathy for secession now to drape their houses with national flags to convince the mob of their loyalty.[41]

Philadelphia was not the only place where patriots intimidated those individuals who disagreed with them. Near Centreville, Indiana, a committee called on one of their neighbors who had expressed his sympathy for South Carolina secessionists "to make an inquest as to his devotion to the Union"; so confronted, he professed his loyalty.[42] At a meeting in Manitowoc, Wisconsin, Democratic newspaper editor Jeremiah Crowley voiced a positive opinion about Jefferson Davis; the crowd shouted him down and within the day he was editorializing about the need to preserve the Union regardless of the cost.[43] A "vigilance committee" in Waupun, Wisconsin, issued a "Warning to Traitors" on April 21, threatening individuals who were dissuading men from volunteering; the committee warned that "the public expression of traitorous sentiments" could no longer be tolerated.[44]

On the East Coast, Democratic editors in New Jersey gave in to popular pressure, even if some did so begrudgingly, and expressed their support for the war.[45] Some of them, concerned about free speech, shared the sentiments of their colleagues in

Rockland, Maine. Before the end of April, the editor of the Rockland *Democrat and Free Press*, probably reacting to overly enthusiastic patriotic expressions in the community, was protesting that his community must respect free speech even as he vowed his support for the Union. Less than a month later, he accused Maine Republicans of trying to "put down freedom of speech, freedom of the press, and free opinion. . . . The papers have advised it; individuals have advised it, and mobs have threatened personal violence and destruction of property."[46] The issue of constitutional rights would be one that antiadministration Northerners would test as the conflict dragged on beyond the quick conclusion that Americans expected in the spring of 1861. In the wake of Fort Sumter, patriotic pronouncement notwithstanding, Sidney Fisher believed that Philadelphia Democrats still hated Lincoln and "will take advantage of any turn in affairs to create trouble."[47]

Fisher remained suspicious because, despite the optimism of many Northerners, there was no promise that political unity would remain the norm after the country went to war. In fact, for some, during the spring of 1861, uncertainty about the future prompted concerns that things would get worse before they turned for the better. Charles Peddle and probably many other Northerners worried how far the secession movement would go before it would end. He feared disloyalty in Missouri and Kentucky, believing that it was a foregone conclusion that Kentucky would secede. So, too, would Missouri, he assumed, an event that would bring about a civil war in St. Louis. Equally unsettling for many Northerners was the April 19 mobbing of U.S. soldiers of the Sixth Massachusetts by Southern sympathizers in Baltimore, something Peddle judged to be "a most dastardly thing." But fear, anger, and excitement produced action in Peddle's community. By April 21, Terre Haute had already "sent two companies, about 200 hundred men from this place" to stop the secessionists and raised home guard units to protect the region from those potential Confederates mustering along the state's borders.[48] The Lincoln administration would deal with the border state crisis, securing Kentucky, Missouri, and Maryland for the Union, although those states would experience different degrees of bloodshed and fratricide before the war ended.

TIME TO ANSWER THE SOUTHERN INSULT TO THE FLAG

The events of the spring of 1861 stirred new martial feelings in the breasts of people across the North that would lead men to turn away from the quiet of civilian life and accept the challenge of putting down the rebellion. As Augustus Ayling observed of his Lowell, Massachusetts, neighbors, "Everybody was ugly and ready to fight the rebels if only given a chance."[49] The firing on Fort Sumter had been an insult to the nation, the Constitution, and the flag, an insult that now required an answer.

Secession continued to mean chaos and anarchy, a destruction of the best govern-ment known to man. Consequently, the government relying on its patriotic citizens "must and will maintain its authority, even if it is necessary to make the rebel States a solitude."[50] Other editorialists fanned the fire of patriotism in their communities with similar warnings and stirring words that promised the Northern states would use all of their resources to vindicate national honor.[51] A Cleveland, Ohio, editorialist made clear the insult was grave and demanded a response. "Men of Ohio!" he proclaimed, "the Flag of our Country . . . has been torn down from its standard, and left to trail in the dust beneath the banner of rebellious host!" He then asked: "Shall it remain there? . . . Ohio must be in the van of the battle."[52] "Patriotic citizen!" demanded a Boston writer, "choose which side you will serve, the world's best hope, our noble Republican Government, or the bottomless pit, social anarchy."[53] Underlying the insult in the attack on Fort Sumter, the Democratic editorialist of the *Pittsburgh Post* continued, "The American flag—the flag of our Union—and the honored banner of a government which is bound to protect the interests of the whole country . . . has been fired into by American citizens, disloyal to the government of the country." Again, such an insult required a response. "No American of true heart and brave soul will stand this," he confirmed, "No American ought to stand it." Despite any sympa-thy a Northern Democrat might have had for Southern complaints, there was now no choice, he continued, because the insult to the flag had international ramifications as well as domestic ones: "we will sustain any administration, no matter how distaste-ful its policy may be to us personally, in proving to the world that the American eagle,—the proud bird of our banner—fears not to brave the wrath of foreign foes, or the mad rebellion of its own fostered children."[54]

Future soldiers understood that they would need to put aside the pleasures of home to address the crisis, and they immediately began to offer their services to their country. Maine resident Abner Small recalled that the shells fired on Fort Sumter "exploded under me" and propelled him into the army. He and his comrades unhesi-tatingly signed their enlistment papers. "Our minds were made up," he wrote, "we needed no persuading." They dropped everything to answer the call to duty. "George Benson left his anvil," Small noted, "Jim Ricker his plow, Frank Pullen his school books, Will Wyman his paint pot hanging to the ladder."[55] Those frontier Michi-gan farmers who learned of Fort Sumter from the horseback rider jumped from the threshing machine and rushed off to enlist even before the messenger had finished his announcement. Anna Howard Shaw, a young girl on the verge of womanhood at the time, recalled, "In ten minutes not a man was left in the field."[56]

Across the North, men and boys could recount similar stories about how the immediacy of the situation drew them from their old routines. One Vermonter "hurd [*sic*] of the surrender of Fort Sumpter [*sic*], dropped his work and the next day shouldered his knapsack and started for Charlestown," while a group of Middlebury

College students left their schoolbooks to join the army.[57] On April 21, William T. Shepherd described to his mother the emotions the crisis stirred in him that he had never before experienced. "Often when thinking of the great question of the day my heart jumps—sending a chill through my veins, inspiring my soul with courage to do anything in the cause of my country & liberty," he told her; "It seems as though I must do something to rescue my Native land from destruction and ruin."[58] The army would be "a Hard life," Shepherd expected, "but anything for my Native Land."[59]

African American Northerners were just as eager as their white neighbors to enter the fray. They met in their communities to proclaim their devotion to the nation and formed voluntary military companies or offered extant organizations to fight for the Union and more.[60] Cleveland, Ohio, African Americans made it known that they were "ready to go forth and do battle in the common cause of the country." The Hannibal Guards of Pittsburgh, Pennsylvania, did not hesitate to volunteer for duty in the state's militia. "[A]lthough deprived of our political rights," they petitioned, "we yet wish the government of the United States to be sustained against the tyranny of slavery."[61]

Black Northerners from across the region joined these Cleveland and Pittsburgh residents in expressing their desire to go to war to save the Union. However, the record of antebellum black abolitionism suggested that they understood very well the kind of Union they expected to save, even if they diplomatically avoided mentioning emancipation. From the outset of the war, the orator, editor, and abolitionist Frederick Douglass made it clear that he believed the conflict was about slavery, that the rebels "mean the perpetuity, and supremacy of slavery" to the point where, if successful, they would "place their iron yoke upon the necks of freemen."[62] Douglass also immediately understood the practical strength that the slaveholding rebels drew from their chattels, and he advocated emancipation as a tool of war from the outset of the fighting. If the government were to "cut off the connection between the fighting master and the working slave," it would "at once put an end to this rebellion."[63]

Black Northerners shared Douglass's view of the war as an antislavery war and believed that they could make a significant contribution to its successful conclusion if only the nation allowed them to fight. On April 27, George Lawrence, Jr., writing in New York City's *Weekly Anglo-African*, suggested that a band of 500 black guerrillas ranging through the Appalachians and along the coast could do more to destroy slavery than white troops ten times their number fighting traditional battles. "We want Nat Turner—not speeches," he wrote, "Denmark Vesey—not resolutions; John Brown—not meetings."[64] Even in the wake of the disastrous battle at Bull Run in Virginia in July 1861, black abolitionist James McCune Smith prescribed immediate emancipation as "The only salvation of this nation."[65]

At the outset of the war, most black Northerners tactfully avoided such incendiary language, but theirs would indeed be an antislavery war, especially if the nation allowed them to fight. In 1861, however, when white men took up arms, they did so expecting to fight a short, white man's war, with the sole purpose of restoring the nation's antebellum constitutional status quo. In Ohio, African Americans, who understood the political limitations placed on them by the state, came forward only to find white authorities opposed to their enlistment. Over a hundred black Wilberforce University students organized a company, but the governor turned them away.[66] Cities across the North had black militia groups ready to fight, but Lincoln's government was not yet ready to embrace their sacrifice, and local authorities had little desire to accept their black citizens as volunteers.[67] Even African American refugees living safe in Canada were willing to return to bear arms in the cause, but failed to secure places in the white volunteer army.[68] As a Cleveland, Ohio, police officer declared, blacks were to mind their own business because "this is a white man's war."[69] Confronted with that reality, most Northern blacks tempered their support for the conflict until emancipation became a declared goal.[70] In 1861, however, at least some of the spurned black men of Ohio pledged to remain committed to the Union cause.[71]

FOUR

RALLYING TO THE COLORS

STATE GOVERNMENTS BUILD AN ARMY

During the 1860 presidential campaign, the new Republican Party, far from relying on a strong centralized national organization, rose to victory on the enthusiasm generated by state contests and local politicians. With secession, President Lincoln faced the national crisis understanding that the Republican governors generally supported the use of force to end the rebellion. Local politicians in Republican-dominated legislatures also declared secession a traitorous attack on a just Constitution.[1] Such patriotic zeal was important, for when Lincoln responded to the firing on Fort Sumter with a call to arms, he needed these men and their states to answer. The one thing the administration clearly could not do at this time was to field an army of sufficient size to meet the challenge of secession without the help of the states.

At the outbreak of the war, the U.S. Army consisted of about 16,000 men. Congress was not in session, and the only legal authority Lincoln had was to call for volunteers to serve for 90 days to put down the rebellion.[2] Legislation would rectify that limitation in the near future, but Lincoln did not hesitate to do what needed to be done, expecting to go to Congress for confirmation of his actions as commander-in-chief. Before long, the national government became more closely involved in raising troops. In the meantime, the safety of the Union was in the hands of local communities that raised companies of men and state governments that organized them into new volunteer regiments.

Technically, the universal state militia system, the backbone of America's defense since its founding, should have been able to provide tens of thousands of men—all the men Lincoln believed he needed—to put down the rebellion. It was, however, a system generally rendered ineffectual by neglect. States expected voluntary companies, private groups that allowed men to drill and to socialize, to complement the statutory militia in times of crisis. Even the best of these units could find themselves generally unprepared for a hard, sustained fight with secessionists, but their existence could provide a core group around which other volunteers answered the call to arms and states formed new regiments.[3] Learning of Fort Sumter's fall, Charles Russell, a factory foreman in Derby, Connecticut, immediately led his volunteer company, the Derby Blues, into the army, contributing to the formation of the Second Connecticut Volunteer Infantry.[4] The men of the Winnacunnet Guards, a unit based in Hampton, New Hampshire, marched as a group into the First New Hampshire Volunteer Infantry.[5] New regiments from Ohio, New Jersey, and Pennsylvania also had volunteer companies as their backbones.[6]

State governments began to pay more attention to their militias when Southern states began to act on their threats to leave the Union, but the firing on Fort Sumter made military matters essential concerns in capitals across the North.[7] Throughout 1861, governors and their states were the primary engines in creating and supplying a force with which to confront the secessionists before a Washington bureaucracy began to deal with many of the usual problems of mobilizing and maintaining an army.[8] Governors such as Oliver P. Morton of Indiana and John A. Andrew of Massachusetts acted vigorously to answer Lincoln's call to arms. While some states were in more favorable financial positions for meeting the crisis, others found it necessary to rely on citizens to help outfit the men who would leave for the front.[9]

Men of means put their personal fortunes on the line to aid their states in defending the integrity of the nation. Sometimes the donations were idiosyncratic. For example, in Connecticut one patriotic family from the shipbuilding town of Mystic offered its yacht to the government for the duration of the war, while a man from Salisbury promised the government 100 tons of iron, just the thing for producing cannon balls. More immediately practical were the material pledges of local Connecticut businessmen, such as the shop owner in Middletown who gave every last stitch of underwear in his store to a local volunteer company or the Hartford tailors who cut cloth for uniforms without charge.[10]

Generally, however, wealthy patriots endorsed bank loans and pledged funds to outfit volunteers or to help the families of recruits who went off to war.[11] Bank officials raced to lend money to their beleaguered states. In Madison, Wisconsin, businessmen and community leaders even competed with one another in making pledges from their personal funds.[12] In the small New Jersey communities of Oxford Furnace and Belvidere, wealthy businessman John I. Blair gave a total of $700 to support volunteers and families.[13] On a somewhat larger scale, on April 16 Governor William Buckingham of Connecticut, his effectiveness restricted by an inadequate public treasury and unserviceable weapons, personally vouched for a $50,000 loan, which would allow him to arm his state's volunteers with modern rifles.[14] Across the Northern states, wealthy individuals also used their own resources to raise and equip military units.[15]

Bankers, businessmen, and community leaders were not exceptions, but the norm when it came to the people's patriotic response to the Southern insult to the national flag; they were simply doing with greater resources what citizens of lesser means were doing in communities of all sizes everywhere. After Sumter's fall, communities quickly gathered to hold meetings to raise money to support the war effort before the federal government began to muster resources of its own. In Morrisville, Vermont, residents at a "very spirited" town meeting passed resolutions "giving their wealth, strength and life if need be to the cause of freedom."[16] Other towns and cities did the same, gathering substantial sums with which to prepare their men for war and to care for the families they left behind. Chicagoans, for example, collected $30,000 with which to purchase equipment for volunteers.[17]

Smaller communities did the same as Chicago, also realizing that they should share the burden of caring for the families that their men left behind. The people of Springfield, Massachusetts, gathered at a town meeting that raised money to equip volunteers and assist their families.[18] Residents of Dover, New Hampshire, resolved to raise up to $10,000 to care for the families of volunteers.[19] Eventually, states with borrowed money and budgets in place developed more formal procurement systems. Their politicians generally directed lucrative contracts to businesses within their boundaries, sometimes mixing personal motives with the needs of the state and winning friends along the way.[20]

In the end, it would be Washington that would centralize the acquisition of the needed war materiel, creating a sizeable bureaucracy unknown before secession and one that would spend more than one billion dollars to supply the men in the victorious armies.[21] And, in the end, it would be Lincoln as the commander-in-chief, through the War Department, who would control volunteers for the terms of their enlistments in those armies.[22] When the dust settled by the summer, however, regimental organizations rallied by their governors continued to nurture the sense of pride that men held for their particular states. After a brief period of allowing men to elect their own officers, the states assumed the responsibility. Officers who led the regiments carried commissions signed by their state's governor.[23] Men mustered under state flags as well as the old national banner, and carried names into the larger army organizations that included their state of origin.[24] Building the volunteer army was federalism in action.

RECRUITING COMMUNITIES

Thousands of young men sought out places in militia regiments at their local armories, visited newly established recruiting offices, or wandered about the countryside hoping to find a place where they could sign up to fight the secessionists. Frequently, the first volunteers rose to the challenge at the end of the patriotic town meetings that were common across the North. On April 20 in Prairie Du Chien, Wisconsin, a Union meeting ended with the singing of the "Star Spangled Banner," "Three cheers . . . for the Stars and Stripes," and men adding their names to an enlistment roll.[25] The pattern repeated itself across the Northern states. In Jacksonville, Illinois, men sufficient to fill two military companies volunteered after its April assembly.[26] Throughout Minnesota, similar public meetings helped ambitious men who wished to become officers raise more companies of volunteers than the state could muster into service.[27]

As men came forward to fill the ranks of new companies of soldiers, it might have been difficult for the reluctant young neighbor or cousin or friend to resist the contagious community desire to answer the firing on Fort Sumter. Northerners could not escape the "military spirit" that Alfred Bellard, a young New Jersey apprentice, observed coming "to a boiling pitch" in the wake of Fort Sumter.[28] Indeed, in April James Madison Bowler joined a Minnesota company without first consulting with his future wife. "So many of my friends are going and the cause is so just," he explained, "that I cannot resist going with them and for the cause."[29]

The pattern of building an army town-by-town and state-by-state proceeded in similar ways across the North. Consequently, men and boys went into the service with friends, relatives, neighbors, and work associates. In doing so, they shaped their companies into martial expressions of the communities they were defending. In small communities, whether defined as a college, a factory, or a town, personal bonds encouraged friends and relatives to accompany one another into the service. On April 19, Augustus D. Ayling of Massachusetts reported that he was in a company that also was home to some of his "intimate friends" and "schoolmates."[30] Students from the state normal school in Bloomington filled the 33rd Illinois regiment, which became known as the "Teacher's Regiment."[31] Wisconsin's Manitowoc County Guards consisted of almost 100 men who had lived and worked together in a small community.[32] And at the outset of the war, Dixon, Illinois, farmers made up the 34th Illinois Infantry.[33]

There were other types of communities that sent groups of their men to war, communities that might have been rooted in geographical locations but also had other personal ties uniting the volunteers. Working men stuck together. A group of Terre

Haute, Indiana, railroad workers, for example, went off to fight, while Suffield in Hartford County, Connecticut, produced a company consisting of cigar makers.[34] Massachusetts shoemakers who had participated in an 1860 rally joined the Lynn Mechanic's Phalanx.[35] And Galena, Illinois, provided enough lead miners to form the 34th Illinois Infantry, aptly nicknamed the "Lead Mine Regiment."[36] Solidarity reigned among some of these groups, with Brooklyn Navy Yard workers pledging family assistance and Philadelphia printers promising to "keep all members . . . in good standing" while they were off fighting.[37]

Young men who had organized to support Lincoln's campaign for the presidency provided another antebellum group that could transfer its loyalties to army units. In 1860, these political activists, known as the Wide Awakes, had marched first through the streets of Hartford, Connecticut, wearing a uniform consisting of caps and capes and carrying torches. The organization, which enlisted men and organized them into military-style units, spread across the state and elsewhere in the North. Such organizations provided a committed core for the recruiting of volunteers in Connecticut in 1861.[38]

Germans also came to the new volunteer army in ready-made organizations prepared to fight for liberty in their adopted country. These volunteers earlier had participated in the Turnvereins, clubs that drilled young men in fitness activities as well as the handling of weapons. The Turners would give the Union cause 16 regiments.[39] The German gymnasts were an interesting example of a social and ethnic community contributing its men to the volunteer army, but other ethnic communities also contributed their men and boys to the Union cause. Irish militia companies in Chicago, for example, eventually brought their members into the 23rd Illinois Infantry, and other ethnic groups residing in that city joined common organizations.[40] Indeed, Illinois provided numerous examples of the ethnic organization of military units that might have given their German, Irish, and Scots members some comfort in familiar surroundings.[41] In the end, states quickly filled their quotas leaving some men wondering if they would miss out on the war and governors complaining that they should be allowed to do more for the Union.[42]

Despite such initial enthusiasm, there were men who were not so quick to leave behind their communities. Some young men felt that their familial and business obligations were legitimate reasons to stay put, at least for the time being. Politics, however, played a large role. Sometimes, entire volunteer companies whose members disagreed with the Lincoln administration's war refused to step forward. In Wisconsin some Democrats had political objections to Lincoln's call and refused to serve, again showing the underlying tensions that were easily overlooked in Northern communities during the spring of 1861. Some Wisconsin volunteer companies consisting of Irish and Germans also disbanded rather than be obligated to respond.[43]

Other communities, even as they raised troops for Lincoln, expected to keep men behind for the legitimate purpose of home defense, suggesting their localism, their trust in their own efforts, and their expectations of the federal government at least at the outset of the war. In April 1861 in Terre Haute, Indiana, the community planned on raising four companies, with two of them ready to go off to war while the remaining two companies would stay home "except in extraordinary cases." The people there expected "squally times along the Ohio River as Kentucky no doubt will go with the balance of slave states."[44] Farther west, Governor Thomas Carney advanced the state of Kansas $10,000 to muster about a company's worth of men to guard the state's border. Lincoln initially did not give him permission to raise more men for local defense, but the state did so later in the war when it feared invasion.[45]

WOMEN AND THE INITIAL RUSH TO WAR

Some wives and girlfriends cautiously urged their menfolk to calm down, to wait and see how things would develop, and, in the meantime, to tend to their own lives. In April 1861, Illinois resident Lizzie Little wrote to her fiancé George Avery, urging him to delay enlisting. "Let some battles be fought, see the power you have to contend with, for I believe it is a fierce one," she advised with some prescience. "The South will not be conquered in a day as some here vauntingly boast but in the end we may hope may we not for complete victory." From her perspective, she offered practical advice. After all, the country would need intelligent men to reconstruct the Union once the war was over, she argued. Wait until "the loafers of our cities, the scum of society show their valor ere the working efficient men take the field."[46]

Voices such as Miss Little's, however, could not withstand the drumbeats and speeches that rallied communities to war. Women could indeed be as patriotic as their menfolk, especially when they offered their sons and husbands to the war effort. In April 1861, Vermonter Ann Stevens witnessed an acquaintance—"a noble woman" she called her—"with red eyes" proclaim that "she will give up her husband for her country."[47] In Boston, a mother watched the Sixth Massachusetts leave for war, her son in its ranks. She remarked, "If the country needs my boy for three months, or three years, I am not the woman to hinder him . . . for if we lose our country what is there to live for?"[48] In the end, women performed a great service by accepting the inevitability of their menfolk's new military commitments, while taking comfort in cultivating a trust in God.[49] When one Wisconsin woman witnessed her husband sign his papers, she said to him, "God bless and protect you, my husband." But another Wisconsin woman whose husband had joined the army exhibited another motivation for men to sign their recruitment papers; she made it clear that her spouse would live an unhappy existence if he had not rallied to the cause. "I would almost despise my husband and would think him a sneak," she said, "if he hadn't gone."[50]

Politicians and editorialists reminded women that they, too, had a stake in the outcome of the conflict and certainly had work to do. Wisconsin women heard Governor William A. Randall ask them to make bandages. "It is your country and your government as well as theirs [the men going off to fight] that is now in danger, and you can give strength and courage and warm sympathies and cheering words to those who go to do battle for all that is dear to us here." Randall, of course, was relying on women to accept their traditional roles of nurturer and nurse. "I commend the soldiers to your kindness, encouragement and prayers" Randall continued, "with full confidence that when occasion calls, many, very many Florence Nightingales will be found in our good land."[51]

Elsewhere, men might note that women could have a significant impact on the morale of the soldiers they sent off to war and needed to show a positive attitude, even if saddened by the forthcoming separation. An editorialist in Troy, New York, remarked, "A woman's gentle encouragement, and high-souled abnegation of herself, can exercise more influence in determining the conduct of a true man, than any other thing on earth." Women will make men better soldiers by giving them their emotional support. "There is not a soldier [that] will enter the field of battle with firmer step and more invincible will," the writer continued, "if the voice of the woman he loves best has cheered him in his departure and he knows she waits to hear that he has done well his part."[52] Indeed, young women in Wisconsin and probably elsewhere across the Northern states were not above cajoling, coaxing, or embarrassing young men into enlisting while they also enthusiastically participated in the local rallies that usually preceded the call to volunteer for service.[53]

While women could not participate in the rush to volunteer, they did what they could to aid their menfolk. When Cleveland, Ohio, women discovered that men at a local camp were without blankets, they promptly collected the necessary items by driving carriages up and down the city's streets alerting people to their purpose; they continued to do so until they had a sufficient quantity to meet the needs of the camp. At the same time, another group of Cleveland women sewed a thousand shirts for volunteers over two days of intense work.[54] Middle-class women in Dubuque, Iowa, took it upon themselves to organize as the Ladies Volunteer Labor Society and sewed uniforms for two companies of soldiers.[55] The women of Winona, Minnesota, provided their local company with what turned out to be the only outfits that came close to marking them as a military unit among all the other volunteers in the First Minnesota.[56] On a Sabbath day back east in Hartford, Connecticut, "A great many ladies served God . . . by serving their country, in making uniforms for its gallant defenders."[57]

Clothing soldiers was but one way that women contributed to the initial rush to arms during the spring of 1861. Nursing sick recruits and feeding their healthier comrades at the various rendezvous camps were other ways of using the skills of homemakers to fight the insurrection. Jacksonville, Illinois, women sewed and baked for the new soldiers at Camp Duncan, first coming together in church groups that developed into more formal voluntary associations.[58] Women from Keokuk, Iowa, brought cakes to soldiers at the training camp, enjoying the break in their own daily routines by witnessing the drills, a practice that wives, daughters, and curious women would continue across the North throughout the war.[59] And when time permitted, women, such as those in Madison, Wisconsin, produced grand banquets for their men before they left for battle.[60] These women could rise to the challenge not only because they had the valuable skills of homemakers, but because they had developed organizations ranging from sewing circles to temperance groups that had allowed them to rally for quick collective action.[61]

FLAG PRESENTATIONS

One of the last things that the women of a community frequently did before their men left for war was to join prominent men in public ceremonies that included the presentation of the flags they had made or procured for the regiments. In 1861, the Second Connecticut received its colors at New Haven. The local Home Guard formed a hollow square before the liberty pole on the town green "enclosing all the ladies who had worked on or were interested in the flags." "Two pretty girls held the flags, assisted by two gentlemen. Mr. Foster made a short and spirited address to the regiment, and their Colonel replied in a few brave words, and then Dr. Leonard Bacon read the twentieth Psalm, 'in the name of our God we will set up our banners,' etc., and made a beautiful prayer, and amid the shouts and cheers of the crowd, the frantic waving of handkerchiefs and flags and the quiet weeping of some who were sending off their dearest ones to all the chances of war, the glittering waving splendors were lifted aloft and the regiment swept on."[62] Regimental flags, blessed by the touch of local women, became powerful symbols of the soldiers' communities and families, reminders of home and reminders of their reasons for leaving it behind.[63]

Flag presentations and farewell ceremonies, perhaps including a last banquet for the soldiers and their friends, could not pass without additional speeches by local politicians and prayers offered by local clergy, reminding citizens and soldiers alike about the reasons for the events they were now witnessing. But eventually, the boys and men of the communities had to leave for the front. Minnesota volunteers left Goodhue County encouraged by the Red Wing brass band.[64] People cheered on the men of the First Michigan Engineers as their train carried them through Michigan and Indiana.[65] Catholic soldiers might have found some additional comfort in the presence of their clergymen involved in the departure ceremonies. In 1861, Irish Chicagoans sent off its Irish Brigade with a mass celebrated by the local bishop, while New York City's Irish Brigade's flag presentation ceremony had several high-ranking churchmen in attendance.[66]

FAREWELL

The women left behind grasped the first reality of war as they watched their menfolk depart from home. As activist Mary Livermore later recalled, they faced it with a heroic demeanor as they tried to mask their own "exquisite suffering."[67] They were losing the company of husbands, brothers, and sons for what might have been the first time in their lives. Women also readily grasped the seriousness of the situation, some perhaps better than the soldier boys they were sending off to war. When one Maine regiment left the state capital of Augusta in early June, they briskly trotted off to the train cars to the sounds of "sobbing mothers, wives, and dear ones."[68] At Jersey City, New Jersey, women at the station "were crying and wringing their hands," while the boys who were setting off to war went to the trains as if they were engaged in a frolic.[69]

Women wept as they said their good-byes, but they attempted to assuage their sorrow by selflessly grasping the larger needs of their country. In April 1861, Ohioan Amanda Wilson fretted about her brother George, encamped and awaiting orders to move to the seat of the war. "Yet," she admitted, "we would not love him if he were not willing to fight for our Country."[70] And as Esther Claflin reassured her husband Gilbert after he left for the army in the fall of 1862, "if by making this great sacrifice we can help the cause of truth and liberty is it not better than living merely for ourselves?"[71]

These were sad times for the home folk, and as waves of enlistment continued to deprive them of family members throughout the war, a new group of women came to understand what their counterparts had experienced in the first rush to arms. In September 1862, Rachel Cormany confided in her diary that when she learned of her husband's enlistment, "I felt an undescribable [*sic*] heaviness in my heart."[72] She became calmer after praying, but "at times still I am overcome, tears relieve me very much, my heart always seems lighter after weeping freely[.] In daytime I get along very well but the nights seem very long."[73]

Rachel Cormany was not alone in her sadness as other women throughout the war knew that they had to adjust to the novel circumstances, whether it was their husbands or sons who left them at home to worry about the future. In May 1861 Lizzie Caleff informed her future husband Madison that thinking about their separation "sends a thrill of sorrow through my heart that is not very easy subdued." After sending off her husband in the spring of 1861, Iowan Emeline Ritner admitted that she "felt as if I had been to a funeral"; nevertheless, "I must train myself, and get used to it."[74] Indeed, a Vermont wife well understood the potential sacrifice that she faced as her husband left for the war. That woman "with red eyes" said "she will give her husband up for her country."[75]

FIVE

SOLDIERS AND CIVILIANS
AS NEIGHBORS

CHANGING SCENERY: MILITARY ENCAMPMENTS

In July 1861, Englishman William Howard Russell returned to New York City after an absence of some months and immediately noticed the "changed aspects of the streets." "Instead of peaceful citizens, men in military uniforms thronged the pathways, and such multitudes of United States flags floated from the windows and roofs of the houses as to convey the impression that it was a great holiday festival." Before the outbreak of the war, he had seen men in uniform walking about the city, but "they disappeared after St. Patrick had been duly honored, and it was very rarely I ever saw a man in soldier's clothes during the rest of my stay. Now fully a third of the people carried arms, and were dressed in some kind of martial garb." Recruiting posters were everywhere as were tailors specializing in military uniforms. Martial engravings filled shop windows. Children walked the streets dressed by parents in the uniforms of French North African Zouaves. And shopkeepers were peddling all sorts of military equipment, no doubt well aware of the increase in the number of soldiers passing their storefronts.[1] Businessman Emile Dupré agreed that before the end of April 1861, New York "look[ed] like an army camp." "There are armed men everywhere," he informed his parents, "everyone carries a revolver, and we're living in an absolute torrent of emotion." The only items people wish to buy, he lamented, were guns.[2]

The onset of the war had quickly changed the way people experienced New York City. Those changes, however, were not unique to that great metropolis as towns and cities across the North witnessed some degree of the same thing. Public spaces from the center to the outskirts of Northern communities especially took on the aspects of a militaristic society. Rallies and flag raisings in town squares and elsewhere in the aftermath of Fort Sumter's surrender turned public spaces into arenas of patriotism. The gathering of volunteers continued to keep them as such. The first wave of volunteers used their towns' open areas first for drilling and then for mustering prior to their transfers to larger encampments.[3] Madison, Wisconsin, had just committed the proceeds from a new tax to refurbish its fair grounds, only to have the area become the site of Camp Randall; sheds once used for livestock became housing for new recruits.[4] The people of Chambersburg, Pennsylvania, watched new recruits take over public and private spaces and a military encampment pop up where there had been none, giving them the opportunity to observe the process of men becoming soldiers.[5]

Mobilization changed the local landscapes as men joined military companies, as military companies consolidated into larger units, and as places once used for peaceful pursuits accommodated the processes. As the war progressed, recruiting demanded more effort than it had during the spring of 1861 and later in 1863 a federal draft prompted enlisting among those eligible men who had previously hesitated. Consequently, good order required officers situated at convenient places to facilitate and to encourage enlistments as well as to teach the fresh soldiers their new trade.

At the beginning of the war, militia armories were the logical places for enrolling volunteers. In 1861 men joined companies at these buildings in Lowell, Massachusetts, Providence, Rhode Island, and elsewhere.[6] New recruiting offices also materialized in urban Philadelphia and Dubuque, Iowa, and in villages such as Rockland, Maine, and North Adams, Massachusetts.[7] Similar offices ran the length and breadth of New Jersey.[8] Even the small state of New Hampshire had at one time 28 recruiting offices.[9]

After the Union disaster at Bull Run in July 1861, a second round of recruiting required a continued military presence in communities that had rarely seen soldiers on their streets before the spring of 1861. Josiah Favill, a recruit turned recruiter, noted that during the summer of 1861 the cities of "New York and Brooklyn were transformed into immense recruiting camps." Indeed, "In all the public squares and parks," he explained, "hundreds of tents were erected, covered with flags and immense colored bills, on which the advantage of various branches of the service were fully stated."[10] By the late summer of 1861, there were over 50 recruiting offices in the New York City area, including Brooklyn and nearby New Jersey cities.[11]

Buildings once used for peaceful purposes deferred to the needs of war by becoming recruiting centers. In Chicago, the North Side Turner Hall, a place that German immigrants used for drill, gymnastics, and intellectual development, became the point of recruiting two companies of new soldiers. Cincinnati's Workingman's Hall also produced several companies for an Ohio German regiment, while in Indianapolis, Union Hall served as a gathering point for volunteers for an all-German Indiana regiment. During the fall of 1862, Turner Hall in Milwaukee remained a focal point of German enthusiasm for the Union, serving as the drill hall for noncommissioned officers. Over 100 Turnvereins spread across the North in 1861 undoubtedly provided a similar familiar military starting point for the new German volunteers.[12]

Thus, public and private property gave way to the needs of war as men mustered for the conflict. New soldiers spilled over into whatever appropriate spaces they could find while they waited to take on the rebels. The great demands of the new volunteer army required that less conventional structures and spaces be pressed into military service for the time being. Some New York soldiers gathered in a Manhattan iron works until they moved up the Hudson River to a flourmill in Yonkers.[13] Connecticut volunteers eventually established a camp in a New Haven park, but first slept in Yale University's Alumni Hall. Other Connecticut volunteers spent the winter months of 1861 and 1862 in a dilapidated New Haven carriage factory.[14]

State capitals as well as other towns and cities conveniently located along good transportation routes became particular and logical gathering points for the new volunteer regiments. Before heading to the front, Maine volunteers camped in a "grove like park" on the "beautiful slopes between the State House and the river" in Augusta, Maine, close to the state buildings.[15] As the people of Maine's capital city understood, the war demanded new purposes not just for vacant lots but for public parks as well. Not far above New York, the war transformed park-like Davids Island in the East River, a seasonal recreational destination for urbanites, into a military rendezvous in the fall of 1861.[16]

New York City, a major transportation hub that witnessed the movement of hundreds of thousands of soldiers through its rail and ship depots, constructed a large building in the park in front of City Hall with a capacity to shelter 2,000 men.[17] The city's parks continued to do great service, with the encampment by City Hall housing 70,000 men during the first year of the war. In 1863 officials closed that location, shifting soldiers to the more convenient waterfront battery, but during the summer of 1864 parks still provided resting places for some of the 40,000 soldiers who stopped in New York on their way to the war.[18] In the midst of all of this martial activity, the board governing Central Park refused to allow musters in that green space of tranquility, even at one point having sheep make use of meadow space in hopes of discouraging an army presence. By the spring of 1864, however, regiments moved onto park property to practice the military arts.[19]

Along with vacant lots, parks, and fairgrounds, recruits transformed farmland near towns into army camps. Civilians watched as soldiers erected shelter in empty fields on private property, as they did at Camp Diven near Courtland, New York, and Camp Knox outside of Rockland, Maine.[20] Turning fields into military camps was a practice that would continue throughout the war. In 1862, for example, a renewed emphasis on raising troops resulted in even more new camps rising up out of empty fields. In August and September, companies of the Third Massachusetts Volunteer Militia, which had previously served for 90 days, gathered at Camp Joe Hooker at Lakeville to return to the fray as a nine-month unit.[21] Earlier in July, Camp Vredenburgh appeared on the Revolutionary War battlefield of Monmouth, near Freehold, New Jersey, no doubt reminding the new soldiers tenting there of their forefathers' struggles to forge the Republic now threatened by the rebellion.[22]

The new military camps quickly absorbed the recruits and just as quickly prepared them in a fashion for war. A number of these sites became permanent fixtures as the need for mustering and training camps continued longer than Northerners had initially expected. Cleveland, Ohio, hosted seven military camps, including Camp Cleveland, which became a temporary home to around 15,000 soldiers who trained on its 35 acres during the war.[23] Camp Randall, established on fairgrounds near Madison, served about 70,000 Wisconsin recruits over the course of the war.[24]

CHANGING SCENERY: HOSPITALS

Just as military camps took over open spaces and buildings once used for civilian purposes, so too did hospitals as communities coped with the more sobering return of injured troops. At the beginning of war, necessity led to the conversion of buildings not especially suited to the medical requirements. Private mansions, hotels, factory buildings, schools, and town halls all became refuges for the men who not too long ago had assembled and trained on other grounds formerly devoted to civilian purpose.[25] In larger cities such as Philadelphia, private hospitals became military hospitals even as patriotic citizens established new facilities in advance of the federal government's efforts to establish a network of purpose-built hospitals.[26]

As the war continued into 1862, Northerners such as Cordelia Harvey became aware of the inadequacies of army hospitals planted closer to the battlefront and argued that soldiers would best recover in the more salubrious and familiar climate of their home region.[27] Also, by 1862, the institutional inadequacies of makeshift hospitals became apparent, convincing the War Department to develop a system of larger general military hospitals in the rear where men might recuperate in more peaceful surroundings.[28] Converted buildings, however, remained in use in communities, reminding civilians of how the necessities of war could supersede the purposes assigned to property in peacetime.[29] The roofless Estes House in Keokuk, at the southeastern tip of Iowa, was still under construction when it became a point of recovery for many wounded soldiers; it grew into a larger military hospital.[30]

In Germantown, Pennsylvania, outside of Philadelphia, the hospital established in the town hall outgrew the original facility to become the Cuyler Army Hospital.[31] Madison, Wisconsin's octagonal Farwell Mansion, built before the war and standing abandoned at its commencement, became an army hospital in October 1863; it also would expand into a larger military hospital.[32]

The need for hospital space even encroached on a few Northern recreational facilities. Indeed, the very locations that made them attractive resorts might have convinced the authorities of their suitability for a new wartime purpose. The army leased Rhode Island's Portsmouth Grove Estate, a resort on Narragansett Bay, in the spring of 1862, with its hotel facilities initially supplemented with tents spreading over the nearby grounds.[33] Eventually, the federal government took over open space as needed to augment a new system of purpose-built military general hospitals, producing efficient facilities such as West Philadelphia's large Satterlee Hospital, "twelve acres of ground" therapeutically "removed far enough from the tumult of the crowded parts of the city" that could house 3,500 men.[34] By the end of the war, the federal government had developed a network of 204 army hospitals across the North with the ability to hold 136,894 soldiers, bringing the war into places that had not previously seen such human destruction.[35]

GOOD NEIGHBORS

Large and small military encampments gave civilians opportunities to see how their boys adjusted to military life in the rapidly growing volunteer army. Men and women visited nearby camps to spend some time with family members before they left the area, to provide the men with small comforts, and to satisfy their own curiosity about military life. Military encampments thus provided civilians with opportunities to put into action their feelings of patriotism by looking after new soldiers, be they their boys or someone else's husbands, brothers, and sons. But patriotism could also be fun, as military camps provided some diversion to the normal routines of life. Throughout the war, civilians found it entertaining to watch soldiers engage in drill, while the recruits happily showed off for the young women in the crowds. People living near military camps also had opportunities to attend free concerts performed by military bands, and they enjoyed the added excitement that military units gave to their local celebrations.[36]

As soldiers welcomed civilians into their social lives, the civilians responded in kind. In June 1864, men from Camp Burnside in Indiana swelled the ranks of the attendees at a Sunday school picnic, making a good impression on the civilians.[37] James Randall recalled well-behaved boys marching in disciplined groups to one Midwestern town to attend Sunday services. Randall had especially fond memories of how the Universalist Church welcomed the soldiers, hardly distinguishing the religious occasion from a patriotic meeting. "When we reached the church its doors would be thrown open, and we marched up the aisle to the music of fife and drum," Randall noted, "to which the minister in the pulpit beat time, while ushers and others made way for us to the most desirable seats."[38]

While there was much to enjoy during camp visits, civilians also at times were shocked by the conditions that their soldiers had to endure while the army, the states, and the nation learned how to organize such large numbers of men. A visitor to Camp Curtin in May 1861 reported that "it was a most shocking scene of filth, discomfort and disorder," and that the men were not adequately fed, leading to "dissatisfied & demoralized" recruits.[39] Such first-hand observations, along with newspaper reports and complaints from soldiers, spurred citizens to do something to ease the problems of their men and boys. Concerns prompted by the inadequate food at Camp Curtin led the people of Berks County, Pennsylvania, to donate supplies to the soldiers stationed there.[40] Connecticut newspapers also spread the word about the ill-treatment of soldiers. Citizens protested and demanded action from their lawmakers, which led to investigations of the governor's conduct of the war.[41]

Sooner or later the soldiers needed to leave their encampments and face new discomforts without the relief provided by nearby civilians. It was usually word of the imminent departure of soldiers that drew out the largest crowds of family and friends who participated in one last celebration to show solidarity with the men, to buck up their spirits, and simply to wish their loved ones farewell. Camps became especially crowded, noisy, and festive immediately before men left for war as families and friends came to say their good-byes. At Augusta, Maine, in 1861 Colonel Oliver Otis Howard met his new regiment amidst the chaos of their encampment where parents, wives, sweethearts, and some drunken soldiers gave a carnival atmosphere to the site as their men prepared to leave the state.[42] Over on the coast at Camp Knox near Rockland, Maine, crowds of civilians gathered to visit the men of the Fourth Maine Volunteer Infantry Regiment before they broke camp. "The camp grounds were thronged with thousands of the people of this and surrounding towns during the morning," a local paper reported. "Many were light hearted and gay, enjoying the beautiful morning and the varying scene before them; but many were sad and weeping, and the bright day was to them, doubtless, one of the saddest which had ever dawned."[43]

During the early days of the war, citizens continued to show their appreciation to the volunteers by feeding them as they moved closer to the battlefields of the war. Along the routes regiments traveled, people turned out with refreshment for friends and strangers passing through their communities. People graciously tended to the bellies of the First New Hampshire as the regiment proceeded to the front.[44] Hartford, Connecticut, butchers and their customers donated a variety of meats, fruits, and vegetables to feed soldiers who would be passing through the city on

Christmas day 1861.[45] Also, grateful citizens frequently paid similar attention to their soldiers upon their return during the war. When the 49th Massachusetts returned to Pittsfield at the end of the summer of 1863, the citizens adorned their streets with flags, constructed arches, and met the soldiers with bands, fire companies, and other local organizations and prepared a feast for the soldiers.[46] In 1864, Milwaukee's residents happily fed men who had reenlisted in the Sixth Wisconsin. More importantly, the city's women formed the Wisconsin Soldiers' Home Association, which established a soldier's home that tended to the needs of over 30,000 hungry, wounded, and ill returning veterans who stopped in the city on their way to their homes.[47]

The enthusiastic send-offs were exciting and the presence of returning soldiers sobering, but in between those events, the home folks thought of the absent men, and not just their own family members. "Our soldiers walk just as naturally into our warm living remembrance, into our prayers, as they would walk into the door of their own homes if they were able," wrote Ohioan Eliza Otis in July 1862 while her husband was away in the service. "I don't see how any really intelligent, loyal heart can forget them, and I don't believe they do." The very fact that a man was a soldier, she continued, "is the key that unlocks all our sympathies, which awakens all our gratitude, and makes [us] remember those whom we have scarcely met as if they had grown up with us by our father's hearth stone."[48]

BAD NEIGHBORS

Military facilities, despite their beneficial impact on some communities, were mixed blessings and provided numerous examples of how soldiers could be problematic neighbors. At Elmira, New York, the boom times created by the military presence there also strained the local postal facilities with so many soldiers, Union recruits, and Confederate prisoners adding their thousands of letters to the mails.[49] The people of Elmira, however, suffered more from the lax discipline of the soldiers who sojourned in their town and on one occasion in 1864 had drunken Michigan cavalry troopers rampaging through the streets.[50] Throughout the war, farmers had to deal with soldiers who stole chickens and fruit or cut down trees on their land for fuel; city dwellers had to cope with men in blue who generally made a nuisance of themselves in their businesses and on their streets. But soldiers were not responsible for initiating all riotous behavior, although when provoked many of their number failed to exercise restraint. In New Haven, Connecticut, soldiers killed a bricklayer who had insulted the wife of one of their number by calling her a whore.[51]

While mothers and sweethearts might call to mind their heroes at the front when they saw blue uniforms, they also witnessed good examples of the kind of bad behavior that confirmed their fears about the negative influence of soldiering on the moral lives of their men. Civilians were especially concerned because they assumed that good men made good soldiers and bad men made bad soldiers, with the latter being incapable of seeing the battle through to victory. Northerners had yet to develop the notion that ill-mannered professional warriors could still fight well and win wars.[52] Now they confronted examples of the fact that not all soldiers were paragons of virtue, even if the war they fought was a virtuous one. This realization troubled them and continued to make them anxious down to the time their soldiers returned from the war during the spring, summer, and fall of 1865.

When soldiers congregated in towns, they looked for liquor, which often made them rowdy and turned them into lascivious creatures. Such a combination of vices caused problems in the communities where these men were stationed. Camp Wood at Fond Du Lac housed some soldiers who were "as wild as bucks, would get drunk occasionally and then would fight at the drop of the hat." On one occasion, the soldiers, "gloriously drunk," wrecked two saloons and ruined other property. A disagreement with some antiwar Democrats—Copperheads as loyal Union men called them—prompted the rampage. "Luckily no one was killed," recalled James Randall, "but the copperheads were driven from town effectively as snakes if the like named were driven from Ireland by St. Patrick." A group of sober soldiers quelled the riot, and the drunken men "got to bed to sleep off their booze." Even the perpetrators admitted "that the whole affair was extremely disgraceful."[53] At times, soldiers, sober or otherwise, were just being patriotic after their own fashion. On March 5, 1863, soldiers from Camp Chase at Columbus, Ohio, joined a mob that destroyed the offices of *Crisis*, a Democratic newspaper. Brigadier General James Copper chastised the soldiers, reminding them that their duty was "to uphold the laws, not violate them." Forgetting your duties as soldiers," he scolded them, "you have become rioters and burglars; and instead of being, as you ought to be, the protectors of the rights of citizens, you have become their assailants." The general warned the men against such future violations of the citizens' "sacred" rights in their "persons and property," but the men went unpunished. The journal, published by the antiwar Lincoln critic Samuel Medary, resumed its activities.[54]

In April 1864, a mob of soldiers ranging upward to 200 in number and many of them drunk rescued an inebriated veteran who the Hartford, Connecticut, police had jailed for fighting. One local reported that the men were "mad with liquor" and uncontrollable, consequently "they had matters their own way."[55] During the summer of 1864, soldiers kept Springfield, Illinois's forces of order busy with their drunken larks, while in Milwaukee, Wisconsin, police required assistance from the army to maintain order.[56] Indeed, the drunkenness that was common among soldiers contributed to the violence that disrupted communities and kept provost guards well employed. In October 1863, in Chambersburg, Pennsylvania, the provost marshal arrested three soldiers "who were found in the Street, near midnight, intoxicated and engaged in riotous conduct, making indiscriminate attacks upon all who passed by."[57] Earlier in the war, Keokuk, Iowa, witnessed an outburst of violence when a proprietor of a saloon attempted to remove some troublesome soldiers. As the local paper reported, there were some soldiers in the town "who are, we are very sorry to say, making themselves very offensive to our citizens." That was reason enough to justify organizing a committee to help keep the peace, but soldiers were not always responsible for striking the spark that caused tension between town and camp to erupt into violence.[58] In November 1862, drunken Keokuk firemen threw rocks at the Estes House, a hotel where convalescent soldiers were quartered. Men poured out of the building to answer the insult and, reinforced by other soldiers in the town, they routed the firemen and citizens who had joined in the brawl.[59]

Liquor and sexual misbehavior appeared to go hand in hand. Milwaukee, Wisconsin, experienced an apparent increase in the activities of brazen prostitutes who found the expanding numbers of "dissipated soldiers" to be good customers.[60] Also, when Jacksonville, Illinois, began hosting new recruits at the county fairgrounds, its less respectable establishments saw their business grow. In turn, the city government increased the police department's authority to deal with the problems caused by drunkenness and prostitution. Despite this diligence on the part of Jacksonville's leaders, one popular local brothel favored by soldiers continued to be the point of origin of frequent fights until it closed near the end of war.[61]

In some communities, problems caused by soldiers worsened as the war continued and less savory characters enlisted to take the bounties offered to enlistees or the fees paid to men who would stand as substitutes for draftees. Desertion became a problem among these soldiers, who once on the run committed crimes against person and property. In early 1865 in Connecticut, for example, authorities caught a group of deserters in possession of stolen property and burglar's tools.[62] Deserters disrupted the peace and quiet of places like Sandusky, Ohio, a railroad depot town, and were problematic in some counties in the Midwest where they banded together to avoid capture.[63] No wonder the editor of the *Indianapolis Daily Journal* made sure to publicize the execution at a nearby camp in December 1864 to warn other potential deserters and bounty jumpers of the fate that was awaiting them.[64]

Other communities increased their police forces to deal with the problem. During the summer of 1863, the town fathers of coastal Belfast, Maine, established a town coast guard not only to provide some protection in case of Confederate raids, but also to quell disturbances caused by soldiers passing through town. The town watch's authority expired in November, but necessity prompted its reestablishment during the winter of 1864 and 1865.[65] Jacksonville, Illinois, civic leaders also responded to problems related to the war by increasing the pay of its law enforcement officers, hiring additional men for its police, and arming its force with large truncheons, which were, according to a local newspaper editor, "about the size of a rolling pin, of hard wood, and heavy enough to fell an ox."[66]

Six

INCOMPLETE FAMILIES

SOLDIERS' WIVES AND GOVERNMENT AID

Military service spread through the class structure of the North, but the majority of families who had to deal with absent menfolk were of the middling sort or the working class. In part, this was simply because there were more men available from such families to fill the ranks.[1] The pay sent home by these soldiers was critical for many of their families; therefore, it became important to make sure that money reached the home folk. The United States Sanitary Commission, the umbrella organization founded to coordinate relief efforts for soldiers in the hospital and the field, pushed for a remittance system by which men could set aside portions of their pay for their families.[2] After July 22, 1861, Congress provided for soldiers to sign documents when receiving their pay that allowed the men to forward to their families a certain amount of their pay, with trustees moving funds through state treasurers and county clerks to the soldiers' dependents.[3]

It was a system not universally employed, in part because Secretary of War Simon Cameron, who had a problematic relationship with the Sanitary Commission, did not wish it so.[4] Consequently, soldiers continued to use the post office and express companies. They also continued to take advantage of informal networks, entrusting money to friends going home on furlough or to officers and chaplains, who either journeyed home with their funds if on leave or were capable of forwarding money through express offices. Connecticut Chaplain Joseph Hopkins Twichell, for example, acted as a northward conduit for soldiers' pay, on occasion traveling home with the money or to Washington, D.C., where he sometimes forwarded thousands of dollars through an express company.[5] Public-minded citizens beyond the trustees associated with the Sanitary Commission also stepped in to help, receiving and distributing funds to soldiers' families in their communities.[6]

As the war progressed, bounties, additional financial incentives offered to encourage enlisting, as well as relief funds created by communities and states, reassured men that they would be able to leave their families in some degree of financial security.[7] These incentives might very well have been the last reassurance married men needed to go off to war.[8] In 1861, in Rockland, Maine, some men at first hesitated to join the army because of their family responsibilities, but were then able to do so with clear consciences knowing the town would help their loved ones through hard times in their absence.[9]

At some point during the war, because of delayed issuance of army pay, irresponsible husbands, financial crises, or bad luck, some families found themselves in need of assistance. Soldiers' wives in such circumstances might have considered any aid they received not to be charity, but an expression of gratitude or even an obligation of their communities.[10] Officials, however, might have had different, sterner views, usually distributing their aid funds in ways similar to antebellum relief measures.[11] Restrictions designed to make certain the relief money went only to the most needy soldiers' families limited the usefulness of the pledges by community leaders to care for soldiers' families while requiring women to embarrass themselves by admitting to being paupers.[12]

Applications for aid frequently required burdensome paperwork as well as a public admission of poverty. Soldiers' wives in Brockport, New York, received assistance from the town, but the Board of Relief there required supplicants to file a new application with appropriate affidavits every month.[13] Also, some soldiers' wives suffered for their community's prejudices. In the Appleton, Wisconsin, area, there were "severe cases of suffering . . . by families of volunteers"; an editorialist feared that the lack of assistance for certain soldiers' families might be "on account of class or nationality." If that were so, he exclaimed, "then, in the name of humanity, how can we expect poor men to fight for our national government?"[14]

Regardless of tight-fisted restrictions, promises made during the optimistic patriotism of 1861 fell before the reality of a long war that drained everyone's financial reserves.[15] Neighborly assistance could help, and many rural women combined their households to weather their wartime poverty. When so many women faced similar difficulties, their numbers strained even those informal relief networks.[16] Families also helped, with many a young wife moving in with their husband's or her own parents' household. Husbands might have preferred that their wives reside with their in-laws, an arrangement often considered by the men as a means by which they could not only economize but also keep alive their own familial authority through their parents. Wives could find such living arrangements financially convenient but less than ideal, as they could create forced familial intimacy wrought with tension, bickering, and emotional discomfort.[17]

Political differences made matters worse, as Iowan Mary Vermilion discovered when she took up residence with her soldier husband's parents in Indiana. Mary hated disloyal Democrats and claimed to be an abolitionist. Yet William's parents were not squarely behind the Northern war effort. Consequently, Mary admitted, "Our ways and views of life are so different from theirs that it is hardly possible that they should have any sentiments or feelings common with me."[18] But in this instance, her husband William, who acknowledged his parents "live a different way to what I want you to live if I can help," urged her to make a change. In November 1862, he reassured her, "If you can be any better satisfied by coming to Iowa—by going to your father[']s and taking money enough with you to make things more comfortable there, go, *you shall have the money.*"[19]

Before the end of the month William was urging her to move out, even as Mary—Dollie to her affectionate husband—became willing to stay lest she hurt his parents' feelings. "Remember that they are old and getting childish," she explained to William. In December, William, however, was now emphatic. "You have no business to stay with traitors Dollie," he wrote; "I don't regard their feelings. They don't regard ours." To make his point, William added, "I'll assure you I want them to know . . . that I act independent of the feeling of all the traitors whether they lie South or North." Now he commanded her to leave his parents behind, and Mary found more amenable quarters eventually returning to Iowa.[20]

SOLDIERS' WIVES AND THE FAMILY ECONOMY

By necessity, then, soldiers' wives took up much of the burden of maintaining the family economy as best as they could and in some places by doing so shifted the norms of work behavior, especially on the farms that still were home for the overwhelming majority of Northerners.[21] Midwestern farms succeeded based on the labor of the entire family, but women performed certain "female" chores while their husbands shouldered others. In Wisconsin, women usually did work around the house, or maintained gardens and chicken coops. Men did the harder farm work. Such a division of labor surprised the European immigrants of the time, who found it normal to have women do work generally assigned to the men in American families.[22] The war, however, changed things. In Midwestern states, probably half of the farm families lost a man to the army, a problem complicated by the enlistment of large numbers of landless laborers who would have contributed to maintaining the region's farms.[23]

The large numbers of farmers enrolled in the army forced farm women into work routines usually reserved for their menfolk. In Kansas, after several years of war, farm owners discovered it was "impossible to obtain a day's labor at any price."[24] Back east in Connecticut, labor was also hard to come by for some women left on their own. Sarah Hirst had a hard time finding hired labor to make up for the work her husband Benjamin had done before he had joined the army. Worried about her well-being, however, Benjamin told her it did not matter, that he "would rather the whole Place was like a Virginia House [run down by New England standards, that is] than that you should hurt yourself."[25]

Benjamin Hirst might not have liked knowing that his wife was doing hard work in his absence, but it was a sentiment shared by other soldiers across the North even when wives presented them with the reality of their financial hardships.[26] Some Iowa wives were too proud to ask for charity, but not too shy to assume the roles of their menfolk who had left behind the demands of their farms.[27] Michigander Mary Austin Wallace, a young wife with two small children, did all sorts of farm work while her husband was in the army, ranging from digging potatoes, sewing clothes, shucking corn, and in one day in September 1862 "chasing Mr. Harrisons pigs out of the corn two or three times" only to have the porcine pests return two days later for two more rounds of chase followed by her delivery of a personal complaint to their owner.[28] In November 1862, Iowan Emeline Ritner and her husband's cousin Lib Alter butchered and salted a pig. "We done it up just right," she assured her husband, adding, "We just had to do it. There was not a man on the hill that we could get."[29] Later in the spring, Emeline found a man to plow the garden plot, but not being able to hire someone to plant the crop and so she and Lib "pitched in and planted it ourselves."[30]

Elsewhere, women did not hesitate to take on masculine work along with their own feminine chores, perhaps discovering that their husbands' work was no more demanding than their own. Poorer women hitched oxen, repaired their fence lines, threshed crops, and did other chores without the assistance of modern farm machinery.[31] More fortunate women could rely on machinery that made their lives a little easier, but it was still demanding work. "Harvesting isn't any harder, if it's as hard as cooking, washing, and ironing, over a red hot stove in July and August," one Midwestern woman discovered, "only we have to do both now." With her brothers, cousins, and most potential hired hands all in the army, "there's no help to be got but women, and the crops must be got in all the same, you know." Another woman working the same harvest with the advantage of a reaper proudly admitted that she was "as good a binder as a man, and could keep up with the best of 'em." Along with their fieldwork and housework, these women also gathered materials for packages for soldiers in hospitals.[32]

There was patriotism even here in the ordinary labors of tending the farm. As the matriarch of these field workers explained, "we can do anything to help along while the country's in such trouble." And as one of the young women in the field made clear, "as long as the country can't get along without grain, nor the army fight without food, we're serving the country just as much here in the harvest-field as our boys are on the battle-field—and that sort o' takes the edge off from this business of doing men's work, you know."[33] Mary Vermilion seconded this sentiment in a letter to her husband declaring, "A sacred cause makes even the humblest labor dignified and holy."[34]

Beyond the usual farm work or household duties, some women took on other tasks once considered beyond their ken and once reserved to the men in their families. Women supervised their husbands' and sons' financial interests, often sharing information with and receiving advice from their husbands. Some of them collected their husbands' debts and invested their pay, with a skill that encouraged the confidence of their menfolk. Ohio physician Myra K. Merrick assumed control of her husband's lumber business after he had enlisted while continuing to tend to her practice and to her children.[35] Michigander Mary Austin Wallace assumed the supervision of the substantial family farm as well as the construction of the house that her husband had begun before he left for the war in August 1862; on top of these responsibilities, she still had the duties of caring for her toddler son and infant daughter.[36] Mary Bradbury of Illinois, a mother of several children, received frequent instructions on how to conduct her husband's business affairs; she accepted the challenge and ended up increasing the family's wealth.[37]

Middling and poorer women with limited resources had little choice but to do as these women did. Esther Claflin made a point of managing the family budget in such a way that she could report a solvent if frugal existence to her husband Gilbert, who was serving with a Wisconsin regiment during 1862 and 1863. In March 1863, Esther informed her husband that over the winter she had "repaired almost everything I can think of" including "11 pairs of summer pants, so I hope they will get through the summer for everyday without buying." She also "mended all of the cotton shirts, which makes quite a pile." Furthermore, she did her best to keep expenses down in other ways because she had "no idea of making a store bill for you to pay if you ever get back, excepting at the shoe store."[38]

Some women took in laundry and did other extra work to make ends meet. Those women fortunate enough to have homes accepted boarders. But as the war consumed more and more men, there became more opportunities to earn money as they filled positions not only on the farm or in the factory. Women found work in government offices and in the schoolhouses across the region.[39] Beyond the farm, one of the acceptable opportunities open to women who needed work was sewing, especially in the production of uniforms for the men in the army. This struggle to provide for themselves and their families led some less fortunate women to make it clear that they wished their husbands to return home as soon as possible. If their men had already given their lives for the cause, those with little in the way of resources expected the federal government to provide them with pensions as compensation for their sacrifices.[40]

WORRIED WIVES MISS THEIR HUSBANDS

For many wives, the very ordinary routines and concerns of daily life were regular reminders of how the war had disrupted their familial tranquility. After her husband left for the army in the fall of 1862, Esther Claflin performed her morning routines only to have them remind her of the absence of her husband. "I had the griddle hot and the pancakes ready to bake," she wrote, "but no Gilbert came." The emptiness of their house was especially apparent to her when all was quiet. "I listened for his footsteps when the house is still at night and once I thought (I don't believe I dreamed it) that he came in at the door so still and came to the bed and kissed me," she once wrote, "and another time I hear his name called away in the distance and yet so plain." Esther had to adjust to the reality, putting aside "these dream thoughts," but the longing she had for her husband did not fade. Even when she attended prayer meetings, she could not shake herself free of such thoughts. "I can't hardly keep my mind on the subject of the meeting," she wrote to her husband; "It is continually wandering away to you in spite of myself."[41]

In early 1863, Esther reminded her husband how much she pined for him while reassuring him, "You may not suppose that I go to bed in my warm bed without thinking of you."[42] Other wives also conveyed their emotional longing for their spouses. In July 1864, Emma Spalding Bryant, another recently married woman, begged her husband John, "Come to your little wife to-night, please? She wants you *so much*." Foolish love letters, perhaps, as she admitted, but she could not help herself.[43] Such affection found expression when husbands came home on leave. In August 1863, after a trip home Madison Bowler joked with his wife Lizzie, "You need not be so fast to lay that little matter all off on me, for you had something to do in the premises as well as myself, and, unless I am mistaken, you would do the same thing over again without much coxing."[44] Consequently, it was not unusual for wives such as Lizzie to realize they were pregnant after a soldier's visit home. Captain George Burchell, a Detroit, Michigan, soldier, left his wife with child during one furlough; returning to his regiment after another visit home, he bragged to another officer, "If I have not made another boy, I assure you it is no fault of mine."[45]

Despite the love shared by soldiers and their wives, there were some families who could not stand the burdens imposed by the war. There were women so desirous of male companionship that they took advantage of the opportunities presented to them while their husbands were in the army. Rumors about unfaithful wives found their way to the front, upsetting soldier husbands who were too far away to check the allegations in person. Some of the rumors were maliciously false. Nevertheless, the war created a climate in which the sexual behavior of married and unmarried women, especially those engaged in nursing wounded soldiers, became subject to greater public discussion. Bawdy married women left alone by soldier husbands could provoke general concern as they challenged their community's norms by amusing themselves with other men. In 1863, a Massachusetts woman wrote to her son, "We hear bad stories, about George Warren Andrews who it is said visits a Mrs. Craft often & stays for days sometimes, who has one daughter eleven years old, & whose husband is in the army." In this instance, there was no secret to keep: "They are the Town talk, at present."[46] New Yorker Ellen Goldwaite informed her husband Richard that an acquaintance, the wife of a soldier, went out dancing at a local beer hall. "Tom had ought to know it," wrote an indignant Ellen, "but no one wants to tell it to him for fear of making him downhearted."[47]

The betrayals of such wives, not to mention the philandering of unfaithful soldiers, probably contributed to the increase in the divorce rate during and after the war.[48] Faithful soldiers' wives, however, believed their marriages would endure and in fact survive the war stronger than they had been before their husbands had joined the army. For Emma Bryant, the absence of her husband appeared to deepen her love for him. "I never loved you as well before in my life I think as these days since you went away," she wrote to John; "My love seems different—warmer, truer."[49] Husbands responded in similar fashion, perhaps lifting the spirits of their wives with their reassuring words. John Pardington informed his wife Sarah their separation taught him "how to appreciate your company and if I ever come [home] the Lord Willing I think I shall not give you any cause again to set up for me nights like you used to." Asking for forgiveness for previous inconsiderate behavior, John made "a faithful Promise before God if ever I get back to you I will live a different life."[50] Wives who missed their husbands constantly worried about the consequences of camp life and battle. The restraints of church and family were missing in the rough-and-tumble lives of soldiers, and wives well understood their men could become unfit for their return to their civilian lives. The Bible and honest friends, however, could keep soldiers on the straight path, and they encouraged them to seek out good company.[51] In July 1863, Lizzie Bowler had a first-hand encounter with the effects of rough living when a neighbor named David Piercy visited home before returning to Camp Snelling in Minnesota.[52] Being a concerned, loving wife, she issued warnings to her husband about what she considered to be his proper behavior even when away from home. In March 1863, reporting on a good sermon she had heard, Lizzie asked Madison if he had "lost your taste for going to meetings and things pertaining thereto and given yourself wholly up to serve your country?" She reminded him that wartime was not the best time to forget about religion. Dangers "soround [*sic*] you on every side" therefore, she advised, "you should remember your Redeemer liveth."[53]

Where gentle warnings, Christian advice, and letters filled with loving concern failed to keep men righteous, threats, so some wives believed, would. Lizzie Bowler warned Madison that if he had taken up smoking cigars, there would be a price to pay. "[W]hen you come home again," she warned, "you and I will have to occupy two beds." Indeed, she advised, "I would rather you would visit the black ladies then learn to use tobacco. Do you hear?"[54] In other cases, inflicting a modicum of guilt might keep absent men on the straight path. Mattie Blanchard was also very disturbed by the bad habits of camp life that might infect once virtuous soldiers. When she learned that her husband was playing cards, she made it clear to him that he needed to give up the game. "[C]ards can do you no good," she warned; "you are a father now and dont bring disgrace upon your childs head."[55]

STRESS

Soldiers' wives did their best to withstand the stressful burdens left to them by their fractured partnerships. The strain could take a significant toll and test the patriotism that had earlier allowed them to send off their husbands with pride. At times, more general printed information of battles, casualties, and campaigns overwhelmed or obscured the specific personal information they wanted about their loved ones, adding further stress to their lives. For Mary "Dollie" Vermilion, the lack of news concerning her husband's safety after a battle in which reports noted significant casualties drove her to distraction. "Last Thursday I heard of the battle at Helena [Arkansas], and up to this minute I have not heard one word from you, sweet pet," she wrote in July 1863; "Do you wonder that your Dollie is almost crazed?" "I fear everything for you are still living, I fear you are wounded and suffering, and I can't get to you. . . . Sometimes, I think you are safe, then again I am afraid to hope for it, almost. A soldier's life is hard, but nothing, it seems to me, can be worse than this suspense, unless it be having our worst fears realized." She feared God was punishing her for loving him too much. When news finally came, "I feared everything bad. I feel like another being now." But the war and her worries continued. The next month she feared the "hard marching and hard fighting out there" where her husband was campaigning. "If you get sick or wounded, my love, way out there what will you do[?]"[56] For New Yorker Ellen Goldwaite, the inadequate mail service between camp and home was particularly vexing. "Dick, the Lord only knows what the Government intends unless it wants the Lunatic Asylums filled up with crazy women," she complained in April 1862. "I think that it is bad enough that the woman has to be deprived of the man's company without being deprived of reading a letter once a week."[57]

Ellen Goldwaite's husband Richard came home in June 1863, bringing her some peace of mind. But in the meantime, she experienced bouts of depression. Ellen frequently wrote what she herself considered discouraging letters, for which she apologized, but the emotional problem persisted. In July 1862, she reassured Dick that he had already done sufficient duty to leave the army. Later in December 1862, she begged her husband to come home by the spring. "Dick, I do not care how much money we have," she assured him; "I would rather have you come home. I would have less dollars and a contented mind—a thing I can never have while you are in the Army." And at the beginning of the new year, she admitted feeling "so low spirited that I cannot write." Ellen found that when she awoke in the morning she had "as heavy a heart as I could have if every one belonging to me was dead."[58]

Other wives shared Ellen's unsettled state of mind and the reason for her depression. Loneliness compounded by the usual vicissitudes of life jeopardized their mental health. The absence of her husband and the burden of being a mother placed a great deal of strain on Rachel Cormany, who suffered from depression throughout the war. Her daughter Cora contracted measles in early 1863, which compounded Rachel's sense of being overburdened. "It seems very lonely to be all alone with a sick child," she confided in her journal; "O! that my Samuel were here."[59] During the fall of 1863, she felt herself at wits' end as she dealt with Cora, recovered but still demanding of her time and her emotional reserves. "Last night & today Cora cried so much that my patience quite gave way—Indeed I wished I had never been born," she complained to her diary in October. "I felt as if I were the most forsaken creature on earth. Indeed I cannot tell how miserable I felt. . . . I often feel my unfitness to be a mother."[60]

Aggravating Rachel's depression was the intense longing she felt for her absent husband, alleviated only when her husband was home on furlough. In March 1864, she noted how the visit raised her spirits and provided some needed physical satisfaction. "O! I was so glad to see him, to be kissed & caressed & to love kiss & caress him," she wrote. However, after his departure, her melancholy returned. "Friends that come in ask me whether I am sick," she wrote. "I look so pale—but I wonder who would not look pale after parting with the dearest friend on earth. I am sure I do not look any worse than I feel."[61]

Visits by soldier husbands were rare, but letters provided another way of maintaining some intimacy with loved ones. The correspondence that proceeded from the home front to the camp and back again strengthened the family ties taxed by war and were cherished by both the soldiers and their families. Wives felt a revived bond of affection in the correspondence they conducted with their husbands. Also, the letters wives received became tangible artifacts of the relationships that they remembered and hoped to continue when peace came. Mary Vermilion would reread her husband's letters when she was feeling depressed or lonely, a practice other wives must have followed given how carefully they had preserved so many collections of soldiers' letters.[62] Writing to a soldier husband might also help bring emotional relief to the suffering spouse. Wisconsin wife and mother Esther Claflin suffered bouts of depression but, she once wrote to her husband Gilbert, "got over having that longing to desire to die." Apparently, her love of family steadied her emotions. "I realize how lonely it would make you, more than I ever did before, and think it has been selfishness on my part to desire it," she admitted; "And these boys need a mother as well as father."[63] In the end, Esther accepted her patriotic duty. "I try to be very heroic and I almost always feel glad that I can suffer with my country. I am willing to sacrifice. I don't wish to be exempt while our country is engaged in this terrible struggle."[64]

Distant and sometimes artless husbands made an effort to cheer up their sad wives by assuring them that steady domestic patriotism was the best way to see them home safe and sound. In May 1864, Ohio cavalryman William McKnight reminded his wife Mary that he was proud of his service and that she should also feel the same. "You may feel proud that you are a Soldiers wife although your own domestic troubles may dround [sic] all such thoughts," he informed her; "I pity you dear."[65] However, a husband's advice could be fairly banal. Benjamin Hirst of Connecticut must have received some discouraging letters from his wife Sarah, who wrote to him "in such a desponding way." Reassuring her that he was engaged in a good cause, he advised her in May 1863 to "Cheer up, don't work so hard around the House but go around and see your Friends." If she saw how other people lived, "you would soon see hundreds of Women, worse of[f] than yourself, and would be satisfied with your own Lot."[66] Earlier in 1862, he reassured Sarah with the promise that their temporary separation will pay dividends in the future because the returning soldiers "shal [sic] know how to appreciate the Blessings of Home, and I think it will make us Wiser and better men."[67] Ben's words might have provided some comfort to Sarah, but she needed more than simple reassurances and advice not to work too hard. Whether the strain of the war or some other problem was the cause, she eventually ended up institutionalized, spending her last years after Benjamin's death in the Massachusetts State Hospital for the Insane.[68]

RAISING CHILDREN AT HOME

Adding to the usual burdens of economic and emotional survival for soldiers' wives were the difficulties that accompanied raising children without a father's presence in the house. Even the youngest family members were aware that something unusual and extraordinary was happening when the war came. As Frank Coffeen, a Wisconsin man, later recalled, "I did not know what war meant . . . except that it was something that made me afraid and then Ma cried every day and Pa was going to war."[69] The young Frank could not help but notice the burden carried by the adults around him and the tension it generated as they waited for news from the front.[70] Other children also remarked on the missing adults in their lives. During the spring of 1863, the Peirce children frequently talked with their mother Catharine about their absent father and, as she reported to her husband Taylor, they "wish for thee to be at home so they could get a kiss and talk to thee" and "they want to see thee very bad."[71]

Even from a distance, fathers tried to exert an influence over the lives of their families. James Goodnow wrote detailed letters to his problematic son Sam in an effort to keep him on track, while urging him to improve himself for the life he would soon face as an adult.[72] The absent father continued to act as a gentle disciplinarian when the son went astray, reminding him that he was obliged to continue to help his ill mother, to study, to be industrious, and to prepare for his own future.[73] Most importantly, he urged his son to be a good person. "I want you to begin now to form the habit of thinking of the rights and happiness of others in all you do," Goodnow advised; "No man can be useful or happy, who studies his own gratification alone."[74]

Depending on the age of the children, this sort of advice could run from work and school matters to the words offered by Silas Browning of Massachusetts to his daughter, whom he reminded to "grow good as fast as you grow tall."[75] Advice, however, required reinforcement with reminders of paternal affection, and fathers offered expressions of affection as well. In January 1863, Ohioan William McKnight expressed his love for his children and reassured them that he longed to be with them. "You are dearer to me than my own life but I don't expect to see you for awhile," he wrote, and, until better times came along, he advised them "to be good little children and do what your ma tels you and when papa comes he wil have such a good little family." McKnight also explained why their family had to endure separation and sacrifice. "I am bound to help fight it out now so that I may have a better Place for you," he wrote; "For if I had stayed I would not felt that I had done my duty to you or my country."[76]

Thus, McKnight and so many other fathers provided immediate lessons on patriotism to their children when they explained their absences. James Goodnow wove into his advice words to shape his son's understanding of the war, thereby helping him grasp the nature of his sacrifice and the importance of the Union. "This is not a war for dollars and cents—nor is it a war for territory," he explained, "but it is to decide whether we are to be a free people—and if the Union is dissolved I very much fear that we will not have a Republican form of government very long."[77]

Rhode Islander Isaac Austin Brooks believed it worthwhile to help his children make sense of the war, teaching them the meaning of patriotism and why one should love the Union for which he fought. He was living a difficult life, he told the children, but "it is the duty of us all, to do what we can for our country and to preserve its integrity even to the sacrifice of our lives, if it is necessary." He further explained that such a sacrifice was worthwhile because "It is a glorious country, and *must* be preserved to our children." Thinking in generational terms, Brooks explained, "It was given to *us entire*, and *we* must give it to you entire and *you* must give it as you receive it, to those who come after you." He reminded them that the United States was "next to your God, in love, and never see it injured, or disgraced, if you have a hand, or a mind, to put forth in its defense." Thus, all of his advice about hard work and good living, he concluded, was necessary to provide their eventual understanding of why they must "love, and serve your country" if he were not to return home.[78]

Children might have appreciated this paternal advice over the long term, but the immediate circumstance required them to pitch in on a daily basis in keeping their families solvent and fed. Almost-grown sons and daughters assumed duties that their years would have required of them regardless of the war, but their efforts took on additional meaning with older brothers, fathers, and farm hands absent from their communities. Esther Claflin could turn to her brother to help with the threshing of her wheat crop, but for the regular farm chores she also relied on her two young sons. The boys sold apples, milked the cow, tended to sheep, and purchased seed, setting their efforts to planting a crop of wheat and oats. In the spring of 1863, they also shouldered the responsibility of working off the local road tax for the family.[79] Some boys even assumed the manly role vacated by their fathers, quickly maturing in the face of the challenges presented by their unusual circumstances, on occasions defending their mothers from Copperheads and Indians while caring for them when they were ill.[80]

For some of the younger children, the absence of fathers hurried them along to more mature tasks, taking on jobs that might not have come until a bit later in their lives. In December 1862, Elton, about 15 years of age and the eldest of the two Claflin boys, was "trying to split rails and do considerable large work"; both of them, their mother judged, "attend to work very steady for boys." But such examples of maturity did not distract the boys from stretching the boundaries of their young lives. By the late summer of 1863, they were rebelling against their mother's control. "You are needed here very much," Esther wrote to their father; "The boys are running wild, and the cattle and colts are getting very troublesome." Furthermore, Elton was "not willing to mind or do anything else."[81] Gilbert Claflin tried to answer his wife's concerns by writing directly to his boys advising them on farm business. He also urged them to continue to improve themselves, while reminding them that their good behavior would make their father happy.[82]

Younger members of the soldiers' families also pitched in to keep their families solvent and fed, going beyond helping with the usual household or farm chores. In the rough Michigan "wilderness," a young Anna Howard later recalled how most of the men in the region, including her two brothers and her father, went off to fight for the Union cause, leaving her family hard pressed. She was but 14 at the outset of the war and vividly recalled her experiences, including her deferred education, while she pulled more than her economic weight, primarily by bringing home money she earned as a schoolteacher.[83]

It was not an easy time for her. "Those were years I do not like to look back upon—years in which life had degenerated into a treadmill whose monotony was broken only by the grim messages from the front," she later recalled. Being so consumed by the home-front consequences of the war meant that she had "no time to dream my dream" of going to college. It was not until the war's end that she would be able to save for her college tuition. Furthermore, young folk Anna's age were old enough to share in the worries of their elders. Anna's isolation meant that she and her family received inadequate details about the well-being of her father and brothers. "At long intervals word came to us of battles in which my father's regiment . . . or those of my brothers were engaged," she later recalled, "and then longer intervals followed in which we heard no news." She learned that one brother was wounded, but "for months we lived in terror of worse tidings" until word finally came of his recovery.[84]

SEVEN

PASTIMES WITH PURPOSE

AMUSEMENTS

In September 1862, Fannie Meredith of Millwood, Ohio, complained that she had little about which to write to her soldier friend. "Every thing is so uncommonly dull her[e]," she explained, "(all on account of this detestible [*sic*] war)."[1] About the same time, Emma Moody, another Ohioan, also apologized to her correspondent for her letter's lack of news. "There is nothing going on," she explained; "Everything is war."[2] Nevertheless, across the Northern states, civilians sufficiently fortunate to have some time beyond what they needed to take care of the necessities of life broke their daily routines in ways that were not all that different from their antebellum entertainments.

Throughout the war, Northerners pursued the normal cycle of social activities that could suggest to soldiers at the front to believe that war was the farthest thing from their minds. The war did not stop elites from spending their money at resorts or on yachting events, horse races, theater, opera, and other exclusive affairs, especially when the economy recovered as the war progressed.[3] Nor did the war stop working men from finding their pleasure where they could, especially in the watering holes common across the land. In Newark and other New Jersey cities, dens of iniquity prospered thanks to an increase in paying customers.[4] Such low entertainment discouraged German immigrant-turned-soldier Wilhelm Francksen. In an unflattering assessment, probably based on his association with the drinking activities of his Milwaukee, Wisconsin, acquaintances, Francksen reported home, "The common man, if he wants something special, goes to a saloon, drinks a lot, and pays for drinks of other people who have to drink with him but don't have anything to do with him otherwise, and it usually leads to killing and murder."[5]

In between the base and the well-heeled, there was a wide range of entertainments available to Americans who had the time to do more than simply survive the stress of war. People continued to enjoy the outdoors, visit the seashore, picnic, attend socials, ice skate, go sleighing, participate in sporting events, and attend country fairs. If the rich had their regattas, other Northerners had more modest times on the water. Many middling Northerners could also afford the time and tariff to attend minstrel shows, circuses, agricultural fairs, band concerts, and sporting activities.[6]

Friends and relatives continued to call on one another or dine together while young people simply walked out together to enjoy some socializing.[7] Women's reading groups and sewing circles allowed occasions for friends and acquaintances to visit.[8] It cost nothing to sing at religious meetings, but it did require rehearsals beyond the time allotted to services, thus providing another avenue for socializing.[9] And all sorts of Northerners, black and white, either as spectators or participants, devoted free time to the increasingly popular game of baseball, with all of its local rivalries adding even more excitement to the games. Even sport, however, was not immune to the intrusions of the war. Fans attended games that sometimes donated the proceeds to soldiers' relief funds. They frequently noticed a team's shifting lineup as players left the diamond to become soldiers, although there were ball players who did not volunteer, especially if they held anti-Lincoln political beliefs.[10]

All classes of Northerners commemorated personal milestones and the usual holidays that punctuated most family routines. In February 1865, Emma Randolph's family celebrated the 25th anniversary of the marriage of her parents after attending church services.[11] Families still celebrated Christmas, putting up trees, while some of them could still make sure children received Christmas presents.[12] In 1864 Emma Randolph continued to enjoy herself singing at Christmas services in Plainfield, New Jersey, and reported a nice tree and presents around it.[13] Earlier in November 1862, even with the disaster at Fredericksburg, Virginia, fresh in their minds, people such as New York doctor John V. Lauderdale celebrated Thanksgiving by attending church services and eating turkey.[14] In December 1862, Wisconsinite Rosa Kellner celebrated Christmas in a modest fashion, but still honored the holiday. She was pleased to buy cardboard and yarn to make bookmarks for her family.[15]

PATRIOTIC RITUALS

Public rituals also provided amusement but with serious purpose that brought communities together, accentuating the connections of the people at war. The ceremonies attending to sending off the boys stretched into the social life of those left behind as the cycle of civic holidays marched through the yearly calendar. Those Northerners who had no family members at the front could not escape the meaning of patriotic rituals on the well-established national holidays that brought together entire communities to watch parades and hear speeches in honor of the Union that their soldiers were fighting to preserve.[16] Philadelphia politicians did not find the funds to support expected celebrations, but instead of allowing the time to pass unnoticed, the people did so on several occasions.[17]

In February 1862, the people of Belfast, Maine, raised flags, made speeches, and sang patriotic songs in honor of George Washington's birthday.[18] In 1862 Massachusetts residents celebrated Fourth of July across the state, reaffirming their commitment to the Union and the Constitution. They participated in parades, listened to music, heard speeches, and attended celebratory dinners. In Boston, the planned Fourth of July celebration the following year was especially joyous, fueled by the excitement encouraged by news of the victory at Gettysburg.[19]

The events of 1862 dampened the spirits of New Yorkers, but some of them still celebrated the Fourth of July, providing a "a tug load of ice cream and cake, and flowers, and flags, and a chest of tea, forty quarts of milk, and butter, and handkerchiefs, papers, and books, to set out a long table and give a treat" to convalescent soldiers remaining on Bedloe's Island. The patriotic Good Samaritans had prepared to serve 200 men, but they found only 40 remaining. Nevertheless, they provided the men with "a glorious feast, the doctor giving his full consent that even the twelve sick ones, in bed should have as much *ice cream* as they wanted." It appears that they did, for one woman estimated that each soldier had a quart of ice cream, cake, and a glass of Catawba wine.[20]

Unplanned, spontaneous victory celebrations also united Northerners in their communities as they enjoyed the success of their troops. Mary Livermore recollected the excitement that followed news arriving in cities in the Old Northwest after Grant's victory at Fort Donelson on February 15, 1862. People spilled into the streets. They left their employment, decked the avenues in flags, rang bells, played music, and attended prayer meetings. The spontaneous street parties extended into the evening with bonfires and did not end "until physical exhaustion compelled an end to them."[21] After word of Vicksburg's surrender on July 4, 1863, reached Philadelphia, the city erupted in celebration.[22] And in the wake of Gettysburg and Vicksburg, people in the small community of Canton Center, Connecticut, made what noise they could.[23]

COURTING

In February 1864, Philadelphian Sidney George Fisher commented upon the popularity of ice-skating in the larger Northeastern cities. It was an activity, he observed, that allowed ample opportunity for flirting between the sexes "besides having the advantage of healthy exercise in the open air." It also provided the older Fisher with a chance to observe "the spectacle of youth, gayety and pleasure" that the young skaters exhibited.[24] Indeed, young Northerners away from the war were happy to act as people just on the brink of adulthood, especially when the sexes had the opportunity to mix. College boys continued to act as college boys. In 1863 in Indianapolis, male students at Northwestern Christian University had "very gay times" as "They have been having a great time gallanting the girls." Their activities were sufficiently obvious and perhaps distracting to their studies that the president of the university "has made rules prohibiting the young ladies receiving calls from the Students." Demi Butler informed her soldier brother Scot about the restriction at the school their father had founded remarking, "I don't know what they will do now."[25]

No doubt the Indianapolis college boys were at an advantage with so many other young men off at war. Helen Aplin reported to her soldier brother that the social life of the young folk of one Vermont town progressed as it had done before the war; the war, however, had upset the antebellum sex ratio in such a way as to place young women at a disadvantage, especially when looking to socialize with patriotic men.[26] Despite the empty chairs, weddings continued to take place. The beginning of the war did not distract young women from worrying about wedding presents and engagements.[27] Sometimes, however, young people bent the acceptable courtship rituals as the circumstances of war altered old norms. Single women boldly initiated correspondence with soldiers when they inserted letters in boxes of supplies that they mailed to men at the front or in hospitals.[28] Some young women answered ads placed in newspapers by soldiers who wished to begin corresponding with women other than family members. Eligible girls, therefore, provided soldiers with opportunities to stay in touch with the more civilized home front shaped by the presence of women, thereby raising their spirits. Single letter-writing women thus did their patriotic duty and, in turn, were able to enjoy the excitement of developing new friendships.[29] Also, for some unattached Northern women who had known the recipients of their letters before the war, wartime relationships through the mails nurtured lasting relationships, moving over months and years from amusing conversations between friends to making plans for a future between fiancées.[30]

There were situations in which the war intensified the normal progression of these things. Some couples consummated their relationship out of wedlock, as was the case with one woman who was in December 1862 "at the point of death having had an illegal child & the father to it is in the army."[31] Many couples married before a soldier left for the front, as a Marblehead, Massachusetts, resident noticed.[32] Other couples married when soldiers came home on leave. Sometimes they married under dramatic circumstances. Nettie Butler and her soldier sweetheart married while he was on leave after his escape from Libby Prison.[33] A sadder nuptial involved a young woman who rushed to the side of her wounded fiancée, married him, and then nursed him until his death.[34]

INTELLECTUAL PURSUITS

The letter writing that cultivated romances and kept families and friends connected became the most common form of literary expression, but not the only one.[35] Men, women, and young people continued their prewar habit of reviewing the events of the day in the journals they kept. Some upper-class diarists such as Sidney George Fisher, Maria Lydig Daly, and George Templeton Strong left behind more than just a schematic of their lives; they composed substantial historical records of the home-front North, including their own intelligent reflections on war, politics, and other matters.[36] Still, diaries composed by common urban folk such as black Philadelphian Emilie Davis and by farmwomen such as Rachel Cormany provided an outlet for their concerns and fears as well as a record of the sacrifices they endured.[37]

The intellectually curious attended lectures, read books, and frequented libraries. In January 1863, the white citizens of Cleveland, Ohio, paid an admission fee and packed the lecture hall to listen to the black abolitionist, newspaper editor, and orator Frederick Douglass, while on the following evening African Americans attended another of his lectures. Douglass always had a purpose when he spoke in public, and in the latter case he called for the recruitment of a black regiment from Ohio. His efforts helped to muster the 127th Ohio Volunteer Infantry regiment, which became the 5th United States Colored Troops.[38] The young, radical, and increasingly famous Philadelphian Anna Dickinson lectured audiences on the crisis of the Union, the execution of the war, abolitionism, and women's rights.[39] On April 11, 1863, on the occasion of the anniversary of the bombardment of Fort Sumter, people attended a New York City meeting at which the German-born scholarly professor Francis Lieber lectured on patriotism, political unity, and slavery promising dire consequences if Northerners did not accept his views on these matters while urging his audience to join together in loyal leagues. "Either the North conquers the South and re-establishes law, freedom, and the integrity of our country," Lieber warned in his dense oration, "or the South conquers the North by arms, or by treason at home, and covers our portion of the country with disgrace and slavery."[40]

Lectures such as those delivered by Lieber reminded Northerners of what was at stake and why they should continue to make sacrifices. Reading, a more solitary pursuit, did the same as it also entertained those who loved books. Libraries continued to attract subscribers and "reading rooms are more frequented than they were wont to be" at the Philadelphia Mercantile Library, "and the books, tables, files and other advantages of the Library, are more and more in use."[41] But even here the war made librarians aware of responsibilities of preserving the materials generated by the conflict. Harvard librarian John Langdon Sibley, a Republican, believed it essential for his library to collect all manner of literature, newspapers, and ephemera, even from antiwar publications and from the South and in doing so provide "one of the greatest favors to the future historian and philosopher."[42]

The newspapers Sibley collected for his library helped reshape old reading habits for some patriotic Northerners, who kept abreast of wartime events as reported in the various newspapers of the North. In New England, for example, newspapers supplanted more frivolous forms of print.[43] Connecticut newspapers increased their circulation during the war, even with the increased advertising costs needed to pay for timely news reports delivered by wire, supplies, and taxes.[44] Mary Vermilion, although admittedly interested in other periodical literature, refused to subscribe to "ladies magazines while the war lasts." Indeed, Vermilion still "read a good deal" while she was away from home staying with a group of women. She frequently spent evenings with some of them reading material out loud, but even here in leisurely reading she found a political purpose. She selected literature that had a decidedly radical bent with the goal of converting other members of the reading circle to her antislavery views.[45]

The home folks in Connecticut eagerly consumed histories and biographies dealing with the war, making Sarah Emma Edmonds's tales of her life as a federal nurse and spy a best seller after its Hartford publication in 1865.[46] Northerners, however, did not completely abandon fiction in their patriotic effort to read for a better understanding of the crisis that enveloped their country, but fiction also catered to the desire of many readers to know more about the war. The war now provided material for writers that attracted an audience already interested in the subject, and according to industry sources a few years of the conflict did little to dampen sales. In 1863, Louisa May Alcott's *Hospital Sketches* brought a fictionalized version of her experiences as a nurse to the attention of the public while Henry Morford's novels described such things as the impact of the first Battle of Bull Run and cowardly officers.[47] Also, a certain class of publishers produced sensational war stories in books and periodicals that attracted a readership, but also introduced story lines that included matters of race and the role of women in the war.[48] Thus, according to industry sources, "the very restlessness and the cravings of the times may lead the public to seek enjoyment in books."[49]

For patriotic Northerners, reading helped them understand how they were to behave in such an unprecedented crisis, setting out clear examples of patriotic and craven behavior, encouraging the former and warning about the latter. Humor and satire as well as romanticism influenced reading material. Satire in cartoons and in print had their fun with men who failed to volunteer or avoided the draft, journalists who missed the reality around them, women who sewed havelocks but failed to grasp the nature of military service, unethical officers, greedy contractors, and just about any other topic upon which the war might cast its shadow.[50]

FUND-RAISING AND FUN

Northerners were not averse to socializing while doing good deeds. Indeed, some of the more exciting amusements enjoyed by them were the social events held for the expressed purpose of cultivating patriotism and raising money for the needs of soldiers and their families. In July 1863, Ohioan Ella Hawn reported a large Union meeting that included speeches as well as a dinner along with instrumental and vocal music.[51] A vocal concert in Clarkson, New York, raised money for soldiers' relief.[52] Women in particular devoted their spare time to organizing such events as ice cream socials, lectures, and dances.[53] In November 1863, Anne Butler and her associates raised money for soldiers' families by holding a wide range of social events, including a supper, a concert, a tableaux, and a fair stretched out over an eight-day period.[54]

Civilians could attend fairs in towns throughout the North sponsored by soldiers' relief organizations, but the larger cities such as Chicago, Boston, Philadelphia, and New York witnessed extravagant events that brought in crowds of people.[55] Men remained happy to organize and lead such efforts, but Northern women shouldered the grinding work of raising resources. Such was the arrangement that propelled into being the nation's dominant relief organization, the United States Sanitary Commission.

During the first year of the war, one could expect the appeal for women of forming "Soldiers' Relief Circles" which would allow women to aid the war effort while providing them with the society of like-minded companions who would "meet once a week, from 1 to 4 P.M., the time to be spent sewing or knitting for the soldier."[56] Such relief circles became part of a much larger and more involved movement of women who aided the war effort beyond their ability to knit socks. In April 1861, some 50 to 60 New York City women came together to establish the Women's Central Association of Relief for the Sick and Wounded of the Army, an attempt to bring order and system to the various local groups of women. Soon that female-founded and controlled organization became a subsidiary of the United States Sanitary Commission, a male-dominated organization.[57]

In June 1861, a group of upper-class men received the sanction of the federal government to act in the area of soldiers' relief, which led to the formation of the commission. Its purpose was, as Mary Livermore recalled, "to do what the Government could not."[58] Prominent men such as H. W. Bellows, who became the organization's president, George Templeton Strong, and Frederick Law Olmsted established the commission expecting to harness the enthusiasm of the local women's groups, guiding them with a more centralized, scientific, masculine—and thus a more efficient and rational—approach to relief, one that eschewed Christian sentimentality and even resorted to using paid agents to promote its agenda. The Sanitary Commission founders also had recognized the inability of the federal government to deal with the needs of sick and wounded soldiers and set about to assist soldiers through a wide range of relief activities, including the recruiting of doctors and nurses for their hospitals. By the end of the war, the Sanitary Commission provided the war effort with relief material valued at approximately $15 million.[59]

The Sanitary Commission's most prominent rival was the United States Christian Commission, founded in November 1861 by members of the U.S. Young Men's Christian Association. That organization raised approximately $6 million for the relief of soldiers and sailors but unlike the Sanitary Commission, the Christian Commission paid particular attention to the spiritual needs of soldiers and sailors as indicated by its extensive distribution of Bibles and religious tracts to military men as well as the thousands of sermons preached and prayer meetings held by its representatives.[60] But as with the Sanitary Commission, the Christian Commission relied on a network of dedicated women to do its fund-raising at the local level.[61]

Thus, the most common and readily accessible activity for Northern women who wished to show their commitment to the Union was the widespread efforts of various organizations to raise money to bring comfort to soldiers at the front and in hospitals or to help to provide for their families at home. From the beginning of the war, home-front women did what they could to help their soldiers and believed that their efforts were comparable in their patriotism with those of the men in the field. They formed hundreds of local organizations to raise money for soldiers and send boxes of necessary items to the front and hospitals. Women came together in the Dubuque Ladies Aid Society to tend to the needs of soldiers and eventually their families.[62] Women in Bridgeport, Connecticut, went door to door to secure donations for soldiers' relief.[63] But even women in more isolated rural areas participated in this great effort to provide some comfort to military men. The organizer of the Marshalltown, Iowa, Sanitary Commission, Majorie Ann Rogers, drove herself to scattered farmhouses to solicit aid.[64]

A group of women living on small farms in Wisconsin some distance from a railroad line donated all sorts of goods to the war effort but decided to do even more using what Mary Livermore called "new and untried methods." They asked farming neighbors for donations of wheat, sold what they collected, and used the profits for soldiers' relief. Their efforts were impressive. "Sometimes on foot, sometimes with a team, amid the snows and mud of early spring, they canvassed the country for twenty and thirty miles around, everywhere eloquently pleading the needs of the blue-coated boys in the hospitals," Livermore wrote. In the end, they gathered and sold 500 bushels of wheat for soldiers' relief, forwarding the proceeds to the Sanitary Commission.[65] Even the children of these active women could participate in what amounted to patriotic play, raising funds through various enterprises and by conducting their own small-scale sanitary fairs.[66]

Such heroic service by adults as well as children continued throughout the war, with some good effect. The Sanitary Commission estimated that there were over 10,000 local societies organized during the war that provided as much as $50 million in donations to various state and private entities.[67] But it was difficult work. Local organizations' efforts lagged after 1863 as women and communities tired or directed their attention to veterans in need of charity and assistance. Women in Newport, New York, curtailed their contributions to the Sanitary Commission because they felt the need to look after the needy families of their hometown soldiers, while women in Chatham, Pennsylvania, devoted themselves to caring for sick veterans who had returned home.[68]

The successful sanitary fairs that women such as Mary Livermore organized combined the familiar elements of the male-run early 19th-century agricultural and mechanics' fairs and the female-dominated fund-raising fairs that began in the United States during the 1820s. The organizers, however, raised their fairs to a more spectacular level.[69] Local fairs proliferated across the North, raising funds by selling goods produced by community members or donated by businesses and manufacturers. The Soldiers' Aid Society of Northern Ohio, for example, sent out circulars, one of which arrived at the late gun manufacturer Samuel Colt's address, requesting donations of artifacts for an exhibit "of Trophies from Battle-Fields, Relics, Curiosities, Autographs, &c." The organizers wished to secure all sorts of flags and military paraphernalia "capture[d] from the enemy or borne at the head of our own triumphant columns," all of which might "stimulate interest in the great struggle through which we are now passing, or gratify the taste of the antiquarian." In addition, the committee hoped to display various hand-made objects produced by soldiers, all of which would be "converted into substantial comforts for Soldiers" by the aid society.[70]

The larger urban sanitary fairs became the big charitable and entertainment events of the day. Chicago, for example, was home to the first major fair, running from October 27 through November 7, 1863. The event opened with a fantastic parade, cannon salvos, and throngs of attendees, many given leave by their employers to miss work. It attracted donations from across the North for sale in its various booths, including all sorts of manufactured goods, pianos, cattle, perfumes, and President Lincoln's signed Emancipation Proclamation, which ultimately secured a bid of $3,000. The fair sponsored musical performances as well as a lecture by the well-known young patriotic orator Anna Dickinson, among other entertainments. People laughed when Mary Livermore promised that the fair would bring in $25,000.[71] Livermore underestimated the draw of her enterprise; the organizers extended the fair's duration, which when concluded had accumulated over $78,000 for soldiers' aid. Other big city fairs exceeded Chicago's success. The organizers of Boston's December 1863 fair could raise admission fees because so many people wished to attend, raising $146,000 in the end. New York's Metropolitan Fair, which opened in April 1864, raised an estimated $2 million and Philadelphia's Great Central Fair, which opened in June 1864, raised well over $1 million.[72] Even smaller cities hosted fund-raising fairs. The people of Cleveland, inspired by the Chicago fair, held one of their own, the Northern Ohio Sanitary Fair, which raised $78,000 in less than three weeks during February and March 1864.[73]

The money spent by the attendees of these fairs indicated that, as Sidney George Fisher judged the Philadelphia Sanitary Fair, they were "well worth seeing." In 1864 Fisher visited his local event and observed large buildings sheltering lavishly decorated rooms, filled with "articles for sale & exhibition in infinite variety."[74] Suitably impressed, he concluded, "These fairs & Sanitary Commission are miracles of American spirit, energy, & beauty."[75]

The sanitary fairs that amused thousands of Northerners and raised funds for the boys in the army were also expressions of their communities' patriotism. They grew out of a certain amount of local boosterism, but they also were an affirmation of a united nation facing the challenge of traitors hoping to destroy the republican promise it embodied at a time when state identities still mattered. Visitors could not attend a fair and escape the fact that along with the clever contraptions and novelties on display there were sufficient flags and other military artifacts gathered in one place to provide proof of the heroism of soldiers fighting to preserve the nation. And it would be a dense individual who walked the aisles of buildings from New York City to northern Ohio and elsewhere who would not be able to witness the results of the sacrifices made by the organizers and contributors.[76]

African American women initially had no soldiers for whom they could raise relief funds because of the North's reluctance at first to fight anything but a white man's war for the Union. Nevertheless, black women did what they could to assist contrabands, the slaves who sought shelter and freedom behind the Union lines. Black communities organized relief efforts for these former slaves gathering in crowded camps. The Contraband Committee of Philadelphia's Mother Bethel Church and other groups relied on the efforts of Northern black women and white organizations devoted to contraband relief. Wives and daughters took on the tasks with which white women had occupied themselves from the outset of the war and did what they could to make their soldiers' lives more comfortable. Antislavery advocate, newspaper editor, and former teacher Mary Ann Shadd Cary most famously went beyond such traditional roles in the women's war effort. Although a resident of Canada who became a British subject in 1862, she returned to the United States in 1863 and worked for contraband relief with the Colored Ladies' Freedmen's Aid Society of Chicago.[77]

Some black and white women who shared Cary's energies required an intellectual outlet and, perhaps, more demanding settings than home-front fund-raising for their war efforts. Before the war, abolitionist women such as Cary spoke out against slavery and now during the war they publicly rallied audiences for the Union. Anna Dickinson, the young Philadelphia abolitionist and stalwart lecturer for the Union cause, earned a reputation as a Northern Joan of Arc. Other more "ordinary" women may have shared Dickinson's patriotic sentiments, but became involved in the nation's political discourse in ways that did not attract as much attention.[78] Mary Vermilion, for example, coped with the travails of daily life, but also entered the world of wartime politics by attending Union meetings, which sometimes were all-day affairs, and reading newspapers; she did not hesitate to express fully her political opinions in letters to her husband.[79]

The enthusiasm of women for the male-dominated national organizations also waned as the female patriots came to believe groups controlled by a distant patriarchal board had a potentially serious flaw in that they lacked the personal knowledge of their soldiers' needs. Women feared that the Sanitary Commission and other such large organizations might misuse or misdirect their material contributions and rightly worried that light-fingered freight handlers and surgeons might help themselves to the things that they had worked so hard to deliver to the front. Women's groups' desire for their independence led their members to resent the controlling hand of national organizations, creating a tension between their patriotic commitment to national loyalty and their deep ties to their local communities. This desire for autonomy often found expression in how local groups ordered their priorities, giving preference to tending the needs first and foremost of soldiers from their communities; it also prompted them to organize local fund-raising events and fairs that they could control.[80]

The women who dominated the organization and execution of fund-raising events walked away from their successes with lessons well learned. Their experiences sharpened their social and political skills while making them even more aware of the limitations that society placed on them. Mary Livermore learned that she and her female associates needed their husbands' signatures to have a building constructed for the Chicago sanitary fair even though they would be using their own resources to pay in advance for the work. The law required no less, their contractor told them, because all their property legally belonged to their husbands. "We learned much of the laws made by men for women, in that conversation with an illiterate builder," she later recalled. "I registered a vow that when the war was over I would take up a new work—the work of making law and justice synonymous for women."[81] Young women who became active during the war could second Livermore's experiences and match her determination to do something about the paternalism they encountered in their work as they moved into the postwar nation; their wartime success in developing and coordinating such an extensive network of female-dominated organizations was testimony to their competence as well as fuel for their rising expectations.[82]

EIGHT

KNOWING WAR

FEAR OF INVASION

For New Jerseyan General Robert McAllister, no matter what civilians did or saw, their efforts to understand war could never reach the level that came with actual experience. "All the men in the army," he wrote to his daughter in January 1863, "who a short time ago were at home speculating, come out now and acknowledge that they knew nothing about it, and that there [*sic*] views are entirely changed." Indeed, he continued, "I wish all such could come and try there [*sic*] hands. It would be a holesome [*sic*] lesson and would teach them wisdom and stop a grate [*sic*] deal of this complaining at home, as well as lessen [*sic*] the dissatisfaction in the army."[1]

Perhaps the general was being unfair to those Northerners who experienced something of the war, even if not in the same way as his campaigning soldiers. Fear, pain, and death, not to mention anxiety and worry as well as the desire to know what their men experienced all could bring civilians closer to a better understanding of the conflict. Also, the dangers of a closer war appeared real to many of them. Those civilians residing near the Canadian border and on the Great Lakes worried about the possibility of Confederate raiders harassing their communities from their northern neighbor or even war with England, Canada's master. As if to prove distance from the battlefields of Virginia offered no absolute protection to the Yankee home front, on October 18, 1864, escaped Confederate prisoners of war, their uniforms hidden under civilian clothes, raided St. Albans, Vermont, harassing the people and robbing three of the city's banks before escaping across the Canadian border.[2]

Earlier in August 1862, the Sioux uprising in distant Minnesota also suggested that some Northern civilians learned the meaning of fear in the face of the threat of violence, even if it did not come at the hands of rebels. Indian attacks in Minnesota triggered panic among residents not only there but also in relatively safe Wisconsin. Families in both states fled their homes in terror, but Wisconsinites panicked beyond all reason. In one town, residents fled, "stampeding like cattle while not an Indian was within fifty miles." Rumors spread of towns burned to the ground, of people massacred by the native horde, of scalping parties roaming the countryside. Consequently, refugees clogged roads with their wagons.[3]

The Sioux who caused the widespread panic were not auxiliaries of the Confederate army. They had their own grievances, but Wisconsin's Governor Edward Salomon believed he could recognize a conspiracy in these events. "I am well satisfied," he explained as he requested more arms from Washington, "that these Indians have been tampered with by rebel agents."[4] Regardless of the irrational behavior, at least a fair number of civilians tasted the kind of fear more frequently experienced by their Southern enemies.[5]

The poorly defended Atlantic coastal states, as distant from the southern battlefields as the settlers of the Great Lakes, were vulnerable to Confederate naval raids, thus prompting some realistic concern among their inhabitants about rebel infringements on their peace, quiet, and trade. Before the war the government had planned an impressive system of forts that, if completed, would have protected harbors from Maine southward from rebels or potential European belligerents. In 1861 many of them stood as inadequate sentinels, unfinished and lacking in weaponry and manpower, victims of shortsighted congressional budgets, until the real threat posed by secession and potential international enemies moved the government to renewed efforts.[6] Federal and state governments tried to rectify the problems of coastal defense, but the occasional Confederate attack on shipping reminded East Coast residents that there was a war in progress.[7]

VIOLENCE AND BORDER REGIONS

Residents of the borderland counties of the free states more than other Northerners had legitimate concerns about their exposure to invasion or to partisan guerrilla violence. Kansans had experienced internal violence before the war between proslavery and antislavery factions. Little changed with the coming of the war, but Missouri's significant rebel sympathies and its own internal civil war did not help matters across the border. During the fall of 1862, Kansas communities along that Missouri border felt "no security for life or property," wrote John Halderman, a state militia commander, "and many, in despair that the Government will afford them aid, are leaving the State or moving back into the interior, abandoning crops, houses, and other improvements to the mercy of the enemy."[8]

Kansans were far from innocent in this border war, with James Lane and his "jayhawkers" making their reputations with forays into Missouri.[9] Federal troops from Kansas also fought rebel sympathizers across the border in Missouri while the Kansas border region remained "infested with bushwackers who kill in the dark, murder, destroy and rob the country of everything they can carry off." This guerrilla conflict only bred fear and hatred. George W. Packard, a soldier in the Seventh Kansas, advised his mother that an end to it would come only after "About two-thirds of the inhabitants of Mo. . . . [were] killed like wolves or as any other venomous wild animals." For Packard, during the spring of 1863 "Murder, robbery, and plunder seem to be the order of the day."[10]

The August 21, 1863, sacking and razing of Lawrence, Kansas, by William Quantrill and his men, however, appeared to be the most shocking example of such border violence. Quantrill's raid was a retaliatory attack for what Kansans had done in Missouri, and it certainly succeeded in exacting vengeance in blood and treasure from the antislavery residents of Lawrence.[11] After the ashes had settled, stubborn residents were determined to stay and rebuild. Nevertheless, some of their number admitted that the massacre had the effect of terrorizing them. After funerals for victims of the raid, a "night of terror and excitement . . . followed." Word had arrived of an imminent attack by Quantrill, which led people to hide in a cornfield through the night. Not long afterward, Lawrence resident Elizabeth Earl admitted that her "nerves" were "so unstrung" by the raid, which had caused unimaginable "distress, and suffering, of our women and children, by the suden [*sic*] death of their Husbands and Fathers." Women left the town "Horrified and will never return," Earl wrote to her mother, and "others have left, thinking by doing so, they can throw off the feelings" resulting from the massacre of friends and family.[12] Far from the Lawrence raid being the end of such cross-border fights, Kansans planned their own vengeance.[13]

Incursions into the border states of Maryland and Kentucky in 1862 caused some concern farther north of those loyal slave states, imparting some sense of the fear experienced by enemy civilians in the Confederacy.[14] In September, Cincinnati had prepared for the worse. On learning of Confederate progress in Kentucky and the approach of cavalry dispatched from Confederate General Kirby Smith's forces, some residents of the city fled their homes. Authorities proclaimed martial law and essentially conscripted all citizens for preparing the city's defense. Men drilled. A few defaulters found themselves arrested by the police. Volunteers converged on the city. As Northerners had done since the beginning of the war, Cincinnati's citizens fed their guests, and the town appropriated local buildings for their barracks. Men built defensive works on the Kentucky side of the river, while other communities along the Ohio River also prepared for invasion.[15]

After two weeks of manning the improvised defenses and a few skirmishes fought on the Kentucky side of the Ohio, Cincinnati's danger passed as Kirby Smith's contingent withdrew southward. Not long afterward, western Confederates under Braxton Bragg failed to do better, stymied by Union forces on October 8 at Perryville, Kentucky.[16] Neither Philadelphia nor Harrisburg or for that matter Cincinnati had to live with the enemy marching down their streets, but the threat had sown the sort of fear common in Confederate communities in the paths of invading Union armies, raiders, and foragers.

THE GETTYSBURG CAMPAIGN

In 1862, despite real concerns about General Robert E. Lee's progress in Maryland during his invasion northward, Pennsylvanians won a reprieve. On September 17, 1862, the Army of the Potomac stopped the invasion with a bloody fight at Antietam Creek near Sharpsburg.[17] The summer of 1863 once again proved the vulnerability of Pennsylvania with a particularly harsh reminder of how the war might spill over into Northern backyards. Incursions above the Potomac River by the Army of Northern Virginia during the Gettysburg campaign of 1863 spread fear among the people of the state. The Army of the Potomac, however, gathered at Gettysburg for a battle that lasted from July 1 through July 3. Lee failed to break the Yankee forces. His army retreated and completed its crossing of the Potomac by July 14.[18] Before the battle and Lee's successful retreat, however, the Confederates gave Pennsylvanians a taste of what an invading army could do.

During June, as during the earlier Antietam campaign, Yankees panicked as a Confederate army threatened Harrisburg, other points in southeastern Pennsylvania, and perhaps, some people worried, even Philadelphia. Harrisburg, the state's capital and a communications hub, as well as rail lines were attractive targets, as the people of that city understood. A prosperous, well-built town on the Susquehanna River, it also had desirable military resources in the Pennsylvania Arsenal located there. Governor William Curtin was well aware of the city's situation and acted accordingly. The prudent governor not only supervised the local defenses but also sent men far afield to scout the enemy. He petitioned Lincoln for troops while calling up Pennsylvania militiamen. "It is our only hope to save the North and crush the Rebel army," he wrote, "Do not suppose for one instant that I am unnecessarily alarmed." In the meantime, officials spirited away important documents while moving the state's wealth to New York for safety. The concerns of the residents of the capital intensified with the sounds of the battle they heard in the distance when on July 3 the artillery of both armies unleashed their power.[19]

Southern Pennsylvanians in the path of the Army of Northern Virginia tried to escape the rebels, either making their way to Harrisburg or at some other point putting the Susquehanna River between them, their portable property, and the invaders.[20] As the rebels approached, Chambersburg businessman William Heyser witnessed, "Suddenly about two hundred more wagons, horses, mules, and contrabands all came pouring down the street in full flight. . . . Such a sight I have never seen, or will never see again." There was no mistaking the panic, as Heyser observed "The whole town . . . on the sidewalks screaming, crying, and running about. They know not where." Heyser joined fleeing Chambersburg residents that night on the journey to Harrisburg, a city he found "in wildest confusion."[21]

The people who remained in Chambersburg, as well as other nearby places such as Carlisle, were able to watch rebels come and go through their streets, breaking into stores and warehouses and taking what they needed or fancied.[22] When the invading army finally returned to Virginia, it had suffered a setback on the battlefield, but by all appearances it had participated in a successful raid. The tens of thousands of animals as well as significant quantities of agricultural and manufactured products seized by the Confederates were sufficient proof. The Army of Northern Virginia would be able to sustain itself for some time off of the bounty appropriated from the civilians north of the Potomac.[23]

The people of Gettysburg, even more so than the surrounding towns, saw exactly what war did to life, limb, and property. They initially watched Confederate and Union soldiers fighting in streets and houses, and they listened to the thundering battle continue south of their town. When the residents emerged from their homes, they viewed previously unimaginable scenes, the consequence of the physical mayhem and destruction of war. The odor of the summertime battlefield was unavoidable, especially with dead and decomposing soldiers and animals an immediate presence on the town's streets, and the task of burying the multitude of human and animal bodies on the fields of battle around the town appeared to be overwhelming.[24] Local residents had no choice but to spend much of their time after the battle cleaning up their community, praying, and recovering from their traumatic experiences. Refugees eventually returned to views of great destruction in the town and its immediate hinterland, hardly able to breathe the putrid air of an atmosphere reeking of death. Soldiers had erased farm boundaries, consumed farmers' pantries, and poisoned wells with dead bodies.[25]

Federal surgeon John H. Brinton recalled the medical emergency that followed the battle, but also the immediate swarm of the curious, who created additional problems for the federal army. "The town of Gettysburg was filled with hospitals and stores for the wounded, surgeons and their assistants, who were coming to see a real battle-ground," Brinton noted, but there were also "newspaper men in abundance, and a crowd of Sanitary and Christian Commissioners, who wandered about everywhere, and kept remarkably good tables at the houses which they regarded as their headquarters." Not only did individuals who had some real or invented purpose for being there arrive on the scene but also "Crowds of citizens" from nearby locales and even far-away Philadelphia. These were not helpful volunteers, according to Brinton. "A great many were in search of relics or 'trophies', as they called them, from the battlefield," Brinton noted, "shot, shell, bayonets, guns, and every sort of military portable property." Trophy hunting was against regulations, but rules did not stop individuals who did their best to evade provost guards. The solution was a practical and necessary one: the Provost Marshal sent those civilians caught in the act of scavenging for souvenirs "out to the field of battle, to assist in burying dead horses,—not a pleasant duty." Despite the complaints of the conscripted gravediggers, the threat of being placed on such a burial detail seemed to have stopped the trophy hunting.[26]

African Americans, unlike their white neighbors, suffered a particularly heinous hardship at the hands of the invaders who acted as slave catchers. Rachel Cormany took particular notice of the fear among local African Americans, whom she witnessed being hunted and captured with the rebels "driving them off by droves." "O! How it grated on our hearts to have to sit quietly & look at such brutal deeds," she lamented; "Some of the colored people who were raised here were taken along— I sat on the front step as they were driven by just like we would drive cattle."[27] News of captured African Americans caused panic in the black population, prompting freeborn blacks and former slaves to evacuate their homes, abandon the region, and seek refuge 35 miles away in Harrisburg or even farther eastward in Philadelphia. Philadelphians opened their churches and homes to the fugitives from Lee's army. In Harrisburg, residents, already frightened badly by the invasion, witnessed black refugees occupying parks, churches, and the courthouse. However, not all African Americans panicked and ran from the rebels; east of York on the Susquehanna River, a company of black volunteers joined in a defense of Wrightsville.[28]

It would not be until March of 1864 that the scattered decomposing bodies of half-buried soldiers would find permanent and suitable resting places in dedicated cemetery ground at the battlefield.[29] In the meantime, the desire for better treatment of the dead and a more sanitary landscape led to the battlefield's reincarnation as a national soldiers' cemetery, a development that would forever make the place a physical reminder of what had occurred there as well as providing the nation with arguably the greatest statement of the war's meaning.[30] The cemetery's dedication was a long affair, but the enduring high point was a short speech—the Gettysburg Address—by President Lincoln lasting only a few minutes.

On November 20, 1863, Philadelphian Sidney George Fisher recorded "a large meeting at Gettysburg" the preceding day, its purpose being "to consecrate a cemetery for the interment of our soldiers who fell . . . at that place." Many dignitaries were present and the famous orator Edward Everett made a "long but common-place" speech "tho well written & appropriate." Lincoln, on the other hand, made "a very short one, but to the point and marked by his pithy sense, quaintness, & good feeling."[31] Editorialists across the land considered Lincoln's brief remarks a master-piece.[32] It would be Lincoln's dedication of the Soldiers' National Cemetery, where he explained the necessity for such bloodshed in Pennsylvania and, indeed, elsewhere across the South, that would make that place unique in the memory of the war. His declaration of the nation's "new birth of freedom" and the necessity to make certain that "the government of the people, by the people, for the people, shall not perish from the earth" were essential reasons for continued sacrifice such as that witnessed at the Gettysburg battle.[33]

About a year after the battle at Gettysburg, the people of southeastern Penn-sylvania once again faced the enemy's wrath. Confederate cavalry peeled off from Jubal Early's army, which was raiding up from Virginia and into Maryland to the outer forts of Washington, to return to Chambersburg. Eager to retaliate for Yankee depredations in Virginia, Early expected to make Pennsylvania communities pay for their army's destructive behavior; his cavalry demanded a ransom but on July 30, 1864, were satisfied with razing the town.[34] And the residents once again came to understand the nature of war by first-hand experience as they surveyed "the black and smouldering [*sic*] ruins of that once happy and prosperous town."[35]

THE JOHN HUNT MORGAN RAID

Farther west Midwesterners had little time to enjoy the federal victories at Vicksburg and Gettysburg. On July 8, 1863, Confederate General John Hunt Morgan with some 2,400 to 3,000 cavalry troopers raided north of the Ohio River, traveling over 1,000 miles through Indiana into Ohio and through the hinterland of Cincinnati until his capture less than two weeks later on July 10.[36] Indianans had realized earlier that the Ohio River offered them little protection from their Southern enemies and always had feared Confederate raiders. Now Midwesterners suffered what was all too common for Virginians and other Confederates in the path of invading Yankees.

Indianans panicked when they learned of Confederate soldiers riding on their state's soil, fearing they would reach Indianapolis, and thousands of volunteers con-verged on the capital to protect it. Confederate raiders "stole a great many horses," according to Kate Starks, and at Corydon, they routed the home guard, killed resi-dents, and set fire to the town. Women and children at Newpoint, Indiana, "went about town screaming & holoring fit to kill themselves & when news came that they were fighting at Summansville & Napoleon and that there was more of their men than there was of ours some of the women like to have went crazy but they were drove back and did not get to come further." By the time federal troops ran Morgan to ground in Ohio on July 26, he and his men had accomplished little but for the destruction of property and the fear they caused among the citizens. Both consequences, however, were significant reminders of how the vagaries of war could bring about the unexpected.[37]

NEWS FROM THE FRONT

Civilians far from these traumatizing yet very localized events could only experience them in a vicarious fashion. Short of being in the path of an invading army or traveling to a battlefield, they might glean some understanding of the costs of war by reading published reports or viewing exhibits of photographs and magic lantern shows.[38] In the wake of battles, citizens scrambled for copies of extra editions printed by their local newspapers, hoping to learn something of the recent events or read casualty lists dreading seeing familiar names among those men killed in the fight. New Yorker Julius Wesslau and other concerned citizens made it a regular habit to scan the papers to keep abreast of events. In December 1864, he reported to his German parents, "The first thing I do every morning is look through the newspaper." The consequences of war were obvious to him, even so far removed from the fighting, with the political implications being made clear on the editorial pages. "Every day there are reports about battles, towns being destroyed, railroads, ships and other property," he wrote, "there are articles that curse the rogues in the government, one screams peace, the next for war, and usually the rabble with nothing to lose screams the most about the government (they themselves elected)."[39]

Hometown journals often recruited local men, some of whom had journalistic experience, to act as their special correspondents, but every soldier who wrote a letter home was a reporter to his own family.[40] Soldiers, as much as any newspaper, educated the home front about the ways of war, military commanders' high and low, the Southern landscape and rebels, slaves and slavery, the campaigns in which they marched and fought, and the death throes of the rebel armies.[41]

Many of the home folk were able to come to an even better understanding of the war when they had the opportunity to see and to speak to their soldiers in person. Throughout the war, individual soldiers such as William Merrill of Andover, Massachusetts, came home on leave bringing with them information that they shared with friends and strangers.[42] After the battle at Antietam Creek in September 1862, Sidney George Fisher, while traveling between Philadelphia and Wilmington, Delaware, "fell into conversation with a young soldier who was wounded" at that fight. The young soldier impressed Fisher with his patriotic enthusiasm and manly bearing and gave Fisher "an account of the battle & of the dreadful scenes that accompanied it, by which he seemed much impressed." The wounded soldier did not spare his civilian traveling companion. "He saw 1,100 men buried at once, in a long trench,"

Fisher continued, "but so hastily was the work done that hands, feet, & heads stuck out above ground."[43]

As the war raged on, entire regiments arrived home at the end of their enlistments or on furlough because of reenlistments, giving people throughout the Northern states opportunities to give them the joy of their communities, celebrating their return with parades, martial music, ringing bells, speeches, receptions, and dinners.[44] Even as communities honored their veterans, the appearance of the regiments might have sobered them, especially if the citizens recalled the day those men had left for the war. In the fall and winter of 1864, Bostonians were eager to celebrate returning soldiers, only to be shocked when they witnessed the greatly reduced size of the regiments.[45] The physical appearance of these veterans might also have given the home folk pause. Members of the 25th Connecticut returned home in August 1863, "a pretty hard looking set" after only a year of soldiering. Friends did not recognize the bearded men, who had dirty uniforms draped on their skinny frames.[46] The homecoming also provided an opportunity for men to inform home folk of the circumstances of the deaths of common acquaintances and to compare notes about local casualties serving in other regiments.[47]

Thousands of Northern soldiers also made their way home because of ill health or wounds, and communities of all sizes tended to them. Convalescing men rested in the expansive hospitals of cities and towns, where they attracted the attention of sympathetic civilians. Wounded veterans became a visible presence on Northern streets in larger towns during the war as they waited for artificial limbs or for trains to their final destinations. Even in small towns such as Nininger, Minnesota, wounded veterans attracted the attention of the people as they hobbled about on crutches.[48]

While on the mend, injured or sick soldiers sought comfort with their families. They frequently had their peace and quiet upset by the visits of curious citizens who wished to learn something about the war from the men who knew it firsthand. Iowan Will Kemper returned home on leave in an exhausted state in June 1863 and then again in March 1865 to recover from his time as a prisoner of war. On both occasions he attracted a stream of neighbors who quizzed him about his experiences. The visitors who called in 1865 in turn saw an ill-but-game veteran who willingly discussed his experiences with them, repeating the same stories over and over as required.[49] Indeed, it would be hard for wounded veterans to enjoy quiet anonymity in their communities; the local press often considered their homecomings to be newsworthy, making their presence known to all of their subscribers.[50]

It would be hard for families of the men still on campaign to miss the reminders of war's cost brought to their communities by these experienced soldiers. They made real the worries they had for their own husbands and sons, but for some of them, those concerns assumed a more universal quality, transformed into wider feelings for all the suffering soldiers. In June 1864, Emeline Ritner expressed her concerns for the hard times all soldiers endured in the service of their country. "I wonder you don't all get discouraged, sick and utterly *fed up*," she admitted; "But, the *true* soldier has the *noble Union & the glorious old flag* in view, and mind, not the hardships of the day . . . There is fighting for the right and right *will* prevail."[51] Crete Garfield wrote to her husband, the future president, James Garfield, explaining that her concern for all soldiers unsettled her. "I cannot think of the horrors this terrible war is planting around our brave boys, I could neither eat nor sleep nor live should I give myself up to the contemplation of the sufferings and miseries of those who are fighting for us," she admitted; "I only make the hours endurable by filling them so full of some employment that I cannot think."[52]

DEALING WITH DEATH

Just as sick and wounded veterans reminded Northerners of the reality of war, so, too, did the funerals of their hometown boys whose families were fortunate enough to be able to retrieve their remains from hospital or battlefield. By the end of the war, at least 360,000 soldiers had given their lives for the Union, killed by the enemy or by disease. Most of these men never returned to rest in their native soil, buried where they had fallen on some distant battlefield or encampment. However, those dead who made the last trip home concluded their journeys with the usual rituals of interment that their families required for their own peace of mind. In 1864, for example, people in Indianapolis, Indiana, in North Adams, Massachusetts, and in Trenton, New Jersey, watched funeral processions for local men.[53] In May of that year, the people of Lowell, Massachusetts, filled the streets to pay their respects as the body of Major Henry L. Abbott was laid to rest with military honors.[54] And in November, Waterbury, Vermont, residents buried a soldier with speeches, a turn-out of an honor guard of 32 soldiers, and an assembly of the local Masonic lodge.[55]

Northerners repeated these scenes throughout the region, usually with elaborate ritual for the more important men of the community.[56] Such ritual required civilians to think about the cause for which the dead had sacrificed themselves, reevaluate their lives, and come to terms with their grief. The dead also reminded civilians of the dangers that their men continued to face on their behalf. Rachel Cormany, whose husband Samuel was in the army, watched a soldier's burial across the street from her home in Chambersburg, Pennsylvania. "The first I ever saw buried," she noted; "I could not help shedding a tear for the brave soldier, perhaps thinking that such may be the fate of my poor Samuel makes me so sad."[57]

Americans had been familiar with death before the war, but the violent and obscene, sudden or lingering faraway deaths brought on by battle or camp sickness were new to most of their experiences. Before the war, death followed an established ritual. People did not normally die among strangers, and the death process provided the kind of structure that allowed family to contemplate the event, grieve the loss, and come to some degree of closure. During the war, this process remained possible for some families, but soldiers commonly died on distant fields, away from their loved ones, leaving them searching for some meaning in the loss that shattered their world.[58]

Often poor communications, unmarked graves, the grim reality of prisoner of war camps, incomplete casualty lists, and the general confusion of war even deprived families of positive knowledge of their soldier's death, leaving them in a nether world of uncertainty. Family members could find some comfort by gathering as many details as possible about their loved one's passing. They desired to know the last words of their loved ones, which would serve as part of the enduring memories of the deceased. They especially wanted to learn that they had died a good or noble death, one that was the consequence of heroic action or one that exhibited the traits of a true Christian.[59]

Families were fortunate to have information about the deaths of their soldiers in the letters of condolence written from someone who had been close to their loved one. The Remley family of Iowa learned of the circumstances of their son Lycurgus's death in June 1863 because his brother George had been nearby. George, a member of the same regiment, had nursed his ill brother for some time in a hospital behind the Union lines at Vicksburg and was able to provide his family with his brother's dying affirmation of his Christian faith in his last words. Lycurgus had asked George to tell the family that "he died in hope of a blissful immortality." George also resorted to the common evangelical Protestant beliefs of the times to comfort his family, consoling his mother that Lycurgus "is a thousand times better off where he is." "God was done with him here in this world and took him home to himself in Heaven, where he is forever free from pain and suffering and misery of Earth," he reassured his mother. George's words probably helped to comfort the grieving Remley family. But if they, religious as they were, had trouble finding meaning in Lycurgus's death, they could find reassurance in the knowledge that it was part of God's larger plan. "He does not willingly afflict the children of men," George wrote, "but makes all things work to-gether for the good of those that love him and put their trust in Him."[60] Still, his mother grieved. Another son informed the father, the Reverend James A. Remley, that news of Lycurgus's death "almost killed her."[61]

By September 1864, George was also dead, killed in battle at Winchester, Virginia. On this sad occasion, the family had to rely on the information provided by one of their son's friends, S. D. Price, the adjutant of the 22nd Iowa Infantry. Price sent George's father two detailed letters explaining the circumstances of his son's death. He informed the family that George was shot down while charging the enemy, not in the later retreat, hence it was a noble death. For some families, knowing that their son had done his duty to his country would have been sufficient, but for the Remleys, a family with a minister at its head, it probably was more important to know that their son had lived a virtuous life. Price reassured them that prior to George's death, their son had maintained his Christian ways.[62]

Most families wished to have their loved ones buried closer to home if it were at all possible. Those who were able traveled the distance to the battlefield to locate their dead; others commissioned proxies to perform the duty.[63] Some family members arrived at battlefields or military hospitals near the front where their loved ones had died only to find that confusion or poor records made it impossible to locate their bodies; others were fortunate to have hospital workers and nurses prepare bodies for transport back home.[64] Even if they could not immediately retrieve a body, families sought information that would make it possible for them to do so at a later date. Thus, George Remley's father wished to know if his boy's grave was marked so that he might locate it in the future.[65]

As the Remleys and other families understood, religion helped the bereaved cope with their personal tragedies. The Rev. Remley reassured his son that Lycurgus "has indeed received his final discharge & is no doubt gone home to his Heavenly father to those mansions which Jesus has prepared for the reception of his 'returned soldiers'."[66] It also allowed for a certain element of fatalism that may have helped some accept what they could not change. When Mary Vermilion's eldest brother succumbed to smallpox after recovering from a battle wound, her husband William advised her, "we must submit to the laws of Him who rules in the Hospital as well on the battlefield."[67] And when a Vermont mother Rachel Stevens learned of her son's death, she advised her daughter "to bear this crushing affliction with the fortitude & resignation of a Christian."[68]

Resignation to the fate of a loved one, however, was not the same as finding meaning in death. Some families might have found comfort in the immediate, positive consequences of their soldier's death that helped lead to an ultimate Union victory, as perhaps Private Oren C. Mudge hoped when he informed Gertrude Howard that her husband had been killed in fighting at Petersburg in 1865. "[I]t was the decicive [*sic*] Battle," he told her; "the rebellion is crushed."[69] For many survivors, knowing that their men died for their country and the Union was sufficient.

NINE

PAYING FOR THE WAR

NEW FINANCIAL BURDENS FOR
GOVERNMENTS AND THE PEOPLE

At the outset of the war, states and municipalities rallied to the flag, raised troops, and put off worrying about how they would pay their bills. The expenses associated with fighting a war, however, could be shocking. At the beginning of the war, the federal government faced millions of dollars of expenses every week, a frightening prospect if the war were to continue longer than the optimists expected. The situation led to additional borrowing and increased taxes on all levels, which by the end of the war, as one pessimistic Democrat lamented, made the United States "no land of rest . . . for the tired taxpayer."[1]

Taxes certainly added to the financial burdens of farmers. In May 1863, after an encounter with a federal income tax collector, Asahel Hubbard, a Whiting, Vermont, farmer, groused about the $15 to $16 he had to pay over and above his $56 in state taxes, which he believed "makes a good smart War tax." Additionally, he complained, he had paid another $50 "last fall for town bounty," a sum he was willing to pay if it helped him avoid conscription.[2] Silas Hall, another Vermont farmer, found that taxation for bounties in his town of Brookfield was just one more thing challenging his ability to balance his budget. His crops were in fine order, although he suffered the usual vicissitudes of the farmer, and he admitted to his soldier son

Edwin, "If you want more money I can supply you a little while longer." However, he warned, "I see the necessity of economy & I hope you will."[3]

Women left to manage the family farms found themselves especially burdened by the additional taxes, an added factor of stress on top of all of their other hardships. Pennsylvanian Elizabeth Schwalm, mother of four children, responsibly tended to her family's finances but still could not always promptly pay all that the taxman required, thus leaving her vulnerable to property confiscation.[4] Mary Herrick considered it unfair of the government to place women in such circumstances. "I am left all a lone I have a small plase [*sic*] and don't want to be taxed to death," she complained directly to Edwin M. Stanton. "[B]y good rights you should pass a law to exemt [*sic*] such as I am from heavey [*sic*] taxes," she proposed for a solution to her and the financial problems of other farm women. She furthered her argument by suggesting the irony that a war fought for slaves would leave her as one. "I think slavery is an abomination in the sight of god [*sic*]," she explained, "that is one reason why I don't want to be a slave to this *war!*"[5]

The burden of taxation went beyond the farmers and also touched the pockets of modest businessmen. In late October 1862, German immigrant Julius Wesslau, a furniture maker in New York, complained to his parents about the tax man's broad reach. "In order to raise money for the war, every little thing is being taxed, so everything we need is more expensive," he explained to the home folk; "There's a business tax, too, and then 3 percent on everything we produce that means about 600 dollars a year for our business." He feared that the government wasted much of this revenue since, he assumed, much of money collected went to collecting the tax.[6] By the end of the war, Wesslau could see how the conflict had reduced the profits of his hard work. During the preceding year his company had a gross income of $40,000, which meant that at a 6 percent tax rate he handed over to the government over $2,400. "Anyone who doesn't agree that this is outrageous doesn't know the value of two thousand and four hundred dollars," he wrote to his family. Audits of untruthful taxpayers, he also noted, led to significant fines.[7]

There was no ignoring the fact that the war required money from Americans who were not used to heavy taxation at any level. Difficulties arose from the fact that the usual prewar ways of financing government proved inadequate during this time of national crisis.[8] The Lincoln administration and the Republican-controlled Congress, therefore, mixed the old and the new as they tried to come to grips with the ever-growing costs of saving the Union. In doing so, they brought the central government much closer to the lives of average Northerners.

During the war the federal government derived significant revenue from excise taxes and borrowed more of what it needed. Tariffs and government bonds covered much of the war's cost, as they had done in the past, with the heavier emphasis on borrowing. Indeed, the federal government covered two-thirds of the cost of the war through borrowing.[9] In addition, the Lincoln government passed indirect taxes and instituted a new income tax. It also engaged in the innovative printing of a paper national currency, known as "greenbacks," and made it legal tender. But even something as old-fashioned as borrowing money had unique consequences in the context of war for future generations. As Democrats reminded the nation, it was a heavy burden or, as Republicans would have one consider it, it left a manageable and worthwhile patriotic legacy.

In the minds of many Republicans, it was a debt that the increased wealth of the Northern population stimulated by the war could readily handle, especially when considering the nation's future prospects. A growing population as well as expanding prosperity in part encouraged by the vast amount of land owned by government with all of its potential abundant riches would make the war debt much less of a burden. In 1864 David Ames Wells made this argument in a pamphlet weighted down with statistics that only an economist or a banker could enjoy. Indeed, Wells believed his data proved "that the country cannot be destroyed, or even crippled, by any *probable* future debt." His reassuring numbers should "induce every loyal man, as he reflects upon our resources as a nation, to '*Thank God and take courage*'."[10] New York resident and German immigrant Jacob Kessler came to the same conclusion. On February 24, 1865, he admitted, "By the end of the war, we will have run up enormous debts." Nevertheless, victory was on the horizon and "The vast resources of this country, the rapid increase in population will make it much easier to pay back this debt."[11]

Taxes, bonds, and a new national currency touched the lives of Northerners in ways that made citizens more aware, and even wary, of their relationship to the federal government.[12] By the end of the war, the Republicans' economic policies had expanded the fiscal and monetary roles of the federal government over states and individuals beyond anything that the nation had previously known. At the same time states and localities dipped into the pocketbooks of citizens unused to such closer-to-home levies.[13] Such financial intrusions required a true and steadfast patriotism on the part of those individuals paying the bill for the nation's preservation.

TAXES

With expenses on the rise as the war progressed, the federal government looked to new sources of income beyond antebellum tariffs and land sales. Congress increased tariff duties regularly, largely for revenue purposes but also to counter British and French protection policies, and the die was cast for higher rates as a matter of policy thereafter.[14] The effect of the tariffs fell unequally on manufacturers and consumers, for consumers paid higher prices for goods protected by the tariffs and tariff rates were set higher on consumer goods than on capital goods.[15]

More indicative of what became the government's aggressive search for revenue was the Internal Revenue Act, passed on July 1, 1861, which imposed specific tax rates for selected industries, such as coal, iron, steel, and paper, and a general *ad-valorem* tax on other manufactures. The law further laid a gross-receipts tax on railroads, steamboats, and express companies. By war's end, Congress extended excise taxes to cover virtually all forms of production, and added licensing fees for professions, except the ministry. Federal taxes touched everything from beer and billiard tables to butchered beef and brokerage bills.

More dramatically, in August 1861, Congress established America's first federal income tax. It set a standard 3 percent tax on annual incomes over $800; it also levied a direct tax on the states based on real estate values that the states could assume and collect as they saw fit. Tax collection was uneven, and revenue needs were growing; consequently, Congress passed a tax bill in July 1862 that broke more new ground by authorizing a progressive income tax with a limit set at a high of 5 percent on incomes over $10,000, while retaining the 3 percent rate on incomes ranging from $600 to $10,000. The law also added a host of other taxes, including excise taxes on many goods and services, stamp taxes, inheritance taxes, and license fees. Congress raised the rates with the Tax Act of 1864, building on the idea that a New York Republican representative had proposed earlier: "that those having a larger amount of income shall pay a larger amount of tax." It raised taxes again in 1865 and adopted new forms of assessments and allowances to improve collections. By March 1865, income taxes alone were bringing in almost a fourth of all internal revenue. Along with excise taxes, they did much to mitigate inflation, encourage public confidence in the fiscal health of the government, and pay for the war. These taxes also put an increasing financial burden on Northerners personally as businesses increased their prices to cover additional costs. The income tax portion of the 1862 revenue act introduced Northerners to a new government agency (the Internal Revenue Bureau), the federal tax form, deductions, and a limited amount of automatic withholding.[16]

Taxation also provided opportunities for wealthy Northerners to practice creative accounting. Some astonished citizens of Dubuque, Iowa, learned of this practice when they perused the published tax rolls and discovered that some of the wealthiest among them had avoided altogether the tax burden. One editorialist wondered how people who had large, well-furnished houses and lived extravagant lives could do so on less than $600 a year. "We wish some of them would set up a school and teach other people the art," he suggested. Indeed, the taxman also took note and warned the dodgers that they had better come clean on their true incomes before he burdened them with penalties, which included a large fine and jail time, on top of what they owed.[17] The problem must have been notable elsewhere in the North, and as Julius Wesslau had noted, the government provided for that contingency. The 1865 federal law also gave Washington's revenue service the power to raise a taxpayers' suspiciously low reported incomes and add a dose of fines on top of what the cheats owed the government.[18]

BONDS AND GREENBACKS

Early in the war, Secretary of the Treasury Salmon P. Chase expected to finance the extraordinary burdens through borrowing. In February 1862, the federal government increased its reliance on borrowing by authorizing Chase to sell $500 million worth of interest-bearing bonds. The government relied on private bankers to sell the bonds, but sales were sluggish, in tandem with Union wartime reverses on the battlefield. Desperate to move the bonds, Chase turned to Philadelphia financier Jay Cooke, who developed a successful plan to market two bond issues that he had received the exclusive right to sell. He launched a sophisticated campaign premised on the principle of self-interest that sold patriotism along with the promise of personal financial gain. He also reached beyond the banking community to tap into the resources of average Americans by appealing to them directly to invest. His approach promised to democratize investment, and to move the bonds. His company and a network of agents used newspaper ads and other printed materials as well as shoe leather to spread the word from cities to isolated farm communities. The result was a financial success for Cooke, but it also had the consequence of convincing many Northerners that their federal government could be a source of financial security for themselves. Big investors bought up the greater share of these bonds, and banks in the Northeast further consolidated their financial and political power nationally with large purchases, but sales offices stayed open into the evening to tend to the needs of working people and the middle class. Importantly, the publicity associated with the campaign alerted even those ordinary people who did not buy bonds that the federal government was offering the investment to them and that the government could have a new role in their economic lives.[19]

The war brought to the Union a new currency that further contributed to the connection of the ordinary person and the national government and the growth of central state power in the economy. At the outset of the war, the federal government coined gold and silver and issued small quantities of paper currency. Americans satisfied much of their currency needs by relying on notes issued by private institutions, regulated, if at all, by the various states in which they were located. Good business required that these banks also regulate themselves, and the notes of functioning institutions were safe for the most part.[20]

This situation often made for confusion and uncertainty about the currency at hand by providing an environment in which the circulation of counterfeit and bad bank notes was common. The suspension of specie payments by banks early in the war heightened a money shortage that threatened to further disorder the nation's finances. All of that changed when on February 25, 1862, the Legal Tender Act became law. The law authorized the Treasury to issue $150 million in U.S. Treasury notes, soon known as "greenbacks" for the green color on the back of the notes, that were legal tender but bore no interest and were not redeemable in gold or silver. The federal government would continue to pay interest on its debt in specie, a promise designed to encourage the purchase of its bonds. Within three months of the bill's passage the first greenbacks were in circulation, and the first money crisis of the war was averted. Two subsequent issues of greenbacks occurred to meet the nation's growing monetary needs and to allow the government to pay its bills. At least in the loyal states, Americans now had the convenience of paper money that had to be accepted in all transactions except the payment of import tariffs.[21] President Lincoln certainly saw value in the new paper, jesting with his treasury secretary Salmon Chase when the government's money appeared tight to crank up his "paper mill" once again.[22]

Further banking legislation made it a burden to use anything but the federal government's greenbacks. By assuming the responsibility of insuring the integrity of money, the federal government sought to cement further the trust of the people in its policies. That such trust was not readily forthcoming amid scandals over the shoddy production of soldiers' uniforms, bounty frauds, cotton-trading corruptions, conscription, and curtailment of civil liberties made gaining faith in the nation's money all the more important. It was no accident that "In God We Trust" was added to American coinage during the war, for it claimed to conjoin the nation with the Maker in the public eye. By federal design, the country ended the war with a uniform and secure currency that shifted monetary policy to the nation's capital.[23] Lincoln summed up the benefits of the new financial programs and the creation of a uniform circulating medium in his annual message to Congress in December 1862, explaining, "In no other way could the payment of the troops, and the satisfaction of other just demands, be so economically, or so well provided for" while saving "the people, immense sums in discounts and exchanges."[24]

The federal government issues also gained credibility during the war because gold and silver strikes and aggressive mining in the West provided much-needed specie. Virginia City, Nevada, and other boomtowns exploded in population and new wealth. As the governor of Colorado wired President Lincoln in October 1863, the territory's loyalty and worth to the Union cause was in the "untold millions of gold to the credit of the Government" deposited in Colorado's "stone vaults."[25] During the war, mining companies dug out enough Western gold and silver to relieve some of the pressure on the federal government's specie reserves, thereby reaffirming the promise of prosperity made in 1864 by pamphleteer David Ames Wells as well as boosting confidence in the Union's ability to pay its debts.[26]

STATE AND LOCAL FINANCING OF THE WAR

States and municipalities coped with financing their war efforts in various ways. Early in the war, officials were able to count on private donations to fund bounty payments to encourage and reward the men who volunteered for military service. As the war continued, such funding gave way to borrowing and taxation, increasing the burden placed on individuals. Wisconsin borrowed money over and above its constitutional limit, liberally interpreting another constitutional provision that allowed it to borrow money to defend the state.[27] Vermont steadily increased its statewide property tax to cover its expenses.[28] Even New Jersey raised its debt load and increased taxes.[29]

Connecticut, on the other hand, hesitated to tax its citizens. In May 1861, Connecticut spent almost $2 million to put five regiments into the field, which the legislature covered by selling bonds. Resistance to any increase in taxation as well as the conflicting economic interests of businessmen, farmers, and small landowners meant that the state also borrowed money to cover the federal government's initial levy on the state. The reluctance to tax Connecticut residents encouraged the legislature to continue to issue bonds to pay the state's war costs until the fear of the consequences of the increasingly large debt, and eventually the sense of security that came with victory, convinced the politicians to increase taxes on businesses and property. By the summer after the victory, property taxes had quadrupled over antebellum figures.[30]

Local communities also had to cope with increased expenses, especially after they began to pay bounties to encourage enlistments. Illinois, for example, gave counties and cities the authority to add new property taxes to their usual assessments, which they were to use for extraordinary wartime expenses.[31] Fountain Green, Illinois, had to borrow money to pay soldiers' bounties and did not hesitate to confiscate property of individuals who failed to pay their share of the debt.[32] Throughout the war, Cape Elizabeth, Maine, met its wartime obligations through borrowing, with the paper it issued in most cases maturing ten to twenty years after the war, increasing its debt from about $13,610 before the war to an 1864 total of $68,729.[33]

The very nature of recruiting soldiers meant an increase in the cost of conducting government business. Nearby military camps prompted a growth in the size of police forces in places such as Cape Elizabeth, Maine, and Jacksonville, Illinois.[34] Increased volumes of records dealing with recruiting and other war expenses required more clerks as well as more space in which to store the documents. Cape Elizabeth officials began the war writing out receipts until they spent money on printed forms and casual record storage gave way to professional procedures.[35]

The immediate costs of conducting war business meant that communities had to economize as well as postpone improvements until victory freed up funds. In 1862, New Bedford, Massachusetts, borrowed money to help pay for war expenses such as recruiting bounties, but also made ends meet by cutting the salaries of town employees including their own, closed an elementary school, stopped lighting the streets at night, and did not fund Fourth of July festivities. School officials steadily reduced education expenses throughout the war by cutting salaries and raising the number of students in each classroom.[36] Budget constraints also forced Madison, Wisconsin, to shutter its high school during the early years of the war; officials closed other schools from time to time and, unable to expand its school system's physical plant, they crammed students into the buildings that remained open.[37] In Wisconsin, county and local governments deferred capital improvements and infrastructure maintenance.[38] Thus, the local public good would need to give way to the exigencies of war, delaying improvements to which municipalities and states might otherwise have directed their attention.

Despite the concerns about war-related expenses, there were some forward-looking individuals who saw the opportunity or the necessity to prepare their communities for the postwar world. Springfield, Massachusetts, began to pave its streets in 1864. Mayor Henry Alexander also secured the funding to build better drainage, which showed visible progress by late 1865 but still left the city in need of a true sewer system.[39] Leaders in New Bedford, Massachusetts, engaged in a debate about civic improvements, arguing that the whaling industry would not continue to sustain the town and that textile mills, essential for the town's economic future, required a better infrastructure. The key appeared to be an improved water supply that would enhance manufacturing in need of steam power as well as provide potable water to the town's citizens. In April 1863, Massachusetts provided the whaling town with permission to investigate the possibility of bringing clean water through a publicly supported system into the town and the political power to make it happen, including the authority to issue $500,000 in bonds to fund the project. The war delayed construction of the water system, but after the peace, the town pursued a less expensive alternative to the one originally proposed. The public water supply finally became available at the end of 1869.[40]

In the past, Congress had reimbursed states for wartime expenditures and states expected the national government to be forthright with its money at this time. In July 1861, the federal government promised to make good to the states the costs involved in mustering their regiments. The law was a confusing piece of legislation that relied on an unforgiving federal bureaucracy in need of exact paperwork, which in turn led to some disputed state claims that remained unresolved well into the postwar period.[41] Connecticut, for example, successfully pursued its claims against the federal government into the early years of the next century, regaining over $2.1 million.[42] Also, at the end of the war, New Bedford, Massachusetts, recouped over $15,000 in war expenses, including money spent on coastal defense. Town officials complained about the Massachusetts state government's reimbursing policies, but accepted the outcome, admitting that such expenses were in fact patriotic and a sign of the locality's "devotedness to our soldiers and seamen."[43]

RESENTMENT AND PATRIOTISM

Northerners reacted to war costs in ways that ran from resentment to acceptance, usually justified by convenience and patriotism. Lincoln's critics, of course, saw disaster looming in his various fiscal and monetary policies. Outraged at how the war reached into their pocketbooks from all directions, they were not wrong in noting how extensive the effort to raise revenue had become by the late days of the war. "We are having good times in paying State taxes, County taxes, Township taxes, City taxes, Bounty taxes, Internal Revenue taxes, tax on Coffee, tax on Sugar, tax on Tea, tax on Calico, tax on Muslin" and, in fact, a tax on everything, complained one cranky Ohio Democratic editorialist at the time of the 1864 presidential election. "We are having 'good times'," he continued longing for a happier specie-backed past, "with our ragged currency, Greenbacks, large and small, Lincoln skins and gilt paper, Lampblack and ink, instead of the good, old fashioned, Democratic Gold and Silver." The government now required tax stamps on all sorts of documents, the editorialist continued in his complaint "and in fact nothing is binding in law unless a Lincoln stamp of some kind is attached." Soldiers die while rich men get richer with their investment in government bonds, he protested, and while the country copes with "a civil war, which has plunged her into debt which will grind all down with eternal and everlasting taxation."[44] Across the border and farther east in the rural Pennsylvania coal country, Democratic newspapers railed against the Republican taxes in a similar vein. "[D]own with public robbers high and low," an editorialist demanded, along with issuing the usual outcry against abolitionists shared by his neighboring Democratic editorialists.[45]

The intrusion of tax collectors into the lives of individuals never before troubled to such an extent produced not only editorial complaints but also satire. In July 1862, *Frank Leslie's Illustrated Newspaper* printed a revealing cartoon showing four tax collectors scouring a bedroom for taxable items, even looking under the dress of the woman of the house, while her husband pleads that he would pay "any amount of tax" if the collectors would "leave his wife's crinoline and other domestic trifles alone."[46] In 1864 New Yorker Timothy Shay Arthur satirized such complainers with his pamphlet *Growler's Income Tax*, in which a patriot convinces Growler that his grievances about a $43.21 income tax—highway robbery, Growler dubbed it—are baseless when one considers the protection the government has provided for his property in the face of the challenges posed by the Confederate military. "Your property is secure," the patriot explained; "You still gather your annual income, protected in all your rights by the strong national arm." And it costs but a trifling sum. In the end Growler admits that he "was striking at the hand that gave protection." Now a convert to the benefits of paying for the war, Growler promised, "If my war tax next year should be a hundred dollars instead of forty-three, I will pay it without murmur."[47]

The added cost of living, however, was no laughing matter for some Northerners, but they found a salve in patriotism. New Yorker George Templeton Strong grumbled about the prospects of taxes as well as paper money destroying his net worth, but concluded, "Never mind. I shall not complain if the nation is saved."[48] A Boston businessman explained to his son in March 1862 that "Taxes are & will be enormous for years to come." Nevertheless, he continued, "We must not flinch from meeting our duty in this trying conflict." Indeed, he continued, good will come out of the conflict. "[T]his war is marking a distinctive character in our young men. We have a country & government not to be assailed but foes within, or foes without with impunity cost what it may in blood, life & treasure." And "Slavery is doomed at all event."[49]

Greenbacks, with their tendency to depreciate in value, continued to trouble creditors such as Strong, who believed that the paper money would destroy "at least half of what property I possess."[50] One Ohioan from Youngstown, carping on the inflationary aspect of circulating greenbacks, wrote in 1864 that the paper money was "one great cheat—one grand swindle" and unconstitutional as well.[51] It was a theme that Democrats would not abandon, Andrew Evans of Ohio reported in April 1863 to his soldier son. Such men "find fault with the '*greenbacks*,' the tax law and in fact everything," except the *Cincinnati Enquirer*, a Democratic newspaper.[52]

Yet, even as greenbacks fluctuated in value and traded at roughly 60 percent of their face value by 1863, many people appreciated the "safety" and uniformity of the notes after the National Bank Act stabilized the currency, especially as private money issued by local banks lost value and eventually became irredeemable.[53] As with their acceptance of taxes, a certain amount of patriotism also went along with the use of greenbacks that appealed to Northerners devoted to the Union. "They are as good as gold," Mary Vermilion wrote to her husband in June 1863. "While I was traveling I often heard people refuse to take anything but 'greenbacks'. I would have declined anything else if it had been offered me." But not only did the use of this new money help Vermilion to define her loyalty, it also allowed her to judge the loyalty of others.

"It is a bad sign to see any one afraid of 'greenbacks'," she observed; "That was one of the signs by which I could always tell the traitors in Indiana."[54]

FURTHERING REPUBLICAN PARTY GOALS WITH LONG-TERM DOMESTIC POLICIES

Republican-sponsored financial and monetary policies, despite complaints from taxpayers, consumers, and political opponents, proved effective in financing the war. They also increased the federal government's power and responsibility over the economy, strengthening a previously weak central state into one able to act on the economic fortunes and future security of its citizens. Disagreements over such policies would continue into the future, but during the war they bound Northerners together in a common interest in the government's actions and its success. Furthermore, Northerners with their very real hardship of 80 percent inflation never bore the burden of the 9,000 percent runaway inflation that ate away at the Confederacy's viability, undermined its legitimacy, and contributed to its collapse.[55]

In the midst of war, municipalities and states looked to the future when they debated and laid plans for clean water projects, road paving, and other infrastructure projects that would improve the lives and economic prospects of their citizens. So, too, did the federal government by enacting a set of bills rooted in the Republican Party's Whig background that dramatically expanded governmental support for agriculture, trans-Mississippi western development, and the spread of public higher education.[56] The sectional crisis required the expansion of federal authority to fight for the nation's survival, but it also provided opportunity. Secession had removed most opposition in Congress to the Republican Party program, thus allowing Lincoln and his allies to fulfill the promises they made in 1860.[57]

Some new programs might not have appeared to be essential to the war effort, but were indications of an active federal concern for American citizens, now possible to put into practice without the obstruction of Southern Congressmen. In 1863, Congressional funding for the free delivery of mail came in response to the public emotional pain witnessed by Cleveland, Ohio, post office employee Joseph Briggs, who watched surprised and shocked postal clients open letters notifying them of the deaths of friends, fathers, and sons. He believed grieving over family war dead should be a private matter. As a result of his advocacy, Cleveland postal workers began to walk the mail *gratis* to the homes of addressees. Other large urban areas followed, thanks to the efforts of the Postmaster General Montgomery Blair, who convinced Congress of the efficacy of the practice, arguing it would pay for itself while providing a boon to unemployed veterans who would be first in line to claim one of the new carrier positions. It was not exactly a necessary wartime expense, but it became popular, was able to survive postwar government retrenchment, and contributed to a united nation.[58]

Another measure, hardly essential for the successful conduct of the war, was when in 1864 Congress set aside some of the nation's western lands for public pleasure by giving land to California to create a state park in the Yosemite valley and the Mariposa Big Tree Grove. Influenced by Frederick Law Olmsted's views on the benefits of public parks, politicians set aside the land in part as a reaction to the butchery of the war. For Olmsted, who managed a gold mine in Mariposa, it was a symbol of the American form of government for which men were now dying: parks for the people instead of the privileged classes revealed the widespread benefits of a republican form of government. It was an idea not without some controversy, since it meant removing land from the productive use of yeoman farmers and businessmen, important constituents of the Republican Party, but the war drowned out the debate and the lands passed to the control of California, a necessity because there was no national park system to administer the land. The preservation of Yosemite was one more indication of how the federal government, with powers invigorated by the war, continued to plan for the future.[59]

Additional programs stood as examples of expansive thinking even in such desperate times as Republicans remained committed to the nationalistic free-labor ideology that had been at the heart of their political party before the war. In May 1862 Lincoln pushed through the new Department of Agriculture, a federal home for scientific farming, despite the fact, as Maine's Senator William Pitt Fessenden noted, there appeared to be no popular support for such an entity. The Homestead Act of May 1862, the Land-Grant College Act of June 1862, and the Pacific Railroad Act of July 1862 also furthered the Republican Party's commitment to western agriculture.[60]

While none of these laws had an obvious immediate impact on the conduct of the war, they revealed the Republican Party's hopes for the future of an emancipated and united America nurtured by its free-labor ideology. Promoters of the Homestead Act believed that agricultural production fed commercial and manufacturing growth, but for some of them, farming was at the heart of the American economy and life.[61] Fulfilling the promise of a law that gave 160 acres of land to undercapitalized settlers who would need to work in an unforgiving environment for five years before securing their claim proved problematical.[62] In Wisconsin, the attrition rate was about one half for those individuals who had made claims during the 1860s.[63] Still, by war's end settlers claimed over 25,000 homesteads, settling large areas of the upper Midwest.[64] Shortcomings notwithstanding, at the time of the law's enactment, people saw it as a promise of a free-labor future.[65] Republican Senator Samuel Pomeroy, who had made his way west to Kansas from Massachusetts, considered the Homestead Act of great significance because the farms established under its provisions will "greatly promote the wealth, strength, and glory of the Republic"; furthermore, "it will secure the entire public domain to human freedom forever!"[66]

The Homestead Act symbolically went into effect on January 1, 1863, the day that Lincoln's Emancipation Proclamation declaring an end to slavery in areas still in rebellion became the policy of the federal government. Equally important, Congress had earlier resolved the issue of slavery in the territories, the bone of sectional contention that had given rise to the Republican Party, banning it on June 19, 1862.[67] To further the free-labor goals, in 1862 Congress passed the Morrill Act and the Pacific Railroad Act.[68] The former provided institutions of higher learning across the land with federal land subsidies to support scientific agriculture as well as the understanding of military science, something sorely lacking at the outset of the war. The latter, also subsidized in part by land grants, would serve the same purpose as the war itself when finally completed by binding together the Union, east and west, in a way that antebellum transportation projects had drawn together the Midwest and the East. The transcontinental railroad promised to complete the great dream of creating a united country and incidentally a national market, thus benefiting those farmers who would make their way into the free lands of the new western territories. In the words of the editor of the *American Railroad Journal*, it also signaled "a new era in the history of our public works."[69] These various pieces of wartime legislation, despite problems of execution and of corruption, appeared to have fulfilled the Republican Party's antebellum promises in the midst of war, further committing the nation to federal support for internal improvements and agriculture, and thereby linking the fortunes of farmers and others to the politics and policies of the national government.[70] Such legislation reaped political and patriotic benefits for the Republican Party, by providing evidence that it was the party promising a better future for the country by laying the groundwork for sustained national improvement and prosperity.

TEN

PRODUCING FOR THE WAR

DECLINE AND RECOVERY

In 1861 and 1862 the Northern economy struggled as it coped with the shock of war. New Jersey and other states suffered because secession deprived them of their old customers in the new Confederacy.[1] Midwestern farmers also had familiar economic patterns ruined by secession. They could no longer transport their wares down the Mississippi River, now running through the heart of the rebellion, a situation that limited access to markets and hurt the prices of their goods.[2] Factories laid off employees and businesses failed. In Philadelphia workers unsuccessfully asked the city to initiate a public works jobs program.[3]

By 1863, however, wartime expenditures in supplying armies and the continued needs of the home market led to a boom that lasted through the rest of the war. Thus, Midwestern farmers rebounded and by 1863, an editorial writer for the Davenport *Daily Gazette* described "truly progressive" agronomists who experimented with diverse crops, concluding "The dawn of Iowa's greatness as an agricultural state is breaking."[4] New Jersey recovered before 1863, even without access to Confederate cotton. Its factories were producing iron, rubber, woolens, and other items necessary for the war effort, sending the state on the road to prosperity.[5] Nimble

Philadelphia manufacturers deprived of Confederate cotton turned their textile machines to woolens while their counterparts in the iron industry moved into war production.[6] New York City clothing and shoe manufacturers reaped profits from government contracts, sometimes wanting hundreds of thousands of uniforms or pairs of shoes in a single order, and the need for equipment spread the wealth to other businesses such as the Singer sewing machine company.[7] Railroads, necessary for transporting all of these things, overcame early fears about the impact of the war, enjoyed an extraordinarily profitable year in 1863, and continued to do well for the remainder of the war.[8]

Such a rebound was visible among smaller businesses not directly connected with supplying the army as people who made money spent money. Karl Wesslau, a cabinetmaker in New York City, informed his German parents in December 1864, "last spring and summer business was very good." By the end at the war, he assessed his situation and concluded: "At the beginning of the war we lost a lot of money, but in the last two years we've made up for our losses and more."[9] In early 1863, Catharine Taylor reported the evidence of renewed prosperity in Des Moines, Iowa. "W. Minson says that there are more buildings engauged [*sic*] to be done this summer in town than he knows of than has been done for the last two years," she wrote to her soldier husband Taylor. "It seems as if money is plenty or more plenty at least than for some time back," she continued, "for the Catholic[s] have got money and subscription to the amount of five thousand Dollars to build a new church."[10] But the money supply was a mixed blessing "because all manner of things have gone up."[11]

Back East in New York City, German immigrant Emilie Wesslau, Karl's sister, complained about the new wartime reality that accompanied the economic recovery. "Food prices have tripled, clothing has gone up even more," she noted, "but we still haven't suffered any want."[12] Emilie might have observed that things could have been much worse. She and other Northerners had to contend with a wartime inflation rate that was less than one-hundredth of that in the Confederacy.[13]

The sustained wartime recovery, although not enjoyed equally by all Northerners, generated a collective prosperity. The gross national product of the region was over $4 billion in 1864, which was more than the total for the whole United States in 1860, and R.G. Dunn and Company reported that only 510 businesses failed in 1864, well below the 5,935 failures in 1861.[14] Millions of fresh acres came under the plow. Factories produced the necessaries of war. Immigrants arrived by the hundreds of thousands. Hundreds of thousands of dollars in army pay contributed to family economies. Railroads added over 4,000 miles of track. All of these things collectively added to the wealth of the loyal states as well as the federal treasury, leading President Lincoln to look to good prospects for a sustained war effort.[15] On December 6, 1864, in his annual message to Congress, the president proclaimed that in every respect the nation was "*gaining* strength, and may, if need be, maintain the contest indefinitely" in terms of both men and material resources, which were "unexhausted, and as we believe, inexhaustible."[16]

AGRICULTURAL BOUNTY

Wartime demand generally provided prosperous times for Northern farmers. Antebellum surpluses and then good wartime harvests combined with poor harvests in England and Europe boosted wheat farmers' sales abroad. In 1860, Michigan exported over 1.9 million bushels of wheat to Great Britain. The very next year, it sent over 24.5 million bushels, peaking at over 27.3 million bushels in 1863 before declining to over 5.8 million bushels in 1865.[17] From 1861 through 1864 the Union exported roughly 203 million bushels of wheat, worth $265 million. As one Midwestern editor proclaimed in late 1861, "Wheat is king and Wisconsin is the center of the Empire."[18] But at the same time, unprecedented English and European demand for other agricultural products further added to Northern farmers' incomes, boosted the nation's balance of payments, and compensated for the loss of Southern markets during the war. Such demand also tied England and France more tightly to Northern interests.[19] American agriculture was already in a state of change, but increased demand required an expansion of acreage and settlement across the North, the wider use of machinery, and greater involvement of American farmers in an international market economy. Small farms remained the norm, but the scale of production was growing. So, too, was the size of debt, as farmers brought more land under cultivation and invested in new machinery thinking the boom years would last.[20]

Citizens who traveled in the agricultural regions of the North would have agreed with Lincoln's assessment of the economic circumstances of their loyal states. Sidney George Fisher, for one, remarked as early as 1862 that in traveling across Pennsylvania he found that "Tokens of redundant prosperity & rapid improvement are visible everywhere" and that the "war indeed has revealed to us & to the world the immense power & unbounded resources of the nation."[21] In 1863, Mary Livermore also witnessed the agricultural bounty of the Midwest as she traveled by rail through parts of Wisconsin and Iowa that appeared to be "a continuous wheatfield." "The yellow grain was waving everywhere," she recalled, "and two-horse reapers were cutting it down in a wholesale fashion that would have astonished Eastern farmers."[22]

Some lone females with husbands in the army and with a young son or two at home or perhaps a brother nearby to lend a hand survived or even prospered in this environment. Farms in fact might not miss a son of military age, since an older father handled the work and might be able to secure some assistance, even if from his younger children. In March 1863, Indianan Mary Hamilton, her two sisters, and her brother helped their father with the threshing of the wheat. It was not something

Mary especially enjoyed since it meant putting off continuing her education but, she admitted, "I do not know what he would do if it was not for us girls."[23] Other families made sure that a son or a brother-in-law remained home to tend to the farm. Such was the case with the unmarried Gould brothers whose sister Hannah, the head of their parentless household, and her husband Marvin Thomas tended the homestead in central New York.[24] In neighboring Ohio, 18-year-old Amos Evans, with older brothers in the army, temporarily took over from his politician father the family farm operations and the care of his mother and younger siblings. The responsibility was large, as would have been the case for most farmers in similar circumstances. He believed he had "almost enough to do for one of my years, yet I will endeavor to act my part, be my lot what it may." Despite being "alone without help" and having "a rough time of it," he trusted in God for success. In addition to the farm work, he also maintained a mill—still considered "the best in the Country"—and kept "up all our own repairs."[25]

At the same time that agriculture demand meant prosperity for so many Northerners, there were small farms that remained beyond the reach of the rising market while others barely survived the war. Throughout the war, family-centric southern Indianans, for example, by choice retained their old-fashioned, low-effort, self-sufficient hog and corn farming, although they welcomed surpluses when they appeared.[26] Other small farmers did not expect to continue to live on the margins but failed to achieve success. There were those farmers who took advantage of the Homestead Act of 1862 who did not persist long enough to register their claims. Also, there were hardscrabble marginal farms that sorely missed the labor of husbands or sons who went off to fight. Such was Anna Howard's rugged, isolated homestead. Anna's father had settled the family on "three hundred and sixty acres of land in the wilderness of northern Michigan" not close to much of anything. Ever the optimist, he was not averse to thinking he could eventually elevate his claim to the level of "a fine estate" that he could pass on to future generations of Howards. The war, however, interrupted such dreams and deprived Anna, her mother, and her younger siblings of the labor of her father and older brothers.[27]

The Howard family members did various jobs to bring in additional income "taking as boarders the workers in the logging camps, making quilts, which we sold, and losing no chance to earn a penny in any legitimate manner." Anna's mother also did sewing, "yet every month of our effort the gulf between our income and our expenses grew wider, and the price of bare necessities of exis[t]ence climbed up and up." The wartime home front made an impression on the young girl, and she later recalled, "It was an incessant struggle to keep our land, pay our taxes, and to live." Labor was in short supply, thus "There were no men left to grind our corn, to get in our crops, or to care for our live stock [*sic*]; and all around us we saw our struggle reflected in the lives of our neighbors."

Anna long remembered an existence that was a "strenuous and tragic affair." "The work in our community, if it were done at all," she later wrote, "was done by despairing women whose hearts were with their men."[28] The Howards survived, but less fortunate families in similar circumstances struggled. Lucy Wheat lost the family farm in Illinois when her husband died and her son left for the army. Wartime inflation compounded her money problems. She complained that the war had brought only "cair, anxiety & trials" and feared that she might have to resort to prostitution to save herself.[29]

MANPOWER ON THE FARM

As Anna Howard witnessed, the high level of soldier recruitment from the rural North made it more difficult to meet agricultural demand, leaving many farms short of labor during the war.[30] The Old Northwest states of Ohio, Indiana, Illinois, Michigan, and Wisconsin, for example, had to continue to keep farms productive while sending to war about 680,000 men who served for more than a short term; on average, every other farm family in those states made due without a worker because of the demands of the military.[31] Back East in New Jersey, where a private's pay beat by one dollar the workingman's monthly wage of $12, employers lost access to 74,000 volunteers.[32] The Gardner, Kansas, area, a farming community on the Missouri border, was doubly troubled. Laborers not only joined the army, but employers also lost "our itinerant population all driven back in the interior for safety" because of the fear of additional raids from their proslavery neighbors.[33]

Thus in August 1863 immigrant German farmer Dietrich Gerstein reported to his brother from his backwoods Michigan farm, "Almost all the single men who work full-time for other people are gone, and the married farmers either don't work for wages or ask for wages that no one can possibly pay."[34] The situation in Gardner, as W. M. Shean, a letter writer to the *Kansas Farmer*, noted in January 1864, was equally difficult, since it was "impossible to obtain a day's labor at any price." As a result, "improved land lies idle from scarcity of labor." Shean urged the state to encourage immigration, which would repay government efforts with farms restored to productivity, "add[ing] to the wealth of the State."[35]

By 1863 the government helped ease the labor shortage with a generous immigration policy. German, Swedish, and Norwegian immigrants started up farms or hired on as farm laborers, pulled westward from eastern port cities by the promise of land made by the government in the Homestead Act and by railroad companies offering credit to draw settlers along their lines.[36] Perhaps an encouraging letter home was sufficient to prompt such emigration to a new land. In May 1864, Karl Wesslau wrote to his parents and siblings, explaining, "These are very good times for people in Germany who want to come over here, [because] it's easy enough to find well-paid employment." Furthermore, assuring them that noncitizen immigrants could avoid military service, he explained, "The government does all it can to encourage immigration, since the war has already cost so many lives that there's a shortage of men."[37] Indeed, in Ireland persistent hard times encouraged emigration, with young men even prepared to serve in the army for ocean passage, a bargain that would have eased labor problems as it eased recruiting demands. The potential emigrants found an advocate in the U.S. vice-consul in Dublin.[38] Despite efforts of foreign governments to discourage emigration, roughly 800,000 immigrants, mostly young northern and western European men, flocked to the Union by the end of 1865.[39]

The farm laborers benefited to a degree from the wartime agricultural expansion and labor shortages, although landowners did better. As Dietrich Gerstein observed, "For laborers here, in fact, times have never been better than they are now."[40] Antebellum Ohio hands had received a yearly wage upward to $150 in addition to their keep; during the war their wages rose to a high of $250 dollars in addition to their living.[41] In 1864, New Hampshire farmers paid female field workers a daily wage of $2 in addition to their board.[42] The proximity of New York farms to the bountiful Midwestern acres and their higher wages forced landowners to pay more than they wished to keep their hands.[43]

To ease the labor shortfall, Northern farmers continued to make use of technology, since machines had already shown their promise before the war. Such machinery proved especially useful on the cereal-growing prairies and plains where reapers and mowers repaid the investment with greater efficiency and a reduction in the manual work force. As the *Minnesota Farmer* boasted after assessing the abundant 1861 wheat harvest, "the addition of one thousand reapers to the already large cutting force, has materially helped to make harvest comparatively easy and of short duration."[44] Investing in a machine also provided some farmers with additional income and a new type of employment, as they traveled their neighborhoods working other farms for a fee. "It is thus," wrote a Cincinnati editorialist in 1862, "that machinery has done the work of thousands of men, who have thus been spared for the war."[45] Between the start and the end of the war, the number of factories producing the needed machines increased significantly, adding weight to the farmers' arguments about agriculture being at the heart of the nation's economy. Before the start of the war, there had been over 70 factories in operation; in 1864, there were 187 works making reapers and mowers and keeping 60,000 employees busy.[46]

The spread of technology allowed farmers' daughters to step into the shoes of brothers who went off to war. Young women wrangling a team of horses attached to a machine to prepare fields for planting or to harvest crops became common sights in Ohio and elsewhere.[47] As Mary Livermore's Midwestern women discovered, the work that they performed in planting, tending, and harvesting crops when their men were away was difficult but manageable, especially with the aid of farm machinery. The work demanded new skills, and the necessity of it forced women to learn them or the farms would fail. Some women took pride in their work. Indeed, one woman boasted that she could do it all and match any man in working a binder.[48]

Women also saw their work as a patriotic duty. The country needed them to take on new roles. For Livermore, these women "were invested with a new and heroic interest, and each hard-handed, brown, toiling woman was a heroine."[49] Conservative Northerners did not always see it that way and protested such activity, fearing it would somehow debilitate feminine minds and bodies.[50] The editor of the *Prairie Farmer* disagreed, assuring farmer fathers that such work would "not compromise . . . [the] dignity and sense of propriety" of their daughters, while the Illinois State Agricultural Committee urged women to put aside their feminine attire and go into the fields to drive the various machines they could easily handle.[51] In fact, farmers' daughters and patriotism could sell farm equipment, or so one manufacturer believed when he advertised in the June 10, 1865, issue of the *Prairie Farmer*. The illustration depicted a respectable looking young woman, protecting her complexion with a broad brimmed hat, in charge of a "Sulky Hay Rake." The character explained her actions by noting her "brother has gone to war."[52]

Although labor shortages and other difficulties caused many farmers to struggle if not fail, discipline, luck, and rising farm prices brought personal rewards, kept farms in business, and fueled expansion. Ovid Butler, president of a college in Indianapolis, for example, invested in cheap farmland in Illinois, which allowed him to reap a fine grain harvest in 1864, despite the burden he had of managing the property on his own. It was not only a way to make money, he explained to his soldier son Scot. "I feel that in these times while so much of the labor of this country is necessarily withdrawn to fill the Armies" it became a patriotic duty "to increase those productions of the earth which are essential to feed and clothe these Armies and the population." Such a person was, in fact, "a public benefactor."[53] Persistence, opportunity, and examples of success, as well as Ovid Butler's style of patriotism, encouraged the establishment of new farms and the expansion of old ones, even in New York State.[54]

INDUSTRY AND LABOR

The demands for farm equipment meant that manufacturers had to increase their production, the requirement of which placed them in labor situations similar to the farmers who purchased their products.[55] Nonagricultural workers such as those men laboring in the farm machinery factories made up an increasingly large segment of the Northern economy by 1860 and grew in size because of the war. They included all sorts of skilled workers and tradesmen necessary in a diverse and vibrant economy and usually spent their time in small shops and mills rather than large factories.[56] Specialized industries blossomed, such as the textile mill in Philadelphia that developed a reputation for "the superiority of its mourning goods."[57]

Industry and transportation joined agriculture in coping with the patriotic enthusiasm of their workforce, especially in the first years of the war. In September 1862, Massachusetts tanner Henry Fowler complained, "Labour is very scarce," the consequence being "I have to do all my work alone which makes a slow job of it." Because of this scarcity, he noted, "Shoe makers are getting better pay than they have had before for years."[58] He was not alone in his predicament. Benjamin Hirst, his Rockville, Connecticut, coworkers, and workers throughout the North left the mills and mines with fewer hands as they answered the call to arms.[59] Fledgling trade unions also suffered, their ranks diminished as their members enlisted, some not to return, while some local organizations disappeared from the record.[60] Even the coal mining area of eastern Pennsylvania sent off Democrats and Republicans, especially from among the Welsh, Irish, and other immigrant populations, to answer Lincoln's first call; it was a display of bipartisan unity that would not outlast emancipation.[61]

Railroad companies struggled to employ enough men to keep the trains on the tracks. In 1863 foremen for the Western Railroad in Massachusetts complained that the company had lost so many men that they could not unload the coal cars, and the Chicago & Alton Railroad stopped service for a time because it had no mechanics to do repairs. The railroad companies countered the appeals of the military by raising pay, getting employees draft exemptions, and matching army recruiting bounties to attract and retain workers, with mixed results.[62] In some places, such as New Jersey, the loss of skilled workers provided opportunities for men and boys not yet masters of their crafts to move up the economic ladder.[63] Consequently, craftsmen were at an advantage in such a market, but laborers benefited as well. When Karl Wesslau encouraged home folks in Germany to emigrate, he reported, "At the moment there are opportunities to earn money like never before" because "these are golden times for craftsmen, workers and soldiers." He estimated, "a laborer can support his family on 4 days of work a week," although the challenges of inflation remained real.[64]

The labor demand continued through the war, despite immigration, and necessity meant employers turned to women and children to help fill their needs. Owners of textile mills, shoe factories, and other businesses used to female labor hired more women and children to the point where their numbers among the North's mill and factory employees increased by 40 percent.[65] The expanding wartime management needs of governments and many businesses also meant an increase in office staffs to handle the information, complete and process all manner of forms, file reports and myriad other documents, manage payrolls, and perform a host of other bureaucratic duties. Women stepped up to fill these needs, but not without being reminded of their economic inferiority by their lower wages.[66]

The women who replaced men as clerks in shops or hired on as office workers in expanding government bureaucracies became the public faces of the feminization of work, something more conservative Northerners found objectionable. In July 1862, German emigrant Johann Diedan noted a shift in Chicago stores because of the war. "Up to now in America it hasn't been the custom to have ladies as store clerks," he wrote to a cousin in July 1862, "but now several merchants have hired young ladies instead of young men who are going to war." His employer planned to hire as many as seven if he "can find the right ones."[67] In Dubuque, Iowa, Florence Healy took on a position as a shop clerk to fill a gap left by the war. Some customers threatened to stop shopping at the store, but Healy's employer endured the challenge with no financial harm to his business.[68] By February 1864, Chicago merchants who resorted to using female sales clerks were pleased with "the uniform tact and integrity of the women employed"; an editorialist expressed hope that the practice would continue.[69] In fact, there were editorialists who saw Healy and other women taking on similar positions as being true patriots. They censured the men who held such "light avocations" when they should be in the army and when there were women perfectly capable of taking their places.[70]

Beyond those "light avocations," women as well as children took up positions in manufacturing, including those businesses that produced war-related products such as armaments. They worked cheaply, under poor conditions, and for long hours. In urban areas, they stretched their budgets as best they could, but on occasion some of them supplemented their income with prostitution.[71] All factory work could be dangerous, even in textile mills and clothing manufacturers, but women and children did obviously hazardous work in munitions manufacturing plants, arsenals, and other military facilities. Two horrific accidents occurred exemplifying the dangers involved in serving the needs of war. On September 17, 1862, an explosion and fire at the U.S. Army Arsenal at Allegheny, Pennsylvania, took a severe toll on women workers there, while on June 17, 1864, a similar deadly accident occurred at the Washington, D.C., Arsenal. On June 20, crowds gathered to pay homage to the Washington arsenal workers at a large funeral procession, which included President Lincoln, and the press called for an investigation of conditions in the government-run plants. Significantly, such accidents, whatever the public acknowledgment of them, did not improve working conditions or women's pay. Nor did they discourage women from seeking employment in such facilities, for the hiring continued throughout the war.[72]

The demand for labor helped workers, but workers, pressed by inflation, did not enjoy their fair share of the benefits of the growing economy. The rift between capital and labor started to become apparent. Workers protested low pay, poor working conditions, lack of respect, and other discouragements. Women were as aggressive as men in demanding pay increases and improvements. They had some success in military factories. Ordnance workers at the Allegheny Arsenal in Pennsylvania and cartridge makers at the Watertown Arsenal in Massachusetts protested layoffs and work conditions and got some concessions, and respect, for their efforts.[73] From 1863 to 1865 seamstresses in several cities threatened work stoppages and made public appeals for support for relief from poor conditions and low pay. They drafted petitions and memorials to Congress, President Lincoln, and Secretary of War Stanton emphasizing their patriotic sacrifices. In 1865 a group of Cincinnati seamstresses, for example, asked Lincoln for fairness as "the wives, widows, sisters, and friends of the soldiers . . . depending upon our own labor for bread [and]. . . . in no way actuating by a spirit of faction, but desirous of aiding the best government on earth, and at the same time securing justice to the humble worker."[74] Such appeals largely failed, and women in certain industries in New York and Philadelphia began to organize.[75]

Other laborers showed their displeasure with their economic situation by organizing and striking. During 1863, trade unions exhibited a new militancy, striking in Boston and elsewhere.[76] In some areas, such as New York City and the mining regions of eastern Pennsylvania, workers' displeasure combined with antiwar sentiment spilled over into draft resistance, violence, and bloodshed.[77]

INTEGRATING THE MARKET

Building on developments started before the war, the North improved its transportation and communication networks, facilitating the growth of an integrated national market. Great Lakes shipping grew during the war to meet the increased demands of moving grain, meat, and lumber to markets, and also kept down railroad rates by offering a cheap alternative. Railroad companies improved their capabilities by upgrading lines, standardizing signaling systems, developing uniform freight-handling procedures, and building connections to link existing lines. Managerial and office efficiencies also improved carrying capacity and delivery. In response to government and market-driven pressures to cut costs and improve performance, the Pennsylvania Railroad completed the first trunk line between Lake Michigan and the East Coast by buying up the Pittsburgh, Fort Wayne, and Chicago Railroad and linking it with its existing system. Creating railroad systems through the acquisition and linking of existing lines became the dominant pattern of railroad development east of the Mississippi after the war.[78]

Further binding markets, and thus the North, together was the continued development of commodity exchanges and wholesalers, helping to further the war's aims by connecting Eastern cities and producers with Midwestern markets, thereby integrating the states into a commercial nexus.[79] As Abraham Lincoln understood, "the United States is well adapted to be the home of one national family," not two or more, as he noted in December 1862, and its "vast extent, and its variety of climate and productions, are of advantage, in this age, for one people . . . [because] Steam, telegraphs and intelligence, have brought these, to be an advantageous combination, for one united people."[80]

The commercial benefits of these connections as well as the war's needs were important not only for farm and factory, but for the development of the urban hubs of commerce for counties and regions as well as the nation. In Rockland, Maine, William S. Cochran had a sail-making business, but shifted his attention to army tents thanks to a government contract at a critical time when the town was suffering from the loss of its Southern lime market. Cochran's business was able to offer new opportunities for unemployed workers, eventually having 500 people on the payroll producing 100 tents a day, totaling 6,000 by the end of the war.[81] As early as November 1861, the benefits to Rockland were apparent. The editor of the *Democrat and Free Press* reported on the impact to the town of having a thriving business within its bounds. "Our streets are filled morning, noon and night with men and women whom he [William S. Cochran] employs," he wrote, "and the wages which they make are equal to the wages of the best of times." The benefits rippled through the seacoast town, where "The needy are not only making a handsome living from the General's business, but our public houses, dry goods dealers, grocers, market shops, and in fact persons in al [*sic*] kinds of business are reaping the benefits of it." Rockland, he concluded, should be grateful to Cochran for this work, and he will be "kindly remembered as long as the recollection of this rebellion exists."[82]

On a much larger scale, Chicago became the great engine and beneficiary of the east–west connection generated by the war effort. In 1861 it was already the western terminus with three railroads connecting the Midwest with the East and other lines fanning out to the farmlands of the prairies. It also had the advantage of being a major port. Its large grain elevators, lumberyards, stockyards, and slaughterhouses attested to its increasingly central place in gathering and processing nature's produce. Its grain and lumber exchanges dominated the markets and brought order to trade by centralizing information flows, providing credit, reducing risk, and promoting planning. During the war, Chicago capitalized on its advantages to meet the Union army's voracious demand for meat and in the process displaced Cincinnati as the world's largest meat-packer. In 1864 Chicago pork packers and railroad executives laid plans for the massive Union Stock Yard that would further transform the meat trade.[83] The unintended consequence of this growth was a foul urban water supply that eventually required new infrastructure investment.[84]

PROFIT MAKERS

If workers could not claim fair shares in the growing Northern wartime economy, their travails certainly helped businessmen, who paid off debts, built up cash reserves, and invested in expansion and improvements. The war thus hastened the shift from relying on credit from merchants to securing capital from profits and from banks.[85]

It also led to greater cooperation between business and government. By late 1861, for example, the Army's Quartermaster's Bureau stepped in to bring order to military procurement and to contract with suppliers on the basis of competency rather than political patronage. The result was more systematic government oversight of production by specifying requirements for the quality and durability of cloth, shoes, and other goods demanded in government contracts.[86] The government's requirements continued to play a major role in wartime economic growth. As one Massachusetts writer noted in August 1863, "In every department of labor the government has been, directly or indirectly, the chief employer and paymaster."[87] Thus, contracts for moving men and freight provided the impetus for the development of William Davidson's river-based transportation monopoly. Political connections and wartime contracts allowed William Drew Washburn to profit from the state's vast lumber resources. The success of the businessmen of St. Paul and Minneapolis led to the recapitalization of the state's foundering railroads and the landing of additional government contracts.[88] Over the course of the war, the federal government spent about $1.8 billion, much of it directed to those businesses that could provide the necessities of a fighting army.[89]

Such expenditures stimulated innovative products. In 1864, the Patent Office issued over 5,000 patents, which was more than any previous year for the whole United States. Most of the new wartime inventions were geared to the domestic market, but many also had military uses. Thus inventions such as washing machines, clothes dryers, rubber wringers, coal-oil lamps, feed bags for horses, improved sewing machines, steam dredges, and stone-cutting machines served both the home front and the armies.[90] Other businessmen benefited from federal spending by expanding their antebellum products, now in demand because of the war. In 1856 Gail Borden had patented a process for producing condensed or concentrated milk. In 1861 he began large-scale production in New York, and by war's end he had improved the process and expanded production dramatically by establishing branch factories and licensing other producers to meet demand. When sealed in cans, concentrated milk was ready-made for shipping long distances without spoiling, making it valuable in supplying troops in the camps and citizens in the cities. The success of condensed milk also encouraged Borden, and others, to experiment with the condensation process for other foods.[91]

Ordinary Northerners might consider it acceptable for these businessmen to make a fair profit, but avarice was bad for the economic life of the nation, not to mention the lives of its soldiers. More disconcerting for some civilians and soldiers were the moral implications of rapacious businessmen taking advantage of a witless government as they steered the country toward the notion of equating national strength with the unfettered, free-wheeling capitalism that became common after the war. Some of these selfish businessmen even proudly asserted that only a fool would join the army when so much money could be made at home. Banker Thomas Mellon, for example, wrote his son that rather than enlist he should understand that "a man may be a patriot without risking his own life." After all, he reasoned, "There are plenty of other lives less valuable or ready to serve for the love of serving."[92] Many of the nation's financiers agreed, including those among New York City's elite.[93]

During the war, however, thoughtful Yankees considered this problem to be more than making unfair profits. Rather, greed could very well be a sign of moral decay or corruption that could threaten the prospects of victory and the very soul of the Republic.[94] One of the by-products of wartime profits was the creation of what the *New York Herald* called "The Age of Shoddy," a neutral term first used to describe inexpensive, inferior cloth that became a disparaging word for substandard goods and lack of patriotism in general.[95] "The lavish profusion in which the old Southern cotton aristocracy used to indulge is completely eclipsed by the dash, parade and magnificence of the new Northern shoddy aristocracy of this period," the editorialist observed in August 1863; "The individual who makes the most money—no matter how—and spends the most money—no matter for what—is considered the greatest man."[96] Thus, the hardworking German craftsman Julius Wesslau observed a year later the extravagance and spectacle described in the *Herald* in New York City, where "The main streets are clogged with fine and glittering ladies and gentlemen." "So while in the field in the South the most horrible war is raging," he pointed out with a degree of irony, "here in Neujork [*sic*] it's one good time after another, at balls, the opera, theaters and other places."[97]

Such a class of conspicuously consuming profiteers irritated those less fortunate Northerners who believed the capitalists' self-absorbed desire to increase their wealth could damage not only their own character, but also that of the nation. Northerners might have exaggerated the numbers of these crass, newly enriched businessmen of the shoddy aristocracy, but the sense that there were men profiting from the war, dragging it out beyond reason, and caring more for money than patriotism troubled them. Philadelphia teacher Carl Hermanns believed Northern forces could handily defeat the Confederacy, "But the men who are at the top and who collect all the millions don't want to turn their men loose, and they are dragging the war out like a lawyer does a court case." He vowed he would not fight "for these cheats and politicians."[98]

Hermanns exaggerated the control the big men of the North had over the progress of the war and their collusion in its delay, as well as the consequences of their bad decision making, but people did notice a greediness abroad in the land. Philadelphian Sidney Fisher expressed his disgust with an acquaintance who had "lost character since the war began" and worried more about his investments than the future of the Union. "Other people, as much accustomed to comfort and entitled to it as he," Fisher judged, "have lost everything or are subjected to severe privation and yet are ashamed to make a complaint." For Fisher, the war tested character and his friend so far had failed the test.[99]

Even soldiers noticed this desire to profit as they moved through the North on their way to defend the nation at the front. The dismayed Indianan volunteer George Squier wrote from Indianapolis after observing all the signs that showed "money is the order of the day." It was hard for him to witness, this "low dispisable [*sic*] cunning used to gain position and position" even as people cheated the government and the selfless volunteer. Near despair, he admitted that he had to "clench my hands to prevent my patriotism from coming out the ends of my fingers."[100]

Such actions could not go unpunished and would have serious ramifications. The Reverend James Remley feared that God would destroy such selfish men and the selfish nation they were making. In November 1862, he complained to his son Lycurgus, now serving in the army, about the "Thousands of private citizens" who were "even now speculating in the public misery and trying to make money out of the blood and dying groans of innocent people." Furthermore, he worried the war was "being prolonged on purpose to give more time to these traders in human wars to carry on their fiendish business." "How much of this," he lamented, "the Almighty will suffer before he destroys a nation I cannot tell."[101]

Grand procession of Wide Awakes at New York on the evening of October 3, 1860. The young men who participated in the Wide Awakes showed enthusiasm for politics and for Abraham Lincoln during the 1860 presidential campaign. Many of them volunteered for the United States Army along with fellow Wide Awakes after the fall of Fort Sumter. (Library of Congress)

Reading war news in Broadway, New York. During the war, people frequently gathered in public spaces to read extra editions as well as regular editions of their favorite newspapers, a practice that facilitated discussion and debate. (Library of Congress)

Recruiting for war: scene at the recruiting tents in the park, New York. Parks in New York City, Brooklyn, and elsewhere became sites of recruiting efforts, changing public landscapes from places of leisure to places of war. Other public spaces would soon give way to campsites and barracks for the new recruits. (Library of Congress)

Unidentified soldier in Union uniform and two women. This picture of a soon-to-be separated family probably depicts a recruit with his mother and sister. When soldiers volunteered, they left behind families that would feel their absence and anxiously pray for their safe return. Such images, often made before soldiers left for the war, were popular ways to preserve visual reminders of absent loved ones. (Library of Congress)

Filling cartridges at the United States Arsenal at Watertown, Massachusetts. The industrial capacity of the Northern states provided a great advantage to the Union war effort. The Watertown arsenal was not unusual in relying on women workers to maintain production as men left for war. The image, from the July 20, 1861 cover of *Harper's Weekly*, was also a reminder of what women could do for the war effort. (Library of Congress)

Station at Hanover Junction, Pennsylvania, 11/1863 (or 1864). Railroad engines, rolling stock, and facilities such as those at Hanover Junction allowed the Northern states' industrial and agricultural output to reach the men in the Union armies as well as civilians on the home front. (National Archives)

Skating carnival in Brooklyn, February 10, 1862. Northern civilians escaped the worries of war amusing themselves as they could, in this case by skating, a popular winter pastime. (Library of Congress)

Bounty brokers looking for substitutes. With the arrival of conscription came the practice of allowing individuals, including wealthy men such as Theodore Roosevelt Sr. of New York, to hire substitutes to replace them in the army. (Library of Congress)

Secretary Chase's March and Quickstep. During the war, composers produced music to commemorate all sorts of occasions and to honor various celebrities. They especially sang praises for the flag and the girls soldiers left behind. They also composed at least a few songs about the country's new paper money authorized in 1862 and commonly called greenbacks. (Library of Congress)

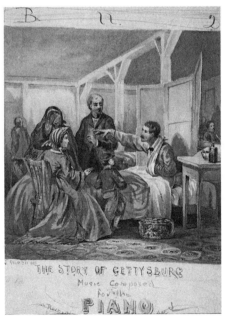

The Story of Gettysburg. Music composed for piano and respectfully dedicated to H. T. Helmbold, chemist. The cover illustration of this song in commemoration of the victorious battle at Gettysburg also illustrates how many civilians came to learn about the experience of battle. (Library of Congress)

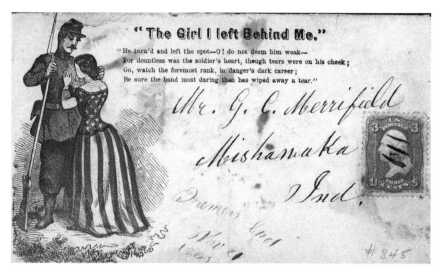

Civil War envelopes. During the war the federal mails carried a significantly increased volume of letters between civilians and soldiers. The patriotically decorated envelopes were one means by which correspondents conveyed support for the war effort. (Library of Congress)

Civil War induction officer with lottery box. The U.S. government responded to the slowing of volunteers and the continued need for soldiers with the Enrollment Act of 1863. A man known to the community drew names from a wheeled or tumbling box, which led some anti-war Northerners to refer to the contraption as the wheel of death. (Library of Congress)

SCENE, FIFTH AVENUE.

HE. "Ah! Dearest ADDIE! I've succeeded. I've got a Substitute!"
SHE. "Have you? What a curious coincidence! And *I* have found one FOR YOU!"

Scene Fifth Ave. Social pressure could play a role in encouraging men to do their duty. (Library of Congress)

Brooklyn sanitary fair, 1864. New England kitchen. Northerners found purposeful amusement in attending sanitary fairs that appeared in cities from New York and Philadelphia westward to St. Paul, Minnesota. Women carried a heavy burden in organizing the fairs, which raised funds for the relief of soldiers and their widows and orphans. The large fair buildings had various departments displaying art, agricultural tools, and other examples of Northern ingenuity as well as relics from battles and extraordinary animals, such as Old Abe, the bald eagle mascot of the Eighth Wisconsin, exhibited at the second Chicago fair along with a large ox named General Grant. (Library of Congress)

The copperhead plan for subjugating the South. The cartoon mocks the Copperhead or Antiwar Democrats and their desire to avoid further bloodshed and talk the Confederacy into peace terms. (Library of Congress)

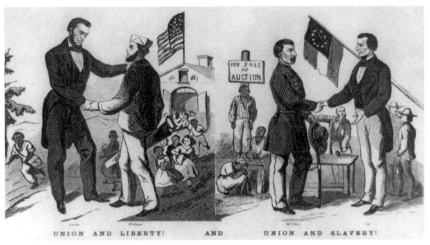

UNION AND LIBERTY!   AND   UNION AND SLAVERY!

Union and liberty! And Union and slavery! During the presidential campaign of 1864, the Republicans stressed their patriotism and associated it with the virtues of free-labor society, while denying any patriotic motive to their opponents and accusing them of being willing to accept reunion with slaveholders. (Library of Congress)

The 26th U.S. Colored Volunteer Infantry on parade, Camp William Penn, Pennsylvania, 1865. In June 1863, the United States Army established Camp William Penn for training units of the United States Colored Troops. The photograph also shows a neatly constructed rendezvous camp, something that became more common as the war progressed as stables on fairgrounds gave way to purpose-built barracks for sheltering recruits. (National Archives)

Arch at Twelfth S., Chicago, President Abraham Lincoln's hearse and young ladies. Lincoln's funeral train passed through Northern cities, stopping to allow citizens to mourn the loss of their president, as it brought the president's body to Springfield, Illinois. (Library of Congress)

Presentation of two hundred battle-flags to Governor Fenton at Albany, New York, July 4, 1865. At the end of the war, one of the last acts of many regiments was to return their battle flags to their states' governors along with the captured flags of the enemy. (Library of Congress)

ELEVEN

POLITICS AND DISSENT

POLITICAL PARTIES

In July 1861 the *New York Times* pronounced that "[p]arty organization is dead," having committed suicide by failing to prevent secession and war. The alternative now was to stand together to save the Union.[1] But Northerners did not euthanize their old party system just yet; rather, they subsumed their political differences into an emotional, shared patriotism that carried them into and through the early months of the war without forgetting who they were. It was one thing for most Democrats to stand with the Republicans, their bitter political adversaries, in the name of the Union, but quite a different thing to give up all political ambitions for their old party. As one Democrat explained, "It is not the administration as an administration, but as the embodiment of our institutions which is entitled to obedience."[2]

Unlike their cooperationist comrades, antiwar or Peace Democrats challenged Republicans from the war's beginning. Holding to their old values of individual freedom and states' rights, Peace Democrats preferred to allow the Confederacy to go its own way, fearing the ambitious desire of some radical Republicans to turn the conflict into an abolitionist war.[3] Even when allied with Lincoln's administration, the prowar Democrats shared the suspicion of their more discontented political brethren when it came to a Republican desire to expand war aims. What was critical for so many Democrats who would willingly set aside partisan bickering was that this war be one of limited ends. As former Indiana governor Joseph Wright and Fort Wayne banker Allen Hamilton advised, "We must restore this Government upon the Constitution alone, without dotting an *i* or crossing a *t*."[4]

Most Democrats thus strove to be a loyal opposition. They would find their work difficult. As the war dragged on, once supportive Democrats questioned the Republican agenda and learned that Republicans had come to assume that any challenges to administration policies revealed traitorous hearts. Throughout 1862 and into 1864, Northern military victory remained elusive, the financial and human costs climbed, and the Lincoln administration's policies, notably concerning conscription, civil liberties, and emancipation, reminded many Democrats that they could offer political alternatives to such a radical expansion of the power of the national government.

During the fall of 1861, fissures appeared in the effort to do away with party politics in Ohio, where Democrats abandoned any commitment to a Union party.[5] Hardly a year into the war, Indiana Democrat James Athon believed such unity tickets, those optimistic efforts to bury party differences, to be on the wane in his own state.[6] Illinois Democrats rejected invitations to join Union parties and sent a majority of delegates to the state constitutional convention.[7] Early military defeats aggravated opposition throughout the Midwest.[8]

In 1862, war weariness and a general sense that the Republicans were mismanaging the war reached into the communities on the East Coast and discouraged citizens further. In January 1862, Massachusetts mother Maria Berry believed "that neither General Burnside nor government know how to act or what to do." She believed she could do better, given her experience as a mother; after all, she wrote to her soldier son, "this Rebellion ought to have been put down long before this time."[9] Later, in November, a Connecticut woman wrote to her husband in the army, "the more I see and hear the less confidence I have in our ever haveing [*sic*] peace restored to us again."[10] Indeed, at the same time, Irish-American New Yorker Rowland Redmond judged the Lincoln administration lacked the intelligence to guide the country, which now "may drift into no one knows what."[11]

The Union army's loss at Fredericksburg, Virginia, on December 13, 1862, did not improve these opinions. Christmas in the wake of that disaster was not a joyful day for Henrietta Parker, a mother from Vergennes, Vermont. She urged her son, Charles, a captain in the Seventh Vermont Infantry, to resign his commission, expressing her disgust with how the politicians were conducting the war. "Managed as things now are, the enemy have and will have the advantage," she complained. "I am sick sick Heart sick, of this War, and I want my Son out of it." She told Charles, "I cannot sacrifice you to this Unholy War, They accomplish nothing but the slaughtering of thousands, and to all appearances it is all they will accomplish."[12]

By the end of 1862, Democrats who had refused to give up their party identity had found renewed energy in their challenges to Republicans who still claimed proprietary rights to national patriotism. Democrats won gubernatorial, legislative, and congressional victories in a number of states.[13] Generally, these victories did not spread beyond old Democratic strongholds nor did they produce extraordinary congressional gains.[14] Nevertheless, the elections gave notice to Republicans that political partisanship endured and throughout the North antiwar Democrats demanded peace.[15] Far from having died with the shots fired on Fort Sumter, the political party system found new life in debates over the conduct of the war and what Democrats considered the Lincoln government's constitutional overreach in suspending habeas corpus, suppressing dissent, and moving against slavery.

There remained efforts to cultivate a united political front, especially during the presidential election campaign of 1864, but unity generally meant accepting Republican policies. The German-born intellectual Francis Lieber and like-minded individuals believed that loyal Democrats should have no objections to reelecting Lincoln. Using rhetoric similar to that found in the orations of 1861, Lieber, a former slaveholder, argued that "in our present troubles" there were no political parties, but only patriots and "traitors to their country in the hour of need."[16] At the October 1864 meeting of African American men in Syracuse, New York, John S. Rock, a black Massachusetts resident, presented the political contest in a way Lieber would have accepted. "There are but two parties in the country today," he reported, "The one headed by Lincoln is for Freedom and the Republic; the other, by McClellan, is for Despotism and slavery. There can be no middle ground in war."[17]

Nominating Lincoln for reelection was not a problem at the National Union Party Convention, as the president's organization now referred to itself. The name change was opportunistic, but at the same time an honest effort to encourage patriots who might still find the Republican name to represent something radical to support their candidates.[18] The party's naming efforts were designed to prove a unity that, if not entirely fictional, was somewhat exaggerated, with the Republicans experiencing some internal dissent.[19] However, in June at their Baltimore convention they emphasized the appeal for a united front, when they replaced the radical vice-president Hannibal Hamlin with Andrew Johnson, a Tennessee War Democrat.[20]

Of course, there still remained a Democratic presidential candidate in the field with noticeable support. Democrats continued to pound Lincoln and his supporters with accusations of radicalism and tyranny.[21] Ohio's *Tiffin Advertiser* made the partisan case for George B. McClellan, the Democratic presidential nominee, by arguing that the Republican Party had given the country "good times" in the form of excessive taxation, government expansion, a "ragged currency . . . instead of good, old fashioned, Democratic Gold and Silver," conscription's "Wheel of Death," and an antislavery war.[22] Democrats insisted that emancipation would unleash a torrent of racial violence, race mixing, and threats to the social order and made the Republicans' proposed constitutional amendment to abolish slavery throughout the land a centerpiece of their campaign.[23]

Democrats approached the campaigning season with some optimism. Unfortunately for their prospects, the Union army's performance improved in time for the 1864 election. Also state elections held in October in Ohio, Indiana, and Pennsylvania suggested a vigorous Republican Party and presented an opportunity to call straying Democrats into the fold of a unity party.[24] Thereafter, the national prospects of Lincoln and his party appeared good. Northerners gave Lincoln an Electoral College vote of 212 to 21 and the assurance that his party would return to Congress in complete control.[25] "The crisis has passed," concluded New York lawyer George Templeton Strong; "My contempt for democracy and extended suffrage is mitigated. The American people can be trusted to take care of the national honor."[26] A resigned Maria Lydig Daly, a Democratic diarist, also acknowledged Lincoln's victory, commenting, "*Vox Populi, vox Dei.* So it must be for the best." Importantly, she added, "All now left us is to put the shoulder to the wheel and do our best to draw the government machine out of the slough."[27] Despite suspicions of rabble-rousing voters and despite the electoral disappointment of Democrats, the 1864 contest demonstrated the nation's commitment to holding elections and to accepting their outcomes.

POPULAR POLITICS

The results of 1864 and of the earlier state and local elections suggested that political parties continued to do the work they had done since the early republic and in an almost universal fashion helped to cultivate an informed if partisan citizenry. "Every man belongs to a party," Dietrich Gerstein wrote in 1860 from his farm in backwoods Michigan as he explained American politics to his brother back home in Germany; furthermore, everyone "has a well-founded opinion about our political situation and can explain his views as clearly as the top *Senatas* in Washington." His Catholic and Old Lutheran neighbors were exceptions, the liberal German Protestant immigrant believed. Exhibiting a prejudice that would especially dog Catholics throughout the war, he concluded, "Those people don't read any papers, they let their preachers do their thinking for them."[28]

Parties held their occasional national conventions, which allowed participants to revive their spirits, roar for a presidential candidate, rant against the opposition's policies, and expand their circles of like-minded acquaintances. The real work of politics, however, was in the states and the communities. Closer to home partisans mobilized support for candidates and sustained party loyalty by making the serious game of choosing a government amusing to their supporters.[29] In 1864 in New Jersey party loyalists formed clubs, assembled crowds in urban areas, canvassed the countryside, and even invested money in buying votes in unpredictable constituencies.[30] Importantly, the parties relied on their newspapers "written free of restraint" to keep readers, "even out on the edge of settlement," "informed about what has happened and what is to be hoped and feared in the near future."[31]

Campaigning was important work, as the activities of the New Jersey Republicans suggested, but also a form of outdoor entertainment matched in oratory and staging only by religious revivals. During the fall of 1863, an English reporter, a somewhat amused and bemused outsider, observed a rally at Carthage, Ohio, that was typical of the times. "[I]t reminded me of a Derby day at Epsom," he wrote home, "only if a somewhat shabbier character with a dash of an Italian masquerade and carnival frolic." The chaotic affair, perhaps a bit vulgar, featured a noisy parade, with people wandering about, eating, and enjoying themselves. Politics demanded orators and the "listless loafers" who listened to them, "cheering occasionally, jeering more frequently; all this in a din of discordant music, the racking fire of great and small guns, and the shrill cries of apple women and vendors of firewater." "For the rest," he continued, "there were children squalling, young people flirting, angry men swearing, drunken men reeling—all the varieties of a swarming, bustling crowd." Republicans hanged a "colossal man of straw with a mask" giving it the likeness of Ohio Peace Democrat Clement Vallandigham; the "zealous" among them then had a grand time "hacking away" at it "with their sabres [*sic*] and poking with their bayonets."[32]

With liquor on hand, such political gatherings along with tavern debates and election day socializing were always one drink removed from violence. During the 1864 election, a soldier on his way home to his wife and sickly child stopped to vote at a barroom serving as a polling station in Nininger, Minnesota. He bought drinks for the crowd of men loitering around the place "and soon all hands began to feel pretty full of talk." A political argument led the well-oiled Democratic disputants to demand the soldier not vote for Lincoln. He ignored the warning. The drunks "caught up fence rails pieces of boards & all sorts of weapons of war that was near & killed him on the spot." The authorities arrested three men and jailed them for trial in St. Paul.[33]

Party supporters when not bloodying one another carried flags, banners, and placards at rallies and in marches. Women and men wore hats, handkerchiefs, scarves, paper collars, and mittens with patriotic symbols and words and political party labels that advertised their loyalty to a candidate, party, or principle. Partisans had access to all sorts of things stamped with political and patriotic symbols, cartoons, and slogans that further brought the war into the home.[34] Even children became politicized, enthusiastically participating in these grownup activities while also loyally wearing their party symbols to school and with the Republicans among them donning the uniform of cloak and cap of the Wide Awake political club.[35] Their fathers passed on political views in the same way that they made Methodists or Baptists of their offspring and with the same understanding of the meaning and consequences of political apostasy. The war might change the control fathers had over their sons who went off to fight, but that did not mean they gave up their paternal obligation. Wisconsin Democrat William Reid engaged his prowar soldier-son Harvey in political discussions, trying to reenforce the family principles from a distance with argument and newspaper clippings as Harvey drifted into Republicanism.[36]

People on the home front could hardly avoid their cause even in executing their daily routines. They sent letters, notices, and other written fare in envelopes embossed with flags, eagles, and other patriotic symbols. As the war progressed, printers added portraits, caricatures, allegories, vignettes of military heroes, images of slavery, and representations of war that expressed more complex political ideas and interests.[37] At the same time, patriotic symbols, especially the old national flag, were stamped on newspapers, magazines, pamphlets, and broadsides as a matter of course.[38] All of these efforts had the serious and successful purpose of stimulating supporters to vote for their candidates, producing high rates of voter participation.[39]

In states with flagging Republican support, men established extra-party fraternities to encourage loyalty to their cause and provide vocal public testimony. During 1863, in New Jersey, the Republican Loyal National League with its fraternal rituals and oaths spread across the state. The organization held statewide meetings in Trenton, which provided the opportunity for Frederick Frelinghuysen to proclaim the loyalty of the state's citizens and the valor of its troops to the approval of the assembled crowd.[40] Farther west in Cincinnati, Lincoln's supporters founded the National Union Association, which sponsored speakers such as the Reverend Charles G. Ames, who in March 1863 exhorted his raucous listeners to give Lincoln their unqualified support, regardless of the direction of his policies.[41] In New York State, Loyal Leagues attracted Union veterans, who made it clear that Democrats were not much better for the country than their old rebel enemies, or as one veteran, a convert to Republicanism, promised, he "would see all democrats in hell before he would vote for one of them."[42]

Earlier during the war, with Republican fortunes flagging because of battlefield reverses, pro-Union businessmen in Philadelphia in 1862 established the first Union League to support Republican candidates and the war effort. As Sidney George Fisher explained in early January 1863, "The conditions of membership are unwavering loyalty and support of the government in all its efforts to suppress the rebellion." By March 11, Fisher considered the venture a success. Other cities would follow Philadelphia's example. But at about the same time, in spite of the show of unity in Philadelphia, Fisher acknowledged the existence of a Democratic club in the city, a reminder that party loyalty survived.[43] The Central Democratic Club, founded in January 1863, provided a philosophical home for antiadministration Philadelphians, who could rely on their new journal, the *Age*, to promulgate their party's views on the war.[44]

Big-city Union Leagues, such as Philadelphia's, were elitist because their agenda required money as well as experienced operators who had the necessary community connections to raise it.[45] The 27 members of Philadelphia's Board of Publications each contributed $250 to subsidize its efforts.[46] Union Leagues in other cities raised regiments and performed other patriotic tasks, but most significantly they did what the Philadelphia Board did so well, publishing reams of pamphlets, tracts, handouts, posters, lithographs, and other literature to defend and explain Republican policies and to promote Republican candidates, which required money. In late March 1863, for example, the Union League of Philadelphia had a reserve of $40,000 and another $22,000 set aside for its publication program.[47] Its Board of Publications alone printed tens of thousands of items, which it distributed to military camps, hospitals, political clubs and reform societies, and other Union Leagues.[48]

If one needed a reminder that politics and parties were alive and well, the Illinois Union League used the antebellum network of Wide Awake clubs, those groups of young men who in 1860 had rallied support to Lincoln, to establish itself across the state. *Chicago Tribune* owner Joseph Medill described his efforts to the president, noting his organization's "somewhat secret . . . but . . . strictly patriotic" actions, with rituals and signs and at least 75,000 members in the state. Democrats also formed secret clubs in Illinois and elsewhere, evincing the continued partisan nature of Northern politics.[49] Open partisanship shaped by club activity also remained common. In 1864, in New Jersey, Young Men's Lincoln Clubs along with Union Leagues contested the election with McClellan Clubs and Democratic Associations.[50]

Secret clubs had not been unusual in American politics before the war. Republicans, however, became concerned when they learned of underground Democratic organizations. Republican suspicions were not misplaced when war opponents found outlets for their views in clandestine groups such as the Knights of the Golden Circle, the Order of American Knights, and the Sons of Liberty, secret societies standing in opposition to the war. In the wake of the first defeat of Union forces at Bull Run in Virginia, antiwar Midwesterners began to organize in secret societies and even go out of their way to intimidate Union supporters.[51] Republicans saw treasonous conspiracies in all such gatherings of Copperheads, antiwar men supposedly as treacherous, sneaky, and vile as the deadly snake, although Democrats claimed they were important bulwarks of the people's liberty against the Republican government's growing power. In fact, Republicans had some reason to worry as some of these antiwar groups skirted legitimate opposition, with the more serious offenses involving Democrats in discouraging enlistments, helping men dodge conscription, hiding deserters, speaking out against Lincoln's policies, and singing "their cursed Secesh Songs."[52]

Fear of traitors and conspiracies could, however, be effective political tools regardless of how extensive they might have been. In Indiana, Governor Oliver P. Morton and other Republicans collected information on secret Democratic organizations, fearing they were plotting conspiracies. The army arrested alleged subversives, and their trials proved to be an excellent campaign maneuver for Indiana Republicans, who were successful in the 1864 elections.[53]

COMMUNITY STRIFE

The lack of tolerance for a conservative opposition to a war probably fostered underground opposition, but it also encouraged political violence, another expression, even if an unsavory one, of the time's popular political activities. Even at a time when Democrats controlled the Indiana General Assembly, the Republican governor Oliver P. Morton and his allies worked to suppress their power. As one Democrat editorialized, the Republicans of the state "have contented themselves with demanding that the Democratic party should quietly give up all their principles, and aid them in carrying out their doctrines." He posed a rhetorical question, well knowing his readership's answer: "Is this right—is this the way to harmonize the people?"[54]

Progovernment editors, vigilance committees, and citizens, taking their cues from Republican politicians who brooked no divergence from the party line, refused to acknowledge the difference between legitimate dissent and treason. Consequently, mobs attacked Democratic editors, destroyed printing presses, and disrupted legitimate Democratic political rallies. In doing so, they contributed to muffling opposition voices without the need for laws, military orders, and other governmental intrusions into their local affairs. In Indianapolis, the editor of the Republican paper, the *Journal*, pointed an accusatory finger at his rival, Democratic editor J. J. Bingham of the Indianapolis *Sentinel*, charging him with having treasonous Confederate sympathies. In August 1861, incited by such rhetoric, Republicans dragged Bingham to the city mayor's office to prove his loyalty by taking a public oath.[55] Ohio Republicans and their supporters boycotted, intimidated, and destroyed Democratic presses in concerted efforts to silence the political opposition.[56] In New England editors and public figures expressing pro-Southern sympathies or too forcefully challenging the Lincoln administration's prosecution of the war were branded as disloyal and treated accordingly, with one Haverhill, Massachusetts, Democratic editor being stripped, tarred, feathered, and marched around straddling a pole. The effect was to stifle criticism and make Democrats cautious in their opposition to Republican policies.[57]

Such intolerance of dissent limited political speech and open debate, illustrating that extralegal action could be effective in limiting the political power of Democrats without official intrusion. An Indiana Democrat admitted to being afraid to express his views because "Some crazy Republicans here in this county don't tolerate free speech." "I hope that Democrats in all parts of the State will be temperate and discreet in criticizing the acts of the administration," he wrote, "Yet we should not consent that good Loyal union men should be mobbed for a free expression of their abhorrence and disaprobation [*sic*] of the acts of [Indiana] Gov. [Oliver] Morton or Pres. Lincoln." Republicans in Indiana continued to use "disloyalty" as an argument against Democratic opponents.[58]

The wartime partisanship spilled over to upset family tranquility and disrupt friendly discourse while breeding distrust and discontent among neighbors. Albert Hancock plagued with antiwar Democrats in his wife's family must have felt the domestic tension when he declared, "it would do him more good to kill one of his brother in laws, than to shoot Jeff Davis himself."[59] Hancock's unhappy sentiments were not actions, but an already unhappy Illinois woman betrayed her abusive husband by spying and informing on him and his circle of Confederate sympathizers.[60] Ohioan Jane Evans, a staunch Democrat opposed to conscription and emancipation, exchanged a pleasant correspondence with her soldier cousin Sam Evans for a time. Their views, however, radically diverged. Sam, once a Democrat, had become an officer in a black regiment and firm in his support for Lincoln, conscription, and emancipation. Their friendship ended, with Sam chastising her for her rebel views while reporting to his father, another convert to Republicanism, that his cousin had insulted him and all Union soldiers.[61]

As with other types of political activities, children carried their affiliations and loyalties with them into their community schools, where arguments over students wearing symbols perceived by Unionist youths to be expressions of disloyalty devolved into fisticuffs in Dayton, Ohio, and Chicago, Illinois.[62] The scholars were enthusiastic partisans, but not much better able to control their elevated feelings than were their parents. Neighbors also turned on one another. In 1862 in Indiana, Unionists denounced vocal Democrats, who ended up being arrested and jailed.[63] In Illinois, they spied on neighbors who were pro-Confederate malcontents, secretly denounced alleged traitors to the state government, and armed themselves in defense against their Democratic neighbors in Clay County; in Indiana after the Union defeat at Bull Run in July 1861, secessionists in the Indianapolis hinterland threatened local Unionists and vandalized their national flags.[64]

Mattie Blanchard of Foster, Connecticut, had to deal with the gloating antiwar men in the community who gathered at the local store and "have a glorious time over the news if it is in favor of the south." These neighbors of hers, she suggested, "ought to be shot" when a time comes for them "to be punished for treason."[65] Even passive disloyalty could earn the wrath of previously cordial neighbors. Emeline Ritner of Mt. Pleasant, Iowa, considered neighbors to be traitors if they failed to support the troops. "When I know a person is a 'copperhead' I *can't* feel that they are *my* friends," she explained to her soldier husband. Rumor had it that one of her neighbors believed that the nation's soldiers would be unwelcome in heaven. "If she was not my nearest neighbor and I knew it was so," Ritner concluded, "I would never have anything to do with her again."[66]

Such heated political feelings could lead to tense and sometimes violent situations for neighbors and communities. Late in the first summer of the war Union loyalists and Confederate sympathizers clashed in three Fairfield County, Connecticut, communities.[67] In August 1863, in the Northfield, Indiana area, a storeowner found his building razed and his stock burned up with it, allegedly because "he voted the Democratic ticket."[68] "Society is fast degenerating into perfect lawlessness," an Indiana Democrat wrote that month, "and from the President down to the humblest citizen the doctrine of force, reprisals and barbarism is fast obtaining."[69]

CHURCHES AND DISSENT

If families and neighborhoods could not escape the weight of wartime politics, neither could the churches that served them and their communities. Politics readily entered churches, and even divided them as they had in the public square. Ministers and congregations took up war issues and confused their political beliefs with God's wishes, much as Republicans assumed that they were the keepers of the nation's true values.[70] In the aftermath of the attack on Fort Sumter, pro-Union congregants of a New Jersey Reformed Church raised a flag at their church. Their antiwar fellow church members insisted they remove the flag. The prowar congregants refused to comply, and the pastor stood by the Union men. Men brought out their weapons, but in the end the church board approved the flying of the old national banner. Ill will remained and almost two years later, the pastor noted "political dissensions of the country have not failed to leave their mark upon the Church." The same issues of dissent and freedom of expression that upset civil discourse also disturbed this New Jersey congregation's Christian peace and that of others across the North.[71]

Catholics tended to be immigrants and Democrats, thus avoiding much of the internal dissension experienced in some Protestant churches, although there were individuals who diverged on issues such as the legitimacy of secession and sacredness of slavery. Some Catholics in Dubuque complained about a political priest, but when confronted with emancipation and conscription, Catholic positions would lead them foremost into strife with loyal Northerners and especially Protestants.[72] Antiwar Catholics dealt with Protestants who had not trusted them before the war. That distrust continued. Pope Pius IX's call for peace did not help matters and neither did the increasingly vocal antiwar stance of the Catholic press. Some Catholic Republicans broke with their fellow communicants over the issue, but if the Catholic press was any indication, by 1864 internal strife was minimal with most editorialists exhibiting discontent with Republican policies.[73]

There were certainly dissident Protestants who, in the manner of the Methodist Edson Olds, argued that Christ blessed the peacemakers.[74] And there were antiwar and Democratic communities that would allow Olds to say what he thought. Indeed, in Iowa, Democrats loathed the preachers who espoused political ideas, which they feared would run to discordant orations on abolitionism and Republicanism.[75] For many Protestants, however, Olds was a sinner and Lincoln's policies were righteous, especially with the addition of emancipation as a war aim. There was little room for dissent when the Northerners were concurrently serving the Lord and the Republicans. "Christian people throughout the North have been praying for this time," Oberlin College student W. W. Parmenter explained to his mother after he enlisted in April 1861; "The conflict is now between Liberty and Slavery, Christianity and Barbarism, God and the Prince of Darkness."[76]

African American churches could not separate their political activities, which favored the Union cause, from their religious functions.[77] They had been involved in the antislavery movement long before the war had begun. When New Haven, Connecticut, African Americans learned of the Emancipation Proclamation, they gathered at their Temple Street Church to celebrate and it was in the Wesleyan Methodist Church of Syracuse, New York, where African Americans met to form the National Equal Rights League in October 1864.[78] By that time, however, white denominations were taking official political stands, which meant that they were also tempting dissent with their rigid commitments. On September 7, 1862, evangelical Protestants of various denominations gathered in Chicago and affirmed the war to be "a divine retribution upon the land for its manifold sins" and only emancipation would allow for absolution.[79] In 1863, the Philadelphia Baptist Association agreed that the end of slavery would confirm the United States' place as the divinely sanctioned "model of the world's civilization."[80] And in 1864, the New Jersey Reformed Dutch Church, which by this time had become an abolitionist church, resolved to support Lincoln.[81] The cause for Union was obvious and good, but once Lincoln stood for emancipation, there would be no separating Republican war aims from God's wishes for these Christians.

Methodists, then the largest denomination in the Union, were especially vigorous in support of the war and the Lincoln administration. They demanded unity on the political issues of the day. In 1863, New York's Methodist Episcopal Conference, after expressing its loyalty to the Lincoln government, resolved that "those who oppose every warlike measure under the pretext of discriminating between the administration and the government, are guilty of covert treason."[82] Earlier in August 1862 the influential Methodist *Western Christian Advocate* made the case clearly in addressing Christian obligations. The choices were as plain to the editorialist as they would have been to any Republican politician: "Shall it be Union, Peace, Brotherhood, Liberty, freedom, and equalizing Christianity . . . [or] disunion, war, selfishness, slavery and a besotted, barbarous, brutalizing, bastard corruption, and the perversion of holy religion?"[83] Condemnations of antiwar positions echoed in other Protestant publications and assemblies. In 1863, the New School Presbyterians, for example, likened the Democrats' criticism of the Lincoln administration's policies on emancipation, suspension of habeas corpus, and limits on the free press to treason.[84]

Preaching in such a heated atmosphere could hardly avoid the political. Protestant preachers wove prowar views into sermons, using biblical texts to support the Union cause.[85] Even Sunday school could be political, as was the case in a Washington, Iowa, Methodist congregation where the minister taught the children that "a Copperhead" was "the meanest thing in the world."[86] Indeed, churchgoers expected their ministers to deliver patriotic sermons, unless they were Democrats. Northern Unionists relied on their preachers to rally their patriotic spirits during low times. Along the way, ministers reminded their congregants to persevere in what was God's work and to be grateful for, as the Reverend Samuel J. Niccolls reminded his Chambersburg congregation in the aftermath of Gettysburg, having a "good and stable government . . . securing prosperity and protection to all alike. This is God's ordaining among us."[87]

Those ministers who were not sufficiently patriotic for their congregations could find themselves with no church. Northern Unionists required their preachers to be part of the war effort, expected them to support the president, and worried about the negative effects that allegedly treasonous ministers could have on the morale and support for the war.[88] Protestant Episcopal, Baptist, Presbyterian, Lutheran, and other church bodies regularly disciplined ministers who preached against the Republicans or encouraged resistance to the war. In the Midwest, where antiwar feelings were common, Unionist-controlled churches punished allegedly disloyal clergy—some of whom had protested their colleagues' overtly pro-Republican preaching—and pressured their Democratic communicants to support the war effort. Over the course of the war years, annual denominational conference meetings in Ohio, Indiana, and Illinois brought 121 ministers to face discipline for disloyalty.[89]

In 1863, the Illinois Methodist Annual Conference meeting in Springfield set a standard when it forced the retirement of Reverend William Blundell. His political sins were many. He had not joined organizations that supported the Lincoln administration. He neglected praying for Lincoln and the Union armies. And he acted immorally when he refused to honor the president's proclamation for a national day of thanksgiving. Furthermore, people had seen him with other disloyal individuals. So eager were the committee members sitting in judgment to reach a decision that they saw no need to trouble Blundell's accusers with requests for evidence, nor did they find it necessary to have the alleged perpetrator of these acts present to face them. The church accepted the committee's recommendation to deny him the right to preach.[90]

Across the North, other ministers came under fire for various types of allegedly disloyal activities, which generally involved supporting Democrats and their values while opposing the Republican Party. Unionists assumed that such views were indicators of the lack of religious virtue. A "Copperhead cannot be a Christian," a minister noted of the beliefs of Unionists; "and he who is not a Christian is not a proper person to preach the Gospel."[91] Congregants, local officials, and eventually the president would not tolerate outright antiwar talk from clergymen. As with unfortunate newspaper editors, disloyal preachers in some states ended up detained, which served to remind other dissidents that silence was a virtue.[92]

Democratic communicants clearly could not have felt welcome in a worship environment where they faced weekly sermons designed to further the Republican agenda and condemn their own political allegiances. In 1864, in New Jersey, pro-Republican preachers frustrated Democratic worshippers and one disgruntled conservative Sussex County man was dismayed to hear ministers "howling for the blood of every Southern man."[93] A Chicago minister concluded one of his services praying for the Lord to save him and his worshippers "from the blackhearted democrats and rebel sympathizers." Others preachers used biblical passages with ministerial authority to interpret scripture in ways to condemn those listeners who failed to agree with the Union cause.[94] Such outspoken partisan ministers could very well make lasting enemies among Democratic congregants.[95] But the congregants were just as likely to direct their wrath at each other, as did those good Christians in one church who held a truce while praying and then "abuse[d] each other out of church."[96] More likely, Democratic congregants might be expelled from patriotic churches, as some Iowa worshippers were.[97] Other frustrated worshippers simply walked away from church discord if they could. In Iowa, there were individuals who left their old churches to avoid its politics or who came together with like-minded individuals to establish churches free of secular debate, usually without having to abandon long-held theological beliefs given the theological similarities of the evangelical denominations.[98]

The preaching expectations loyal Unionists had of their ministers combined with all of their displays of civic patriotism—flag raisings, rallies, recruiting events, odes to the Constitution, days of mortification, and days of thanksgiving—to nurture a civic religion, a syncretism of political and religious beliefs that they could not easily unravel. Patriotic clergy encouraged this development, preaching that God had ordained the Union and those individuals who attacked it challenged God's will. Once the nation passed through this test, even if it required stifling opposition voices, it would be better for the sacrifices endured, confirming the United States, as Hartford, Connecticut, Congregationalist preacher Horace Bushnell wrote, as "God's own nation, providentially planted, established on moral foundations."[99] It also would mean a dominant Republican Party well into the future.

TWELVE

EMANCIPATION, CONSCRIPTION, AND DISSENT

EMANCIPATION

With victory still far from certain, Lincoln's preliminary emancipation announcement on September 22, 1862, and the actual promulgation of the policy on January 1, 1863, disturbed further the war-weary Northerners while invigorating those among them more inclined toward abolitionism. Far from abolishing slavery across the land, the president promised to end slavery only in areas that remained in rebellion and outside of the protection of the Constitution on the first day of 1863. Despite limitations, the Emancipation Proclamation signaled the beginning of the end of slavery, something that caused blacks throughout the Northern free states to rejoice.[1] The Reverend Henry Highland Garnet, a black abolitionist, christened the proclamation "the most able, manly and important document ever penned by man."[2] In Harrisburg, Pennsylvania, African Americans considered the document to be the commencement of "a new era in our country's history—a day in which injustice and oppression were forced to flee and cower before the benign principles of justice and righteousness."[3] It was for Northern African Americans a signal, a start, not an end in and of itself. "After the feast, comes the reckoning," wrote editorialist Robert Hamilton in the *Weekly Anglo-African*. In November 1862, in advance of the final proclamation, the Attorney General Edward Bates had issued a judgment that reversed the federal government's stand on black citizenship, pronouncing "free men of color, if born in the United States [are]. . . citizens of the United states." Consequently, Hamilton argued, "why should we not share in the perils of citizenship?" It was time to join the army and fight. It was time to help the freed slaves.[4]

There were white Northerners who agreed that the war had now become a contest of freedom battling slavery. As an editorialist writing in the *Chicago Tribune* believed, the proclamation returned America to the vision of the founders, a nation that was "the seat of justice . . . where each man, however humble, shall be entitled to life, liberty and the pursuit of happiness."[5] But at the same time, their more conservative neighbors questioned the political efficacy and the constitutionality of Lincoln's action. In New Jersey, for example, Republicans generally rallied to the president and editorialists blessed the proclamation as an historical act of essential justice. There were moderates in Lincoln's New Jersey party, however, who worried about the implementation of the proclamation, and there were conservative Republicans who denounced it.[6]

Elsewhere, moderate Republicans, unlike more abolitionist-minded radicals, took the proclamation to be a war measure, designed to help hurry along the defeat of the Confederacy. For Connecticut governor William A. Buckingham, abolition was secondary to what he regarded as the chief purpose of the proclamation, namely to have an additional tool with which "to overpower the rebellion, even if it interferes with and overthrows their much-loved system of slavery."[7] Such an interpretation could keep weakening Union coalitions from fissuring, a harder proposition given the progress of the war and the antiblack feelings of so many white Northerners, but it could not keep enthusiastic Democrats from taking political aim at what many white Northerners viewed as a wrong shift in the government's direction.

Across the country, there remained conservatives, especially among the Democratic opposition, who believed Lincoln lacked the constitutional authority to emancipate slaves. The proclamation, they argued, overrode legitimate restraints and his actions placed his government "in rebellion," thus making the war "a contest for subjugation."[8] Other antiemancipationists did not wish to see the war for the Union sent along a detour of social experimentation. In 1862 in Centre County, Pennsylvania, opponents of the Lincoln administration had warned their constituents that the government was steering the nation toward an abolitionist war.[9] Now it had come to pass, with all of the dire consequences predicted before now reiterated by the opposition. In New Jersey the proclamation added weight to the fear that Northern states would soon be the destination of every absconding, Southern black man, woman, and child. Consequently, the proclamation added a new energy to partisanship, troubling even its advocates about its impact on voters and the future successes of the Republican Party. It was not an imagined concern given the favorable outcome for Democrats in electoral contests in New Jersey and elsewhere.[10] In fact, the inauguration of a Democratic governor in New Jersey and another in neighboring New York provided the occasion for the crowds to protest Lincoln's proclamation.[11] Thus, Republican Senator John Sherman of Ohio referred to it as an "ill-timed proclamation."[12]

The negative reactions to the proclamation tended to see Lincoln's action as an attack on the rights of white citizens, especially since the federal government earlier that year had passed the Militia Act of July 17, which threatened conscription if states failed to meet volunteer quotas.[13] Also, Lincoln's suspension of the writ of habeas corpus throughout the Northern states followed closely on the heels of the Preliminary Proclamation.[14] In November 1862, a Quincy, Illinois, editorialist warned, "The people will teach the abolition tories that there are other interests beside those of the negro, that should claim the attention of those who are selected to make and execute the laws." These abolitionists, he continued, "were not satisfied that the war should be prosecuted for the white man, and the rights of the white man, but have persistently clamored for it[s] prosecution for the interests of the inevitable negro." Beware, he warned, they also "raise the howl for the emigration of these negroes into the northern States," and expect to force "hundreds and thousands of them into Illinois."[15]

Earlier in October, the editor of the Milwaukee German Catholic newspaper *Seebote* worried that now German and Irish immigrants would end up being "used as fodder for cannons" to secure the abolition of slavery and in the end find themselves "annihilated, to make room for the Negro."[16] Catholic Irish Americans, generally Democrats, opposed the proclamation on constitutional grounds but also feared that the administration was in fact expecting to displace their workingmen with the freed slaves.[17] Indeed, in July 1862, there already had been a clash between black and Irish workers on the Chicago docks, sparked by black longshoremen underbidding Irish longshoremen to unload one vessel.[18] The prominent Catholic cleric Archbishop John Hughes, who supported a war for the Union, made it clear that his communicants, when confronting forced military service, had no intention of "carrying on a war that costs so much blood and treasure just to gratify a clique of Abolitionists."[19]

CONSCRIPTION

Regardless of their views, Northerners still had to win the war either to effect emancipation or to reestablish national unity. During 1862, Northerners responded to recruiting rallies with much less enthusiasm than they had at the war's outset. This was a problem that continued into the next year. In 1863 through the fall, Massachusetts failed to muster a significant number of new black and white recruits, with a decidedly antiemancipationist view in the Irish community contributing to the slow pace of enlistments.[20] That otherwise vigorously pro-Union state was not alone.

To help rectify the situation, the government explored other means to raise the necessary manpower, most significantly the recruitment of black men. During late 1862 and early 1863, the army began its tentative approach to enlisting both former Southern slaves and free Northern African Americans. There remained in the North at this time racism enough to prompt the consideration that such an effort would in the end do more harm than good, especially in the wake of Lincoln's promulgation of the Emancipation Proclamation. New Jersey conservatives objected to the implied equality of having black men under arms and continued to argue that the United States was a white man's country still fighting a white man's war.[21] In July 1863 Sidney Fisher was distressed because "The abolitionists are trying to make what they can out of the enlistment of Negro soldiers & are likely to cause a reaction & injure their own cause & the real interest of the Negro." Furthermore, he believed, "The orators claim equality for the Negro race, the right of suffrage, &c. All this is as absurd as it is dangerous."[22]

African Americans who went off to fight as well as those who remained at home understood that the war should bring to their community those very things Fisher feared. John Rock made clear in his 1864 Syracuse, New York, address that black soldiers were fighting for "liberty and equality." "We ask the same for the black man that is asked for the white man," he declared; "nothing more and nothing less."[23] Earlier in 1863, John Abbott, an Illinois African American serving with the 55th Massachusetts Infantry, explained his efforts to the home folks in a similar way noting, "Our motto is, that every man is born free and equal, and that equality we are fighting for . . . until we get it."[24] Military service was just a start, according to Frederick Douglass: "Once in the United States uniform and the colored man has a springing board under him by which he can jump to loftier heights."[25]

Ironically, because wartime conditions had provided some Northern black men with greater economic opportunities, they were generally less enthusiastic about joining than they had been in 1861. Also, given the Philadelphian Fisher's attitude, one shared by many Northerners, the legitimate fear that they would not be treated as well as white soldiers or that they would be fighting for a country that would not recognize their rights as humans and citizens dampened their eagerness to enlist. Nevertheless, Northern blacks joined the army, although about 80 percent of the approximately 180,000 men who served in the U.S. Colored Troops were former slaves from the Confederacy or Union border states.[26]

These black troops made a difference, but there still came a time when the need for soldiers outstripped the voluntary responses of citizens. The July 1862 Militia Act attempted to answer that need. The act allowed states to draft men for nine months' service, but also reserved for the federal government the power to intrude into the affairs of states and conduct a draft if the states could not fill assigned quotas with volunteers and lacked the machinery to conscript the men needed. The government put the law to the test in August when it called for 300,000 men to serve for nine months. This call for militiamen was in addition to an earlier July 2 call for 300,000 volunteers for three years of service.[27] Also, in July, Congress hoped to encourage enlistments from immigrant communities by speeding along the citizenship process for honorably discharged volunteers.[28]

The militia draft of 1862 left raising troops primarily in the hands of the states, and the use of bounties helped limit the need to force men to serve. However, that effort was only a prelude to the Enrollment Act of March 1863, which placed the conscription of troops squarely under the authority of the federal government through the Provost Marshal General and the various assistant provost marshals general that he appointed to enforce federal authority in communities throughout the North. Neither law was as oppressive and burdensome as it might have been, and there remained ample opportunities for individuals to avoid conscription when the president used the latter law to call for drafts on four occasions. Not only did the states and the federal government offer some exemptions, but the law of March 1863 also provided an opportunity for a conscript to purchase his way out of service with a $300 commutation fee. The conscript could also find another individual who would serve in his place for a fee, but the commutation fee initially held in check the cost of substitutes. The commutation fee remained in place until the government rescinded it on July 4, 1864.[29]

States and localities worked hard to avoid the unhappiness of involuntary service. Incentives, patriotic harangues, and shame led Northerners into the army in 1862, saving most states from the necessity of a draft. Pennsylvanian Samuel Cormany admitted after deciding to answer the call, "The fear of being drafted, if I did not volunteer—had possibly some weight in inducing decission [*sic*]."[30] So it was throughout the North. Publicity in favor of volunteering, some of it false, saved Iowa from the militia draft.[31] New Jersey, a state where Democrats held a goodly amount of political power, avoided a draft in all but one town in 1862 by filling its quota with volunteers.[32] The men of Springfield, Massachusetts, were subjected to calls for patriotic service to save the town from the humiliation of a draft. But as in other communities, the bounty offered by the town might have been an important determining factor.[33] In the end, only seven states did not meet their quotas and the War Department secured more men than it had expected.[34]

Conscripts could not claim bounties, and their fellow volunteer soldiers usually looked down on them, which were additional forceful incentives for enlisting. Communities borrowed and taxed themselves to raise money while bidding against one another to induce men from outside of their boundaries to enlist under their quota requirements. Also, commutation fees and substitutes were not so far beyond the reach of working men that they failed to take advantage of those options. Men subject to conscription banded together in draft insurance clubs, pooling their resources to pay the costs if any of their members were called and wished to avoid service, as did the ten Indiana men who in February 1865 each pledged $200 to supplement Indianapolis funds for the purpose of buying substitutes if any of their number were conscripted. Communities also subsidized the fees and substitute payments of men who wished to avoid service.[35]

Substitute brokers embarked on a new business as they secured replacements for draftees, which often led to dishonest or at least questionable practices. Brokers in New Jersey found a good source for their inventory among European immigrants new to the state and unfamiliar with the circumstances into which they had just landed.[36] Before too long, legal draft evasion was sufficiently common to elicit little comment except from the veterans at the front and Republicans such as newspaper man Joseph Medill, who expected political consequences favoring "The copper-heads [who] are gloating over the prospective harvest of votes they will reap against the bill that 'puts the rich man's dirty dollars against a poor man's life.'"[37]

For the first two federal drafts, when the commutation was still available, Northern men used it liberally; 85,000 of the 133,000 men required to serve in the army paid the fee.[38] On August 2, 1863, George A. Morse, of Woodbury, Vermont, informed his brother that most of the drafted men in the town paid their $300. "[Y]ou know the dra[f]ting law is the meanest law that ever was made," he added by way of editorial comment sharing Medill's concern with the war becoming a poor man's fight; "if they wanted men why did not they draft men and not money[?]"[39]

Groups of potential draftees also eagerly sought out substitutes. In May 1862, with speculation that a draft was on the horizon, Middletown, Rhode Island, men made plans to head off conscription. Sarah E. Fales kept her son in the First Rhode Island Volunteers apprised of their efforts. "[S]ome of the men have be[e]n terribly frightened" by the prospects of being drafted. "[T]hey met at the townhouse again last week not to raise recruits but to raise money to hire men to go for thim [*sic*] . . . Father says there will be no drafting as long as there is a dollar left in the town, what do you think of that for patriotism and love of country[?]"[40] The quest for substitutes, with ever-intensifying competition among Northern communities and, thus, ever-increasing cost for able-bodied men, continued through the last year of the war. Again, this option provided those men who wished to avoid service a way out of the draft; indeed, of the almost 232,000 men selected in the lotteries, more men caught in the relatively low yield of the various calls furnished substitutes than were actually drafted into the army. Over 28,000 provided substitutes as opposed to the over 26,000 men who were drafted into the service.[41] Jacob Philster, a Cincinnati businessman, understood the role played by self-interest and in January 1863 urged Senator John Sherman to attend to it. He warned Sherman that whatever the government did with conscription, it had to continue to appeal to the two sides of Northern nature, "patriotism and cupidity"; just be sure to encourage bounty payments and to allow commutation, he advised.[42]

There were a number of reasons why Northerners could support conscription even if it proved to be a burden to part of the population. Some of them found patriotic virtue in conscription, as it was a means by which citizens could pay the debt they owed to a nation that had given them an environment of liberty. Other Northerners accepted the draft, believing that it could be a good way to spread the burden of service beyond the ranks of the poorer members of society. Some Republicans feared that conscription was the only way for their party to maintain political power as so many of them volunteered while less enthusiastic Democratic voters stayed at home.[43] There were, however, many Northerners who found drafting men into the army obnoxious and did their best to avoid conscription. Upward to 50,000 men probably illegally dodged conscription before the 1863 federal draft, and 161,244 men illegally avoided the subsequent federal drafts.[44]

There was no mystery as to why they pursued such action, according to Philster. "The Draft fix it as you will is distasteful to the American mind," Philster reminded Senator Sherman. It was simple, he continued, explaining, "we don't like the use of arbitrary power, and our republican education make[s] us resent it naturally, and disapprove of its use except in cases of last resort, as the Rebellion."[45] Even as a last resort there were Northerners who objected to conscription, finding philosophical and political fault with the practice. Understandably, pacifists, who opposed the war from the outset, quarreled with the notion of forced military service, used moral suasion to try to convince society to stop the violence, and provided information to potential conscripts who wished to avoid service.[46] Other Northerners believed that conscription was an extraordinary and unconstitutional act, with commutation fees and substitutes favoring those citizens who had money, while leaving their poorer constituents at a disadvantage. Businessmen and farmers in need of labor would suffer, politicians protested, as would the poorer families of the men called to service. Democrats also viewed the draft as an unprecedented burden imposed by the federal government, circumventing the states' role in raising troops as well as abridging the personal liberties of the men conscripted. One Dubuque, Iowa, editor labeled the draft unconstitutional, an act of despotism and "military slavery."[47] Julius Wesslau, a German immigrant residing in New York City, agreed. He complained about the 1862 militia draft, explaining, "[I]f I was unwilling to be treated like a piece of government property in Prussia, I am just as unwilling to do so here."[48]

The Democratic Party, as the loyal opposition, accepted conscription as law, but antidraft individuals were less likely to go along with it, even to the point of resorting to violence.[49] Direct opposition to the draft assumed various forms. In August 1862, in Dubuque, Iowa, some dissenters took preemptive action and left their homes in the Irish neighborhoods when they became concerned with the possibilities of a draft.[50] During 1862, in Pennsylvania, there were more signs of the tension that a widespread draft might promote. In mining areas dominated by Democrats and

Irish immigrants, men refused to cooperate with the process, hid from officials, and sometimes threatened government officials.[51] The problems in the mining communities of Pennsylvania endured into 1865. People there continued to give shelter to draft dodgers and deserters, while doing violence to federal agents, the very men who were supposed to conduct the draft.[52] In 1862, in Brown County, Wisconsin, armed Belgian farmers threatened Senator Timothy Howe in Green Bay, but the senator escaped the mob.[53] Elsewhere in Wisconsin the German and the Luxemburg Catholic populations rose up against conscription, most significantly in Port Washington, where resisters, their courage fueled with liquor, seized conscription records, ran officials out of town, and destroyed the houses of men involved with executing the draft. The army intervened and arrested many of the offenders, who in the end avoided punishment.[54]

Federal officers encountered resistance as they went to the homes of eligible men to sign them up for the coming draft. In June in Chicago, enrollment officials confronted snarling dogs and angry wives and suffered the indignities of having chamberpot waste tossed on them from second-floor windows; officials encountered the worst inhospitable acts the city had to offer in the poor Irish neighborhoods. Clever Chicagoans, if tapped for service, went "slinking off . . . like whipped curs" for the proximate safety of Canada or, as many of the travelers said, "to see their Canadian uncles and aunts."[55]

In June hundreds of troops accompanied by artillery put down a protest in Holmes County, Ohio, while in Indiana, draft resisters killed two enrollment officers.[56] But it was the actual federal draft of 1863 that provoked resistance and violence throughout the North, most famously in New York City where protestors ran riot through parts of the city. From July 13 through July 16, a mob, primarily from the city's Irish working class who resented the economics of the war as well as the new federal war aim of emancipation, destroyed property, razed a black orphanage, and committed mayhem and murder. "These people committed every atrocity imaginable," complained Karl Wesslau, "for three nights in a row the city was lit up by the burning buildings." Furthermore, Wesslau continued, "Everyone thought the government here was really spineless, and the parties attacked it and made fun of it."[57] At least 105 and perhaps 150 individuals lost their lives in the riot, including soldiers shot or brutally beaten by the mob and one black man who committed suicide lest he fall into the hands of the rioters; property damage amounted to millions of dollars of claims.[58] Poor New Yorkers raised themselves up in violent protest, but according to Sidney Fisher, it was the Democrats' "incendiary harangues" that "have inflamed the people and given to the rabble a pretext for disorder." Fisher was not one for allowing freedom of speech in dangerous times, and now here was more proof of the treasonous intentions of "These demagogues" who "are determined to cause anarchy in the North, if they can, in order to serve the South."[59]

The New York riot in particular frightened many Northern communities worried that they would have to suffer similar events when it came time to draft men. Some communities experienced violence, but quelled the disturbances quickly. In Boston, on July 14, Governor John Andrew's quick response with troops supplemented with patriotic Harvard alumni who were in town attending their reunion at a local hotel kept things under control, as did calls for quiet by local politicians and priests.[60]

Other communities experienced unfounded panic. In Northampton, Massachusetts, the home folk were fearful of violence in late July because rumor had it that conscription would provoke an outbreak of aggressive resistance. "[T]he old grannies run up & down the street saying there was surely going to be trouble doing just the thing to create a disturbance," one veteran soldier wrote, apparently tickled by what he considered to be the comical response to the violence in New York City. Watching the home guard patrol the streets "was fun & I enjoyed it." The men of the guard had pledged to "fight to the death," but to save them the trouble he and two companions gathered up and secreted their weapons to keep them from hurting anyone. He assured his correspondent that "no resistance will be made by the conscripts to reporting when ordered in this section" because most of the men called up will "be exempted for disability or pay their mony [*sic*]."[61]

The experience of the resisters in the Pennsylvania districts and elsewhere, however, indicated that opposition to the draft was no laughing matter in many communities and frequently a much more complicated affair than the rejection of forced military service. Working men, and especially German and Irish Catholic immigrants, in Northeastern cities, Vermont quarries, Pennsylvania mines, and the Old Northwest states who tended to vote Democratic believed that conscription was just one more unfair burden from the Lincoln administration, conflating the draft with such government policies as emancipation, their own economic difficulties, and labor problems. They resented the war, fearing that it favored the interests of the wealthy, the war profiteers, and blacks over their own. New York City rioters, for example, worried that if they were drafted black men would displace them in the workforce. The Pennsylvania miners had been very much engaged in labor protests for the usual reasons found among workers who tried to unionize throughout American history.[62] In Iowa, the draft opponents who organized the Independent Military Company of Mounted Riflemen in July 1863 had already been involved in tax protests and probably had been voicing their objections to the war from a much earlier date.[63] And residents of Holmes County, Ohio, believed they were defending their local liberty from the encroachments of the Lincoln administration's expanding, intrusive central government.[64]

Significantly, resistance to the draft in these and other places was not simply an individual affair, but rather an expression of the values of entire communities. Northern communities throughout the region, including their leading men, had learned the particulars of legal draft avoidance from the first threat of conscription.[65] But even where extralegal or illegal resistance materialized, it did so usually with the support of families and neighbors.[66] From late 1864 into the fall of 1865, military forces arrested 2,810 deserters and 3,743 draft evaders in the eastern Pennsylvania mountains. The military received some assistance from local Unionists in this effort, but such numbers could not have existed without significant community support for the dissenters.[67]

Federal authorities, either openly or undercover usually within the Provost Marshal General Bureau, tracked down and dragged into court deserters, dodgers, and those citizens who aided them.[68] In New Jersey, 37 individuals over the course of the war were convicted of such crimes.[69] But in some communities, sympathetic jurists helped the defendants brought into their courts. In Iowa, on one occasion in July 1863, two resisters ended up in prison only to be freed by the county judge when he signed a writ of habeas corpus. They in turn filed kidnapping charges against the assistant provost marshal general and the men who had aided him in making their arrest.[70]

DISSENT AND CIVIL LIBERTIES

There were many reasons to complain about Republican policies as far as Democrats were concerned. Conscription, however, aggravated antigovernment dissent, making it more vociferous and more violent, thus encouraging like reactions from those policy makers they criticized. Not only did conscription threaten to undermine individual choice, it also represented an extension of federal power throughout the Northern states in ways that emancipation, another problematic unconstitutional act, or taxation, another example of government overreach, did not.[71]

The conflict caused by the federal government's draft, however, was also part of the larger national problem of dealing with dissent and freedom of speech in a democratic nation during a time of crisis. Republican politicians and Union generals tried to tamp down opposition in the troublesome regions, but even within the federal government concern for disloyalty meant administering oaths of loyalty and a continued suspicion of concealed prorebel sympathies in the various nooks and crannies of the government. Any division, Northern Unionists believed, "weakened the efforts of the government." For Sidney Fisher, who pondered such things in August 1861, even a peace party made up of Democrats "is really an alliance with the rebels of the South and playing into their hands."[72]

At the beginning of the war, officials fearful about treasonous sentiments within the government meant having all employees of the federal government in Washington and elsewhere take an oath of future loyalty if they wished to keep their jobs. These employees still had to be careful with their speech and concerned about the difficulties outspoken family members could cause them. Postmaster General Montgomery Blair checked on loyalty within his department, ridding it of those individuals who did not measure up to his scrutiny. Secretary of the Interior Caleb Smith reviewed pension records and deprived individuals of their coming payments if they or a family member had spoken out in any suggestive disloyal way. A congressional committee investigated charges of disloyalty shielding informers from defendants; by the end of 1861, the committee claimed to have discovered over 300 disloyal government workers in various Washington departments.[73]

From the first days of the war, the federal government wished either to censor publications that supposedly undermined the security of the nation or use such information to identify disloyal civilians. Postmasters confiscated letters addressed to individuals within the seceded states and sent them to Secretary of State William Seward, who oversaw problems of disloyalty early in the war.[74] In August 1861, the government arrested Pierce Butler, a Philadelphia resident with Southern connections, for corresponding with secessionists. Sidney Fisher, however, believed it was because "He has expressed . . . the strongest opinions in favor of the Southern cause and wishes for its success in earnest language." It was understandable, Fisher concluded, and justifiable, rationalizing "in times such as these that alone is sufficient to justify his arrest."[75]

The government also tried to control the flow of information beyond personal letters. The Post Office excluded from the mails what it determined were treasonable newspapers, and the government actually closed papers it deemed disloyal or disruptive to the war effort. In August 1862, P. Gray Meek, the recently mobbed antiwar editor of the Centre County, Pennsylvania, *Bellefonte Democratic Watchman*, was dogged by a warrant accusing him of "*inducing men not to enlist in the army*." A friend felt obligated to remind the community that this charge was nothing but character assassination. Furthermore, he cautioned, "Remember, this is a free country; and so long as a man is guiltless of treason . . . he has a right to the free expression of his opinion."[76] In September 1862, however, Lincoln proclaimed such antiwar actions, along with draft resistance, unlawful.[77] Unionists approved of such measures believing Democratic newspapers as well as antiwar speeches gave comfort to the enemy. They suggested to Confederates that the North was divided in its war efforts, according to Philadelphian Sidney Fisher, and they "thus encourage the enemy to preserver [*sic*]." After living through two years of war, he concluded in 1863, the Confederacy had benefited a great deal from Democratic dissent, "for the hopes inspired by speeches, newspapers and notes of northern Democrats, the rebellion would have been quelled long ere this."[78]

Shutting down a newspaper, especially in heavily Democratic areas, however, could backfire. In early June 1863, General Ambrose Burnside closed the *Chicago Times*, a vigorously anti-Lincoln paper, whose editor Wilbur Storey was given to scurrilous ad hominem attacks on the president, a man he labeled "so foolish an old joker." The military action provided further opportunity for Storey to attack Lincoln and Burnside, whom he now dubbed "The Beast of Fredericksburg," a reference to the slaughter his army experienced in that battle. The popular reaction threatened an outbreak of violence. Handbills rallied thousands of supporters to the streets "to resent this military interference with freedom of the press." They faced off with Republicans. Lincoln asked Burnside to lift his order, and eventually the crisis passed.[79]

Beyond making disloyal statements, newspapers regardless of party affiliation gave away too much information about the Union army, its strengths, and its movements to their readers and thus to the enemy, a problem with which the government and the military struggled until the army had much more good news than bad to share with Northern readers.[80] Such restrictions required supervising the flow of information over the North's telegraph lines, something the president could do with the authority granted him by Congress in January 1862.[81] During the war the Associated Press (AP), already the principal wire service before the war, gained a virtual monopoly of war news spread by the telegraph thanks to a special arrangement with the federal government. In 1862 the War Department imposed censorship on the telegraph to prevent reporters from sending information that might compromise military matters while it also fed exclusive news from Washington to AP reporters. Major newspapers with correspondents in Washington had the means to get their words out, but papers relying on AP reporters received information from the capital with a decidedly pro-administration and pro-Republican slant.[82]

Concerns over the destructive consequences of dissent also prompted the Lincoln administration to suspend the writ of habeas corpus at various times during the war. This procedure allowed the government to imprison individuals without formally charging them at a time when Lincoln's administration broadly defined disloyal speech. In March 1863, Congress reinforced the president's claim to executive authority when it passed the Habeas Corpus Act authorizing him to suspend the writ when he believed "the public safety may require it."[83] Republicans believed using such tactics was essential in times of war. Constitutional niceties were for after the fighting stopped. This view became particularly powerful in the minds of people such as Connecticut's Horace Bushnell, who equated morality with loyalty to the Union cause. For Bushnell, it was better to "fight our nation's enemies and destroyers." Once victorious, he reasoned, "then if we can, it will be the time to mend the abuses of the laws."[84]

The most famous of antiwar dissidents subjected to harsh treatment at the hands of the Lincoln government was Ohio politician Clement Vallandigham. Vallandigham, a Peace Democrat, ran afoul of General Ambrose Burnside's April 1863 order that broadly defined treasonous speech. Burnside, commander of the Department of

Ohio consisting of the loyal slave state of Kentucky and the free Midwestern states of Ohio, Indiana, Illinois, and Michigan, deemed it his duty to stamp out dissent within his jurisdiction. On May 1, 1863, the politician tempted the government with an oration at Mt. Vernon, Ohio, highly critical of the government's war aims and its threats to the Constitution. Vallandigham's chief complaints were not new, but echoed old oppositional grievances concerning emancipation and conscription wrapped in his claim to constitutional rights of free speech, one that no arbitrary military order could undermine. In the end, he warned the crowd that the government would soon enforce conscription in order to conduct not a war for the Union, but "a wicked Abolition war, and that if those in authority were allowed to accomplish their purpose, the people would be deprived of their liberties, and a monarchy established."[85]

Vallandigham was arrested and imprisoned, charged with treason, tried and convicted by a military commission, and exiled to the Confederacy, even though he urged voters to work within the political system to change the country's course. The Lincoln administration, far from quieting dissent with its attack on Vallandigham, provoked criticism that made the Democratic politician into a martyr at the hands of "this wild storm of fanaticism," as one Iowa editorialist called Republican policy. Democratic politicians organized rallies in defense of Vallandigham and questioned whether the Republican Party's true purpose in conducting the war was to undermine the liberties of the Northern people.[86]

Republicans tended to paint opposition to the Union cause with the blackest brush possible, but they did witness some events during the war that appeared to justify their anxieties. From the beginning of the war, some Midwesterners discussed establishing a confederacy of the states of the old Northwest Territory. Confederate agents made contact with sympathetic Midwesterners, and members of the Sons of Liberty in Illinois were receiving financial assistance from them. Sons of Liberty in Indiana had hidden a cache of arms, which was discovered when they were arrested. And there was an incompetently planned effort to free Confederate prisoners of war from Camp Douglas in Chicago. The latter conspiracy, its dangers exaggerated by the local press, led to the arrests in early November 1864 of 150 people, most of whom were not guilty of treasonous activity. An editorialist for the *Chicago Tribune* stoked enthusiasm for Republican politicians as he anxiously explained that the affair gave loyal people what "the Northern allies of rebellion are capable of." The people of Chicago "have had a glimpse," he continued, "of the reality which awaits them if these sympathizers with treason can once clutch the reins of government." In the end, the Chicago conspiracy arrests, if they did not actually improve the security of the city, provided an electoral boost to Lincoln and his party in the presidential election on November 8.[87]

THIRTEEN

THE TRANSITION FROM WAR TO PEACE

A JOYOUS VICTORY

The presidential election in November 1864 following on the heels of their army's victories signaled the beginning of the end of the war for many optimistic Northerners. The people of Massachusetts sensed a happy conclusion to be on the horizon and on January 4, 1865, the state's legislature made it clear. "By the election of Mr. Lincoln, it has been settled, that from ocean to ocean, from Aroostook to the Rio Grande, there shall be but one nation," Jonathan E. Field, president of the state senate, proclaimed. Importantly, he also noted that the united country would be a different, better kind of place compared to its antebellum self. Anticipating the abolition amendment that Congress would send to the states for approval at the end of the month, he noted that the country would soon be free of slavery. "The breeze that opens . . . [the national flag's] folds," he declaimed, "will cool the brow of no unpaid toil, will fan the cheek of no slave."[1]

The spring's developments rewarded Northern anticipation. As they had done in 1861, Bostonians awaited news of military progress on the streets, expecting editors to post information as soon as it became available. When the wires brought news of the fall of Richmond, they and residents in surrounding communities rang church bells, listened to speeches, fired salutes, and watched parades.[2] "Isn't it Glorious?"

wrote Caroline Woolsey, "New York has stood on its head, and the bulls and bears of Wall street for once left off their wrangling, and sang Old Hundred."[3] Stockbridge in the western part of Massachusetts celebrated "with guns drums, bells, and bonfires." In the evening, "bonfires blaze . . . and gun powder and bad tobacco smoke made the night as gloriously hideous as the most enthusiastic could desire." Nearby Pittsfield missed out on artillery barrages, but "the fire worshippers had to console themselves with rockets, &c., of which the display was good."[4]

Shortly thereafter, Northerners understood that with Lee's surrender on April 9, the war was virtually over. The rebel government had disintegrated and, according to George Templeton Strong, "Napoleon could hardly save Joe Johnston's army," the other major Confederate force east of the Mississippi River.[5] Public joy spread across the North providing opportunities for communities to identify with the war effort, to socialize, and to memorialize the long-awaited defeat of what so many of them had considered at one time Lee's invincible army. On April 10, the Unionists of Fort Wayne, Indiana, were especially pleased with how victory unfolded on the home front at the expense of their wartime political enemies. They announced the surrender of the "Rebel City of Fort Wayne," a Democratic, antiwar stronghold. Fort Wayne put on a celebration that matched the jubilant activities of the bigger Northern cities. Loyal citizens finally were able to raise a national flag above the courthouse, something that had been missing during the war. Businesses closed, and the usual celebratory noise filled the town. "The Copperhead funeral," as a telegram from Union citizens reported, was "largely attended."[6] Indeed, next door in Ohio, according to Andrew Evans, Copperheads had turned quiet in their opposition to the war effort; the recent success of the federal government "has taken the wind out of their sails. You can hardly get on[e] of them to jaw back to a union man."[7]

As Ohioan Cornelius Madden explained to his father on April 10, 1865, "This is the glorious day that we have been looking forward to, with longing eyes, for the past four years and now it has dawned in all its brightness."[8] Later in April, Charles Hale declared in an editorial printed in the *Boston Daily Advertiser* "that the sub-stantial principles of American liberty shall go down unimpaired to all time."[9] Those principles now included a nation free of slavery. As another editorialist explained to readers in the Hartford, Connecticut, area, Southerners "commenced the war to perpetuate slavery" and now "The institution is smitten in the dust, and the chains of the bondmen are broken forever."[10]

African Americans in the North had believed this goal to be the war's purpose from the beginning, and they rejoiced in the defeat of the Confederacy. Northern blacks had watched their men put up with insults, fight hard, die, and finally march as conquerors into Confederate cities. Their communities had fought what Frederick Douglass called "a double battle," one against Southern slavery and another against

Northern prejudice.[11] By their own efforts, African Americans had won their place as citizens.[12]

Earlier, Lincoln's Emancipation Proclamation of January 1, 1863, had prompted widespread celebration among the black communities of the Northern states. There were other hopeful signs during the war. In February 1865, Illinois repealed its black codes excluding black immigrants and court testimony against whites. As the Reverend A. T. Hall declaimed at a meeting of African Americans in Chicago, "The Legislature were the instrument in the hands of God of wiping out the records of injustice. The status of the colored race had become materially changed."[13] Now, African Americans expected to secure victory in the home front war acknowledged by Douglass, with the help of their white allies.[14] As one black Ohio veteran affirmed, "We will not revert to these acts of oppression again," while a comrade in another black regiment proclaimed, "liberty and equality have been purchased at too great a sacrifice" to be lost in the peace.[15]

Northern blacks, however, were cautious in victory. In Kentucky and Delaware, their brethren remained enslaved at the end of the war, although the Harrisburg blacks assured those unfortunates that "the rod of your oppressors will eventually be smitten by the omnipotence of truth . . . the fires of freedom shall light your hill tops, and your valleys shall be made vocal with the songs of liberty."[16] The Thirteenth Amendment, which assured the constitutional end of slavery, was still making its way through the states as the Union army rolled up the last of the resisting Confederate forces. Therefore, even with the Confederate surrender, African Americans continued to fear that the rebel masters of the South would renew their fight at some future time, much to the detriment of black people.[17]

DAMPENED WITH SORROW

Contemplating the celebrations he expected would sweep the nation, Cornelius Madden reminded his father that he had predicted that the war would make Lincoln "a second Washington in the history of our beloved country and thank God we have lived to see that Solved completely."[18] However, Washington had died a natural death in his own bed. That was not to be Lincoln's fate. As Mary Livermore recalled, "From the height of this exultation the nation was swiftly precipitated to the very depths of despair" when Abraham Lincoln fell to an assassin's bullet.[19]

Confederate sympathizer and popular actor John Wilkes Booth shot Lincoln on April 14, Good Friday, as the president watched a play at Ford's Theater in Washington, D.C. The president died the next day, and Northerners' celebrations turned into mourning ceremonies. The news of the assassination made people "dumb with grief," but united in their anger and sorrow.[20] Furthermore, as black abolitionist Frederick Douglass understood, the assassination was "a stab at Republican institutions."[21]

Communities, only recently filled with excitement and joy, now engaged in collective mourning for their martyred president. Easter Sunday, a great day of joy on the Christian calendar, became one of sorrow.[22] Sarah Gay, of North Hingham, Massachusetts, attended church services, noting a flag at half-staff and the church "draped in black crape." "[E]very thing looks mournful," she reported to her husband, who was still in the army.[23] In Burlington, Vermont, "Many stout-hearted men were seen to weep" at a church service and the mourning continued the next day.[24]

Northerners were already used to mourning, but Lincoln's death was extraordinary, its impact wide-ranging in part because Lincoln's reputation had risen to new heights after his 1864 reelection. New Yorker George Templeton Strong wrote only a few days before Lincoln's death that the president's "name will be of high account fifty years hence, and for many generations thereafter."[25] Editorialists now eulogized Lincoln, praising him as being second only to George Washington among America's presidents. "The bullet that pierced the head of President Lincoln touched the heart of the nation," editorialized the *Cincinnati Commercial*; "No event since the death of Washington has so filled the land with sorrow."[26]

At the same time that people recognized their martyred president's greatness, they also intimately experienced his death perhaps because of his ordinary, familiar qualities. Ann Eliza Smith, the wife of Vermont's governor, told her husband, there is a sense of personal loss. . . . Kind merciful man, he will sure find mercy with God."[27] "I felt as tho I had lost a personal friend," Philadelphian Sidney Fisher noted, "for indeed I have & so has every honest man in the country."[28] As the editorialist in the *Kansas Farmer* explained, Lincoln's death brought with it "a real personal sorrow." In his mind, the shared trials of the war created intimacy between the late president and the people. "Each man," he wrote, "feels it as a personal bereavement, for we had looked to our President as a personal friend."[29]

After the surrender of Lee, people in New York City began to debate the fate of Jefferson Davis, the rebel president. Some of them expressed a desire to hang him "on a sour apple tree." Others argued for mercy, joining a debate that individuals pursued across the river in New Jersey and elsewhere through the North.[30] There remained some Northerners who continued to call for pardoning what Caleb Mills of Indiana called "the *rebel rascals*." But citizens across the country joined him in setting aside notions of mercy for the defeated South, now demanding "vindictive justice."[31] The "astounding event" of Lincoln's assassination stoked those feelings, Mills thought, thus breaking "up the delusion, & opening the eyes of the public to the folly, & madness of such feeling just taking hold of an unreflecting multitude."[32]

Frederick Douglass considered the assassination a God-given opportunity for embarking on a harsh Reconstruction.[33] Soldiers in the field were preparing to pursue with hard hearts the Confederates who were still under arms.[34] But even Northern

Democrats would need to be careful. New Jerseyan Emma Randolph assumed all Democrats were somehow accomplices in the assassination. "I feel a stronger hatred than ever for the poor Copperheads," she explained; "now they have stooped so low as to murder our loved and honored . . . President."[35] Some bitter individuals, sharing Emma Randolph's feelings, directed their anger at the closest proxies of the moribund Confederacy, all of whom they presumed were connected at least by association to the dastardly act. Victor Klausmeyer believed that tensions ran so high that "even the smallest incident could have led to all the rebel prisoners and rebel-sympathizers having to pay for this crime with their own blood."[36] The mayor of Philadelphia advised all Democrats to display proper symbols of mourning on their homes, "an external mark of respect to the popular sentiment." Otherwise, he warned them, "he would not be answerable for the consequences."[37]

Indeed, there were some remarkable if not widespread examples of grief-fueled violence. Northerners aimed their vengeance at individuals who did not show proper respect for the slain president, expressed pleasure in his death, or cheered for Jefferson Davis.[38] Cincinnatians besieged Junius Brutus Booth, Jr., the assassin's brother, in his hotel.[39] Indianans in Middletown tarred and feathered a man "who expressed his gratification" with the assassination, while New Yorker Unionists tarred a house on Fifth Avenue for "having not been put in mourning."[40] Clevelanders beat a man who suggested that Lincoln "ought to have been shot long ago."[41] They also chased from the city a prominent local architect, J. J. Husband, for the same sin, and then chiseled away his name from the cornerstone of the county courthouse that he had designed.[42]

Across the land outraged citizens attacked known Copperheads, indiscreet men who cheered Jefferson Davis, and imprudent paroled Confederates in ragged uniforms whose offense was to be on the streets in the only clothes they owned; they also destroyed antiadministration presses.[43] Newspaper editors soon urged calm, and called for angry people to let the law take its course.[44] Northerners, however, would have their blood satisfaction in learning that soldiers killed Booth as he was attempting to make his escape through Virginia and that later in the summer the government hanged four of his accomplices while sending four more conspirators to prison.[45]

On April 19, the day of Lincoln's funeral in Washington, shops and schools closed across the North. Citizens staged funeral processions and black-clothed figures crowded into churches decorated with portraits of Lincoln to attend memorial services, walking past lowered flags and buildings draped in black crepe, listening to tolling bells.[46] Northerners unable to pay their respects to Lincoln in Washington did so at stops in cities along the funeral train's route to Springfield, Illinois, Lincoln's final resting place. As many as one million Northerners passed Lincoln's open casket before the president was interred on May 4. Northerners unable to attend formal viewings lit bonfires and gathered to pray along the funeral train's route while farmers doffed hats as the cars passed by their fields. Springfield, Illinois, was host to tens of thousands of visiting mourners, many of them arriving on overburdened special trains, many of them unable to find places to stay, and many of them passing through the statehouse and in front of the catafalque only to return the same day by waiting trains. But even as they mourned and demanded justice for the heinous act, Northerners attempted to make sense of Lincoln's martyrdom. Many could not fail to acknowledge the proximity of Lincoln's death to Good Friday and Easter: a victim of fanaticism bred by slavery, he died to atone for the nation's sins.[47]

DEMOBILIZATION

The Reconstruction that many Northerners believed to be essential for securing victory would require a continued display of the power of the federal government in the defeated Confederate states. However, soldiers and their families, as well as a government and its taxpayers hard pressed by the war's cost, thought there would be no need for it. Disbanding of the victorious armies was first and foremost an obvious sign of the shift to peace, and the government pursued it with vigor. In June 1865, the War Department mustered out Maine's remaining coast guard companies, an admission that the threat of ocean raids had ended.[48] It was a small event, but still a sign of the return to peace. However, it was the Grand Review that most prominently signaled an end to the need to defend the nation from rebels. On May 23 and 24, a crowd of people in Washington saw first-hand evidence of victory and the nation's desire to return to peaceful business when it witnessed over 150,000 soldiers parade on Pennsylvania Avenue. The war was certainly over, and the volunteers wished to go home as soon as possible.[49] Civilians who witnessed the two-day parade, however, also learned that demobilization had its risks. Men from Sherman's western regiments fought with men from the eastern Potomac army; men from both armies raucously celebrated their survival; and there were disturbances involving soldiers on their way home.[50] Despite these incidents, many Northerners probably agreed with Samuel Cormany, who believed that he and his fellow soldiers "will be better citizens" because of their wartime experiences.[51]

Consequently, cities feted the returning heroes. Governors and mayors made speeches, communities staged parades, and families engaged in their own personal celebrations that "were next to heavenly," even while confidence men, pickpockets, "agents and bad women played their arts on unwary" soldiers lingering in camps or walking city streets.[52] When Samuel Cormany returned home in August 1865, his wife Rachel rejoiced. "Joy to the world," she proclaimed in her diary, "I am no more a war widow—My Precious is home safe from the war."[53] There would remain personal problems and economic issues as veterans adjusted, but their transition to civilian status was a process, not an event, that proved ultimately to be a successful one for most men.[54]

The federal government had final say concerning which regiments would make their way home and when they would do so. However, just as states had raised troops, they also involved themselves in aspects of the demobilization process. New Jersey's Governor Marcus Ward visited his state's soldiers in Virginia on several occasions to help hurry their demobilization.[55] Other governors contacted the War Department to speed along the mustering out of their home regiments.[56] Connecticut provided transportation for its soldiers, assisted them with their records, and helped them secure back pay, bounties, and pensions.[57] Governors also performed the politically essential task of receiving regimental flags from returning regiments, offering words of praise to the men as they did so; they also wisely sponsored some sort of celebration for the regiments, at least in the early days of the summer of 1865.[58]

All told, 800,963 men left the volunteer army before the middle of November 1865, with reductions continuing into the next year.[59] In July 1866, Congress reorganized the army, reducing its size to 54,302 men, with further reductions not far off in the future.[60] For a time, thousands of African Americans remained on duty because of their later enrollment dates and thousands of soldiers remained in the old Confederacy, but their numbers would not be sufficient to stem the growing stand against the government's Reconstruction measures there. The last of the volunteers went home at the end of 1867, while the regular army shifted its attention westward.[61] Soon most of the reorganized regular army still in the rebel South was on duty in Texas dealing with Native Americans, not intransigent ex-Confederates.[62]

A FURTHER REDUCTION OF EXPENDITURES

Within weeks of Lee's surrender, on April 29, 1865, the Quartermaster-General's office stopped spending money at a pace required by war. Orders went out to discharge chartered ships and "all ocean transports not required to bring home troops in remote departments"; suspend all but essential railroad construction; stop buying horses, mules, and wagons; and end any construction of barracks or hospitals, unless most essential.[63] This one department reflected the larger governmental desire to reduce its wartime budgets as quickly as possible. The president and Congress now exercised postwar frugality, with Congress enthusiastically reducing military expenditures through its Joint Select Committee on Retrenchment.[64]

With a smaller reorganized professional military, the federal government no longer needed its hospitals, rendezvous camps, prisoner-of-war camps, and mustering out facilities, not to mention its civilian suppliers. Thus, landscapes once made over for war began to return to their normal peaceful purposes. Shortly after the end of the war, a New York City recruiting depot near City Hall returned to parkland and during the summer, the federal government began to liquidate property in the city, including horses that ended up pulling city streetcars.[65] In Indiana, by 1868 the fairgrounds at Indianapolis that had become Camp Morton returned to its original peacetime purpose, although the military had denuded the land of its trees. Officials sold off the buildings, and the city did its best to restore the property to its previous recreational purpose; the federal government eventually made good on almost $10 million in damages to the grounds.[66] Camp Randall at Madison, Wisconsin, disappeared as people bought up the wood from its demolished buildings. Towns and cities, once centers of military activity enlivened by the novel society engendered by the regiments and once disrupted by the bad behavior of some of the men in their ranks, returned to their old routines.[67]

In upstate New York at Elmira, officials released Confederate prisoners, dismantled entire buildings, and sold surplus material to the locals. All traces of the military post and prisoner of war camp were gone by the end of the year.[68] The process of dismantling the infrastructure of war repeated itself across the Northern states as soldiers and prisoners made their way home. By the middle of July, for example, property at Ohio's Camp Chase was on the auction block, its only worthwhile attraction for buyers being the windows in its buildings; the structures eventually found new use as fencing for the final resting place of its dead inmates.[69] In December 1865, officials sold off the buildings at Chicago's Camp Douglas. The property ended up in private hands, and the city eventually grew over the site.[70]

After the spring of 1865, the army, no longer fighting bloody battles, did not require its extensive system of military hospitals. During the war, the government had developed a network of general hospitals away from the battlefields with a capacity of 136,000 beds.[71] At the end of June 1865, there were still 204 general hospitals caring for over 71,000 soldier-patients and while a few of them continued operating after the war, most of them discharged their patients and closed down.[72] As with military camps, the government went about shedding the unnecessary property. A few hospitals remained in service for the regular army, but others were sold, dismantled, or set to other purposes. The government shut down Philadelphia's Satterlee Hospital in August 1865 and by the end of September had auctioned off anything of value.[73] By the end of 1865, Keokuk, Iowa's Estes House hospital returned to peaceable use and in 1866 was home to various businesses.[74] The government planned to shutter Madison's Harvey Hospital, but Cordelia Harvey was able to turn it into a soldiers' orphans' home, a purpose it fulfilled until it closed in 1874.[75] Otherwise, with few exceptions, the army's general hospitals shared Satterlee Hospital's fate.

Elsewhere, officials shed all types of burdensome property once considered essential for the war effort. The War Department quickly sold off the extensive network of telegraph lines it had required for conducting the war, discharging most of the civilian employees who had operated it.[76] Within a couple of months of war's end, the Brooklyn Navy Yard was crowded with ships on the market.[77] The Ordnance Department eventually sold off millions of dollars worth of weaponry that found its way to the French, Turks, and private concerns, some of which had originally provided guns to the government during the war. By the early 1870s, the army's Quartermaster Department, which had spent over $1 billion during the war years to produce a winning military, had supervised the sale of materiel worth about $66 million, including various items ranging from those ships, telegraph lines, and weapons to blankets and shirts.[78]

If the government no longer needed these military resources, it no longer needed the bureaucracy that had supervised their care once it had divested itself of the surplus. At the outset of the war, the entire executive branch of the federal government employed under 1,300 clerical staff.[79] Over the course of the war, the bureaucracy had grown to accommodate the movement of reams of paper, including the multiple copies of military documents of which the War Department was so fond as well as documentation dealing with new taxes and pensions for veterans.[80] Before war's end, the Quartermaster's Department alone employed 100,000 civilians nationwide.[81] By late April, according to clerk Victor Klausmeyer, the War Department had already begun the process of "winding things up" with its "expenditures . . . to be reduced as quickly and as much as possible."[82]

In early May, Klausmeyer was among the discharged government clerks. The Quartermaster's Department quickly cast off thousands of superfluous workers, reducing its civilian workforce to 4,000 within a few years after the surrender. Other departments did the same, and the government continued the reduction into the near future.[83] Redundant government workers would need to find places elsewhere, as did Klausmeyer. The unemployed clerk improved his circumstances by marrying a widow and establishing a successful insurance business in Baltimore, undoubtedly taking advantage of the presence of a large German population.[84]

The government also rid itself of civilian workers who had helped produce the stuff of war. The Brooklyn Navy Yard immediately reduced its workforce by 600 men, followed by 2,000 terminations at the end of the year.[85] The armory in Springfield, Massachusetts, had employed 2,300 workers during the war; when peace came, the government sacked all but 300 of them.[86] However, the government had no intention of disarming the nation and the Springfield Armory adapted. The armory met the War Department's wish to alter muzzle-loading rifles turning them into breechloaders; it soon employed 500 men necessary for supplying a modernizing force with new weapons.[87] Furthermore, the Ordnance branch of the War Department concerned itself with having proper facilities for storing powder and arms, the continued production of gun carriages for coastal defense, and the further development of reliable rifled cannon.[88]

NORTHERN TRANSITION TO THE POSTWAR ECONOMY

In some areas, such rapid demobilization placed a strain on the once booming wartime economy. Soldiers worried about their prospects, prompting government and private citizens to do what they could for them. New York City, for example, established job registries that connected veterans and employers and in 1866 and 1867, William Oland Bourne sponsored left-handed writing contests for amputee veterans in order to prove their competence at clerical work.[89] Milwaukee, Wisconsin, philanthropists established an employment agency in anticipation of the needs of returning men.[90]

Soldier Taylor Peirce's wife promised him that "There is all sorts of work to do here and plenty of money to pay for it with so I feel confident thee will find something to do if thee is only well enough to work when thee gets home." Peirce was especially anxious about his prospects. His brother-in-law, looking out for family, had already found the veteran a job in an insurance company, but the veteran ended up making his livelihood as an engineer.[91] Some young soldiers, hardly adults when the war began, started new lives from scratch, purchasing land, going to school, marrying, and attempting to find domestic tranquility. Older farmers returned to their properties and tried to reconstruct normal lives for themselves and their families, while others sold land, moved about looking for better prospects, and reestablished themselves in new communities.[92] Indeed, after the war not only veterans but also Americans in general were on the move within and between states, a process that had always been part of the country's nature. New opportunities out West, despite its dangers, had great appeal and would absorb the free-labor ideology as well as the people of the reunited nation.[93]

If the government no longer needed its army, it no longer needed the manufacturing capacity to supply such a large fighting force. Weapons producers, textile mills, and other manufacturers now weaned themselves off their wartime government contracts.[94] As a consequence, Connecticut's industries cut payrolls, its ports suffered from a decline in trade, and the state's residents coped with inflation.[95] Economic troubles, however, varied throughout the North and hobbled different sectors of the economy in different ways. Successful businesses, towns, and individuals adapted to new circumstances, doing what was necessary to meet the economic challenges of peace. The Ames Manufacturing Company of Chicopee, Massachusetts, which was particularly famous for its swords, had increased its workforce to meet government contracts for cannon. After the war, while sword manufacturing continued, it eventually found profit in making bicycles.[96] In early 1866, Camden, Maine, eager to encourage business within its boundaries, provided a substantial incentive to an anchor factory and iron works with a five-year municipal tax exemption.[97]

Springfield, Massachusetts, experienced a decline in the labor force at its armory, but investment and innovation kept people working.[98] New Bedford, Massachusetts, developed a thriving textile industry in the aftermath of the war that replaced the whaling industry as its economic engine of growth. In 1866, Wamsutta Mills was running at full capacity to meet demand.[99] Postwar Connecticut, despite its war production setbacks, gained new positions in the insurance industry.[100] Individuals also remade themselves in the wake of war, finding new opportunities in businesses, professions, and politics, areas in which they had not engaged before the war, as well as in new places where the opportunities presented themselves.[101] In Dubuque, Iowa, there was a growing demand for skilled factory workers, which appeared to suit the returning veterans, now well trained in the discipline required by such work.[102] In the St. Paul and Minneapolis region of Minnesota, the economy did very well after the war, as migrants moved into the state; in 1866 the area's railroad men built their businesses, sparking additional economic growth.[103]

CIVILIAN ORGANIZATIONS AND DEMOBILIZATION

Workers associated with the United States Sanitary Commission anticipated the end of the war months before Lee's surrender. But even with victory there remained work to do. As the army mustered out its volunteer forces, there were soldiers in the ranks who required the help of the United States Sanitary Commission. Returning veterans also placed demands on it and other charitable organizations.[104] Soldiers' Rests, common along veterans' travel routes, provided places for men to pause in their journeys, but with the completion of military demobilization these oases, after tending to tens of thousands of homeward bound men, would soon become unnecessary.[105]

As late as May and June 1865, Chicago was home to a second successful Northwest Sanitary Fair, raising money to help soldiers and their families and to pay organizational bills. It was a remarkable way with which to wrap up the wartime sanitary fair phenomenon. The fair outstripped the earlier event in that city with its size, sophisticated organization, and attractions, which included popularity contests for generals and Chicago belles—voters paid a dollar for each ballot cast—and the sale of pictures of the Eighth Wisconsin's "somewhat rapacious" eagle mascot, Old Abe.[106]

A parade opened the Chicago festivities on May 30 as well as an oration by Governor Richard Oglesby that celebrated the accomplishments of the Northwestern Sanitary Branch of the Sanitary Commission. The governor also reminded his listeners, "The object for which these wonderful labors have been chiefly performed has substantially passed away." The nation had suppressed the rebellion, and "The soldiers of liberty, the brave, noble, scar-worn soldiers are returning home, to be citizens again and soldiers no longer."[107] The fair netted $300,000, but as the governor suggested, it was an exclamation mark at the end of a wartime movement that had amused and distracted many citizens while allowing them to do good in crisis times.[108]

Eleemosynary work ranging from housing and educating soldiers' orphans to helping former soldiers find work or secure pensions began during the war and continued after its end.[109] As the nation returned to peace, however, the great wartime philanthropic organizations demobilized just as the War Department was doing. They collected, organized, and bundled their records and eventually shuttered their doors. During July and August 1865, the Woman's Central Relief Association ended its work and closed its offices; other associations eventually followed.[110] The United States Christian Commission, which during the war had worked to keep soldiers faithful to their Christian beliefs, formally concluded its business with a meeting in February 1866.[111]

In July 1865, the United States Sanitary Commissioner issued a circular alerting its affiliates that the time to end was at hand, a significant task indeed given the thousands of associated aid societies and the several branches it had established in major Northern cities. During the fall of 1865, it maintained some staff to deal with outstanding business, but it was time to sell off property and balance the books.[112] It lingered on into the next decade, when in 1878 it completed tending to its records. It finally shut down once and for all in early January 1879, but with the end of the war, its grand purpose had already passed.[113]

As Mary Livermore later recounted, the wartime experiences of women had taught them the restrictions placed on their lives by male patriarchy. Consequently, as Georgeanna Woolsey Bacon noted, women who had learned to value their own efforts and abilities during the war "were not willing to fold their useful hands when the war was over, and let the old order of things reestablish itself."[114] She and her sisters Abby and Jane remained active in eleemosynary work and especially in the developing nursing profession.[115] Other white middle-class women as well as Northern black women ventured south to teach freedpeople, taking advantage of a unique experience created by the end of slavery.[116] Even so, Northern women activists came to resent the fact that their male wartime associates slighted their causes while concentrating on advancing black rights.[117]

With the end of slavery, it appeared as if William Lloyd Garrison and other abolitionists had achieved their ultimate goal. Garrison's demobilization of the antislavery movement, or at least what was immediately under his control, meant the termination of his seminal abolitionist paper, *The Liberator*. He expected that the Thirteenth Amendment would become part of the Constitution, rendering his American Anti-Slavery Society a success and consequently an anachronism.[118] The organization would be as Garrison said, "an anomaly, a solecism, an absurdity to maintain an anti-slavery society after slavery is dead."[119] Garrison believed the rhetoric and tactics used to attack slavery during the war would not be effective or appropriate in dealing with the postwar issues involving the freedpeople and their advancement. In May 1865, at the meeting of the American Anti-Slavery Society he proposed to end its existence, but failed to carry the day. That day would come on April 9, 1870, after the states ratified the Fifteenth Amendment, an achievement that came in part because its membership believed such a goal was an important one.[120]

In the spring of 1865, Garrison did not propose to ignore the needs of the ex-slaves.[121] As indicated by some of the successes of Reconstruction, white abolitionists did not abandon working for greater rights for blacks when the war ended.[122] Their Northern black allies, however, better understood the complexities and the vagaries of freedom that required continued and constant efforts to overcome obstacles founded on deeply held white racial prejudice. Not only did they expect a better world for their brethren in the South, but also for African Americans in the North that placed them on par with their white neighbors, especially in the political arena.

For men such as Charles Lenox Remond and Frederick Douglass, the end of the war and the eventual confirmation of emancipation with the Thirteenth Amendment were opening acts, with much more drama yet to come. Attitudes of whites, for one thing, had to change. At the May 1865 meeting of the American Anti-Slavery Society, Remond argued that the needs of the ex-slaves certainly came within the purview of the society. Furthermore, Remond maintained, the abolition of slavery did not mean the nation accepted African Americans as the equals of white citizens.[123]

Frederick Douglass, also at the May meeting, argued, "Slavery is not abolished until the black man has the ballot." Understanding the power to make law would be the power to define freedom, Douglass presciently continued: "Legislatures of the South retain the right to pass laws making any discrimination between black and white, slavery still lives there." Garrison's society was obligated to tend to this goal as part of its mission. Southerners would oblige the law and even the new constitutional amendment when it passed through the states, but slavery would continue. "They would not call it slavery," he advised, "but some other name." Indeed, he warned, "you and I and all of us had better wait and see what new form this old monster will assume, in what new skin this old snake will come forth next."[124]

Douglass remained well aware of the shortcomings of law when confronted with entrenched racism.[125] In the aftermath of the war, even as politicians advanced the cause of African Americans in the North and South with legislation and constitutional amendments, problems persisted in the victorious states. In August 1865, African Americans in Evansville, Indiana, were victims of a race riot and Democrats in the state vocally opposed equal rights for them, considering such a move the ushering into the state a "calamity," according to one editorialist, degrading white laboring men while "compelling . . . [them] to become worse than a slave."[126] Also shortly after the war, New Jersey Democrats made it clear that they still expected the political process to be reserved to whites and, despite some dissenters, even Republicans in that state reassured voters that black suffrage was not on their immediate postwar agenda.[127] Across the North, African Americans continued to find white men standing in opposition to their claim of the franchise, as well as all other basic rights.[128] African Americans understood that freedom won was not freedom secured, that even in victory there still remained a battle before them.

* * *

The Northern home front emerged from the war not so much as a new place and people, but as a renewed society still confronting the challenges connected to the war's legacy. The region had escaped the physical devastation that its enemies had endured, and therefore did not have the proximate evidence of what the war did to the landscape, society, and the economy. Victory had reinforced the people's sense of mission, giving them a confidence in their abilities to solve future problems. Within the war generation's lifetime, cemeteries, monuments, parades, and the veterans themselves would all serve as the region's physical reminders of what Northerners had accomplished. But they also would act as the reminders of what a virtuous republic could accomplish and what a great nation should be.

Most Northerners were happy to get on with their lives. However, as African Americans understood in 1865, the war was as much a beginning as it was a conclusion, or at least it was a dramatic milestone in the life of a nation always in the process of striving to meet the promises laid out in its founding documents. Words such as "freedom" and "equality" took on new meanings as laws and constitutional amendments reminded the nation that slavery had died and that the black population expected to take an active part in guiding the future of the reunited nation. Rebuilding the erstwhile Confederacy, settling new Western lands, dealing with new industrial enterprises, exploring new roles beyond the old national boundaries, and welcoming hundreds of thousands of strangers into the country meant dealing with a multitude of concerns all in some way related to the blessings of a united nation and in many ways issued challenges to black and white Americans. The question then became how victorious Northerners would shift their attentions to these tests while striving to preserve the fruits of victory, how they would help the nation to maintain the purpose and the promise of the democratic government they had sacrificed so much to save.

NOTES

INTRODUCTION

1. Quoted in David D. Van Tassel, with John Vacha, *"Behind Bayonets": The Civil War in Northern Ohio* (Kent, OH: Kent State University Press, 2006), 65.

2. Louis P. Masur, ed., *The Real War Will Never Get in the Books: Selections from Writers during the Civil War* (New York: Oxford University Press, 1993), 124.

3. Ibid., 165.

4. Ibid., 167.

5. Quoted in Earl J. Hess, "'Tell Me What the Sensations Are': The Northern Home Front Learns about Combat," in *Union Soldiers and the Northern Home Front: Wartime Experiences, Postwar Adjustments*, ed. Paul A. Cimbala and Randall M. Miller (New York: Fordham University Press, 2002), 129.

6. Quoted in Van Tassel and Vacha, *"Behind Bayonets,"* 65.

7. Free African Americans living in the free states were Northerners, too, sharing in most of the experiences of their white counterparts, ranging from economic hardship to family separation and death of loved ones at the front. However, they faced a special kind of war in which slavery was always the chief cause of the war, emancipation was always a goal equal to union, and race and prejudice always visibly set them apart in their Northern communities. Immigrants and their children, Germans and Irish in particular, shared the Northern war experience, as well, but as with African Americans had some unique experiences, which deserve special consideration. Consequently, in chapters throughout this volume, African Americans and ethnic Americans receive distinct treatment because of these unique circumstances.

8. Jeffrey D. Marshall, ed., *A War of the People: Vermont Civil War Letters* (Hanover, NH: University Press of New England, 1999), 40.

9. Abraham Lincoln, "Message to Congress in Special Session," July 4, 1861, in Roy P. Basler, ed., *The Collected Works of Abraham Lincoln*, 9 vols. (New Brunswick, NJ: Rutgers University Press, 1953), 4:438.

CHAPTER ONE

1. For politics before the war, see Sean Wilentz, *The Rise of American Democracy: Jefferson to Lincoln* (New York: W. W. Norton and Co., 2005).

2. Steven R. Weisman, *The Great Tax Wars: Lincoln to Wilson—The Fierce Battles over Money and Power That Transformed the Nation* (New York: Simon and Schuster, 2002), 14; Bray Hammond, *Sovereignty and an Empty Purse: Banks and Politics in the Civil War* (Princeton, NJ: Princeton University Press, 1970), 16–17; Leonard P. Curry, *Blueprint for Modern America: Nonmilitary Legislation of the First Civil War Congress* (Nashville: Vanderbilt University Press, 1968), 4–5; Richard Franklin Bensel, *Yankee Leviathan: The Origins of Central State Authority in America, 1859–1877* (Cambridge, UK: Cambridge University Press, 1990), 101–5; Richard N. Current, *The History of Wisconsin*, Vol. 2: *The Civil War Era, 1848–1873* (Madison: State Historical Society of Wisconsin, 1976), 156; Cindy Sondik Aron, *Ladies and Gentlemen of the Civil Service: Middle-Class Workers in Victorian America* (New York: Oxford University Press, 1987), 5.

3. Curry, *Blueprint for Modern America*, 180; Hammond, *Sovereignty and an Empty Purse*, 48; Weisman, *The Great Tax Wars*, 14; Heather Cox Richardson, *The Greatest Nation of the Earth: Republican Economic Policies during the Civil War* (Cambridge, MA: Harvard University Press, 1997), 104.

4. William J. Jackson, *New Jerseyans in the Civil War: For Union and Liberty* (New Brunswick, NJ: Rutgers University Press, 2000), 20, 40; William Gillette, *Jersey Blue: Civil War Politics in New Jersey, 1854–1865* (New Brunswick, NJ: Rutgers University Press, 1995), 11.

5. Current, *The History of Wisconsin*, 2:157–58.

6. Michael H. Frisch, *Town Into City: Springfield, Massachusetts, and the Meaning of Community, 1840–1880* (Cambridge, MA: Harvard University Press, 1972), 43–45.

7. Don Harrison Doyle, *The Social Order of a Frontier Community: Jacksonville, Illinois, 1825–70* (Urbana: University of Illinois Press, 1978), 81.

8. John Niven, *Connecticut for the Union: The Role of the State in the Civil War* (New Haven, CT: Yale University Press, 1965), 330–31.

9. Current, *The History of Wisconsin*, 2:183–84.

10. Weisman, *The Great Tax Wars*, 15.

11. William W. Freehling, *The Road to Disunion*, Vol. 2: *Secessionists Triumphant* (New York: Oxford University Press, 2007), 349–51.

12. William B. Hesseltine, *Lincoln and the War Governors* (New York: Alfred A. Knopf, 1948), 5–6; Fred Albert Shannon, *The Organization and Administration of the Union Army, 1861–1865*, 2 vols. ([Cleveland, OH]: Arthur H. Clark Co., 1928; Gloucester, MA: Peter Smith, 1965), 1:15–50. For a discussion of the Republican Party and federalism, see Michael

Les Benedict, "Abraham Lincoln and Federalism," *Journal of the Abraham Lincoln Association*, 10 (issue 1, 1988): 1–46.

13. Historian Phillip Shaw Paludan in his study, *"A People's Contest": The Union and the Civil War*, 2nd ed. (Lawrence: University Press of Kansas, 1996), 10–11, stresses the significance of the local connections of Northerners.

14. Donald C. Elder III, ed., *Love amid the Turmoil: The Civil War Letters of William and Mary Vermilion* (Iowa City: University of Iowa Press, 2003), 47.

15. Ibid., 112.

16. Kenneth Carley, *Minnesota in the Civil War: An Illustrated History* (St. Paul: Minnesota Historical Society Press, 2000), xviii.

17. Quoted in Andrea R. Foroughi, *Go If You Think It Your Duty: A Minnesota Couple's Civil War Letters* (St. Paul: Minnesota Historical Society Press, 2008), 306.

18. Ibid., 5–6.

19. On the significance of economic opportunity, its connection to Northern ideas about American freedom, and its influence on the new Republican Party, see Gabor S. Boritt, *Lincoln and the Economics of the American Dream* (Urbana: University of Illinois Press, 1978, 1994), and Eric Foner, *Free Soil, Free Labor, Free Men: The Ideology of the Republican Party before the Civil War* (New York: Oxford University Press, 1970, 1995).

20. Ulysses S. Grant, *Personal Memoirs of U.S. Grant*, ed. James M. McPherson (New York: Penguin Books, 1999), 110–34.

21. Elder, *Love amid the Turmoil*, 1–6.

22. Foroughi, *Go If You Think It Your Duty*, 4–5.

23. Paul W. Gates, *Agriculture and the Civil War* (New York: Alfred A. Knopf, 1965), 274.

24. For example, see Doyle, *The Social Order of a Frontier Community*.

25. Current, *The History of Wisconsin*, 2:55–56, 71.

26. Ray Allen Billington and Martin Ridge, *Westward Expansion: A History of the American Frontier*, 6th edition, abridged (Albuquerque: University of New Mexico Press, 2001), 117–19.

27. Nancy Grey Osterud, *Bonds of Community: The Lives of Farm Women in Nineteenth-Century New York* (Ithaca, NY: Cornell University Press, 1991), 21–30.

28. Walter D. Kamphoefner and Wolfgang Helbich, eds., and Susan Carter Vogel, trans., *Germans in the Civil War: The Letters They Wrote Home* (Chapel Hill: University of North Carolina Press, 2006), 279.

29. Carl F. Kaestle, *Pillars of the Republic: Common Schools and American Society, 1780–1860* (New York: Hill and Wang, 1983), 75–99; Earl J. Hess, *Liberty, Virtue, and Progress: Northerners and Their War for the Union,* 2nd ed. (New York: Fordham University Press, 1997), passim. Don Harrison Doyle provides an excellent example of the nature of community building and the role of these institutions in a new town, Jacksonville, Illinois, in his study *The Social Order of a Frontier Community*.

30. Rhonda M. Kohl, *The Prairie Boys Go to War: The Fifth Illinois Cavalry, 1861–1865* (Carbondale: Southern Illinois University Press, 2013), 1–4; James M. McPherson, *Battle Cry of Freedom: The Civil War Era* (New York: Oxford University Press, 1988), 31.

31. Richard F. Nation, *At Home in the Hoosier Hills: Agriculture, Politics, and Religion in Southern Indiana, 1810–1870* (Bloomington: Indiana University Press, 2005), 186–200.

32. Phillip Shaw Paludan, *The Presidency of Abraham Lincoln* (Lawrence: University Press of Kansas, 1994), 6; Gary W. Gallagher, *The Union War* (Cambridge, MA: Harvard University Press, 2011), 42–43; Margaret E. Wagner, Gary W. Gallagher, and Paul Finkelman, eds., *The Library of Congress Civil War Desk Reference* (New York: Simon and Schuster, 2002), 69–70, 73–76.

33. James Oliver Horton and Lois E. Horton, *Black Bostonians: Family Life and Community Struggle in the Antebellum North* (New York: Holmes and Meier Publishers, 1979), 2. Also see Patrick Rael, *Black Identity and Black Protest in the Antebellum North* (Chapel Hill: University of North Carolina Press, 2002).

34. See C. Peter Ripley et al., eds., *Witness for Freedom: African American Voices on Race, Slavery, and Emancipation* (Chapel Hill: University of North Carolina Press, 1993), and Jane H. Pease and William H. Pease, *They Who Would Be Free: Blacks' Search for Freedom, 1830–1861* (New York: Atheneum, 1974).

35. W. Jeffrey Bolster, *Black Jacks: African American Seamen in the Age of Sail* (Cambridge, MA: Harvard University Press, 1997), 158–89.

36. Horton and Horton, *Black Bostonians*, 10–12.

37. Graham Russell Hodges, *Root and Branch: African Americans in New York and East Jersey, 1613–1863* (Chapel Hill: University of North Carolina Press, 1999), 187–270; Eric Foner, *Gateway to Freedom: The Hidden History of the Underground Railroad* (New York: W.W. Norton and Co., 2015), 46–62; David Gerber, *Black Ohio and the Color Line, 1860–1915* (Urbana: University of Illinois Press, 1976), 5.

38. For wealth distribution of Northerners by race, see Table 1.2 in Rael, *Black Identity and Black Protest in the Antebellum North*, 22.

39. Paul A. Cimbala, "Mary Ann Shadd Cary and Black Abolitionism," in *Against the Tide: Women Reformers in American Society*, ed. Paul A. Cimbala and Randall M. Miller (Westport, CT: Praeger, 1997), 24–25.

40. Leon F. Litwack, *North of Slavery: The Negro in the Free States, 1790–1860* (Chicago: University of Chicago Press, 1961), 64–112; V. Jacque Voegeli, *Free but Not Equal: The Midwest and the Negro during the Civil War* (Chicago: University of Chicago Press, 1967), 2.

41. Litwack, *North of Slavery*, 94–95.

42. Voegeli, *Free but Not Equal*, 2.

43. Hodges, *Root and Branch*, 232–33.

44. C. Peter Ripley et al., eds., *The Black Abolitionist Papers*, Vol. 5: *The United States, 1859–1865* (Chapel Hill: University of North Carolina Press, 1992), 62.

45. Ibid., 59.

46. Litwack, *North of Slavery*, 3–63.

47. Ripley et al., *The Black Abolitionist Papers*, 5:74.

48. C. Peter Ripley et al., eds., *The Black Abolitionist Papers*, Vol. 2: *Canada, 1830–1865* (Chapel Hill: University of North Carolina Press, 1986), 3–46.

49. C. Peter Ripley et al., eds., *The Black Abolitionist Papers*, Vol. 4: *The United States, 1847–1858* (Chapel Hill: University of North Carolina Press, 1991), 128; also see pp. 126–30.

50. Mark Hubbard, ed., *Illinois's War: The Civil War in Documents* (Athens: Ohio University Press, 2013), 18–19.

51. Wagner, Gallagher, and Finkelman, *The Library of Congress Civil War Desk Reference*, 72–73; Kamphoefner and Helbich, *Germans in the Civil War*, 2.

52. Walter Licht, *Industrializing America: The Nineteenth Century* (Baltimore: Johns Hopkins University Press, 1995), 68–69.

53. Jocelyn Wills, *Boosters, Hustlers, and Speculators: Entrepreneurial Culture and the Rise of Minneapolis and St. Paul, 1849–1883* (St. Paul: Minnesota Historical Society Press, 2005), 76–77.

54. Kathleen Neils Conzen, *Immigrant Milwaukee, 1836–1860: Accommodation and Community in a Frontier City* (Cambridge, MA: Harvard University Press, 1976), 63–125.

55. Thomas Dublin, *Women at Work: The Transformation of Work and Community in Lowell, Massachusetts, 1826–1860* (New York: Columbia University Press, 1979), 145–47.

56. Robert L. Bee, ed., *The Boys from Rockville: Civil War Narratives of Sgt. Benjamin Hirst, Company D, 14th Connecticut Volunteers* (Knoxville: University of Tennessee Press, 1998), 12.

57. Tyler Anbinder, *Nativism and Slavery: The Northern Know Nothings and the Politics of the 1850s* (New York: Oxford University Press, 1992), 3–51.

58. William B. Kurtz, *Excommunicated from the Union: How the Civil War Created a Separate Catholic America* (New York: Fordham University Press, 2016), 22–28.

59. Susannah Ural Bruce, *The Harp and the Eagle: Irish-American Volunteers and the Union Army, 1861–1865* (New York: New York University Press, 2006), 7–41.

60. Michael S. Green, *Politics and America in Crisis: The Coming of the Civil War* (Santa Barbara, CA: Praeger, 2010), 84–85; Kamphoefner and Helbich, *Germans in the Civil War*, 2–7.

61. Kamphoefner and Helbich, *Germans in the Civil War*, 2–5.

62. Ibid., 278.

63. Ibid., 39, 40–41.

64. Ibid., 38.

65. Christian Wolmar, *The Great Railroad Revolution: The History of Trains in America* (New York: Public Affairs, 2012), 55–56.

66. Edward Chase Kirkland, *Industry Comes of Age: Business, Labor and Public Policy, 1860–1897* (Chicago: Quadrangle Paperbacks, 1967), 342; Bee, *Boys from Rockville*, xvii–xxviii.

67. Paul W. Gates, *The Farmer's Age: Agriculture, 1815–1860* (New York: Holt, Rinehart and Winston, 1960), 274; David E. Schob, *Hired Hands and Plowboys: Farm Labor in the Midwest, 1815–60* (Urbana: University of Illinois Press, 1975), passim.

68. Stacy Dale Allen, ed., *On the Skirmish Line Behind a Friendly Tree: The Civil War Memoirs of William Royal Oake, 26th Iowa Volunteers* (Helena, MT: Farcountry Press, 2006), 33.

69. Bee, *The Boys from Rockville*, xxvi–xxvii.

70. James M. McPherson, *Ordeal by Fire: The Civil War and Reconstruction*, 3rd ed. (Boston: McGraw Hill, 2001), 28; Gillette, *Jersey Blue*, 13.

71. Michael H. Fitch, *Echoes of the Civil War as I Hear Them* (New York: R. F. Fenno and Company, 1905; Salem, MA: Higginson Book Company, 1998), 17–19.

72. Mark Hoffman, *"My Brave Mechanics": The First Michigan Engineers and Their Civil War* (Detroit: Wayne State University Press, 2007), 8–17.

73. Bee, *The Boys from Rockville*, xxi–xxiv.

CHAPTER TWO

1. For a discussion of the concept of disunion in the United States, see Elizabeth R. Varon, *Disunion! The Coming of the American Civil War, 1789–1859* (Chapel Hill: University of North Carolina Press, 2008). For a brief look at the events leading up to secession during the 1850s, see Eric H. Walther, *The Shattering of the Union: America in the 1850s* (Wilmington, DE: Scholarly Resources, 2004). The classic treatment of the events around the immediate secession crisis remains Kenneth M. Stampp, *And the War Came: The North and the Secession Crisis, 1860–1861* (Baton Rouge: Louisiana State University Press, 1950), but also see Nelson D. Lankford, *Cry Havoc! The Crooked Road to Civil War, 1861* (New York: Viking, 2007).

2. For Republican ideology, see Eric Foner, *Free Soil, Free Labor, Free Men: The Ideology of the Republican Party before the Civil War* (New York: Oxford University Press, 1970). For the understanding that restricting the expansion of slavery would lead to its ultimate demise, see James Oakes, *The Scorpion's Sting: Antislavery and the Coming of the Civil War* (New York: W. W. Norton and Company, 2014).

3. Mary A. Livermore, *My Story of the War: The Civil War Memoirs of the Famous Nurse, Relief Organizer and Suffragette* (New York: Da Capo Press, 1995), 85.

4. Glenn C. Altschuler and Stuart M. Blumin, *Rude Republic: Americans and Their Politics in the Nineteenth Century* (Princeton, NJ: Princeton University Press, 2000), 157.

5. Russell B. Nye, *Society and Culture in America, 1830–1860* (New York: Harper & Row, 1974), 366–68; David W. Bulla, *Lincoln's Censor: Milo Hascall and the Freedom of the Press in Civil War Indiana* (West Lafayette, IN: Purdue University Press, 2008), 85; Louise L. Stevenson, *The Victorian Homefront: American Thought and Culture, 1860–1880* (Ithaca, NY: Cornell University Press, 1991), 42. On the spread of print culture and its connections to a developing American identity, see especially Trish Loughran, *The Republic in Print: Print Culture in the Age of U.S. Nation Building, 1770–1870* (New York: Columbia University Press, 2007). Ford Risley neatly summarizes the rise and spread of newspapers and magazines in antebellum America in his introduction to *Civil War Journalism* (Santa Barbara, CA: Praeger, 2012), xiii–xvi.

6. Daniel J. Boorstin, *The Americans: The National Experience* (New York: Vintage Books, 1965), 124–34. It is worth noting that people living west of the Mississippi River often suffered a time lag in getting news. The telegraph lines extended only to Fort Kearny in Nebraska Territory in 1860 so that news had to be carried by horse farther west. News of the firing on Fort Sumter, for example, did not reach San Francisco until April 24, ten days after the April 14 surrender of the fort. See Alvin M. Josephy Jr., *The Civil War in the American West* (New York: Vintage, 1993), 236.

7. Jocelyn Wills, *Boosters, Hustlers, and Speculators: Entrepreneurial Culture and the Rise of Minneapolis and St. Paul, 1849–1883* (St. Paul: Minnesota Historical Society Press, 2005), 69–70; Kenneth Carley, *Minnesota in the Civil War: An Illustrated History* (St. Paul: Minnesota Historical Society Press, 1961), xxi.

8. Bulla, *Lincoln's Censor,* 85.

9. Richard N. Current, *The History of Wisconsin,* Vol. 2: *The Civil War Era, 1848–1873* (Madison: State Historical Society of Wisconsin, 1976), 176–77.

10. Walter D. Kamphoefner and Wolfgang Helbich, eds., and Susan Carter Vogel, trans., *Germans in the Civil War: The Letters They Wrote Home* (Chapel Hill: University of North Carolina Press, 2006), 141.

11. Edmund J. Raus Jr., *Banners South: A Northern Community at War* (Kent, OH: Kent State University Press, 2005), 6.

12. Stuart Murray, *A Time of War: A Northern Chronicle of the Civil War* (Lee, MA: Berkshire House Publishers, 2001), 21–22.

13. See, for example, Georgiana Woolsey Bacon and Eliza Woolsey Howland, *My Heart toward Home: Letters of a Family during the Civil War,* ed. Daniel John Hoisington (Roseville, MN: Edinborough Press, 2001), 18; Jonathan W. White, ed., *A Philadelphia Perspective: The Civil War Diary of Sidney George Fisher* (New York: Fordham University Press, 2007), 59–61.

14. Richard F. Miller and Robert F. Mooney, *The Civil War: The Nantucket Experience including the Memoirs of Josiah Fitch Murphey* (Nantucket, MA: Wesco Publishing, 1994), 10.

15. Murray, *A Time of War,* 28–29.

16. Livermore, *My Story of the War,* 86.

17. David D. Van Tassel with John Vacha, *"Behind Bayonets": The Civil War in Northern Ohio* (Kent, OH: Kent State University Press, 2006), 27.

18. James H. Moorhead, *American Apocalypse: Yankee Protestants and the Civil War, 1860–1869* (New Haven, CT: Yale University Press, 1978), 24–41.

19. Quoted in ibid., 24–25.

20. Ibid., 25–26.

21. White, *A Philadelphia Perspective,* 64.

22. Alvin F. Sanborn, ed., *Reminiscences of Richard Lathers: Sixty Years of a Busy Life in South Carolina, Massachusetts, and New York* (1907; reprint ed., Whitefish, MT: Kessinger Publishing, 2010), 91–111.

23. Michael S. Green, *Freedom, Union, and Power: Lincoln and His Party during the Civil War* (New York: Fordham University Press, 2004), 61–62.

24. Ted Tunnell, ed., *Carpetbagger from Vermont: The Autobiography of Marshall Harvey Twitchell* (Baton Rouge: Louisiana State University Press, 1989), 24.

25. "The Strength of Secession," *New York Daily Tribune,* November 28, 1860, in Howard Cecil Perkins, ed., *Northern Editorials on Secession,* 2 vols. (New York: Appleton-Century, 1942; Gloucester, MA: Peter Smith, 1964), 1:107.

26. William G. Le Duc, *This Business of War: Recollections of a Civil War Quartermaster* (St. Paul: Minnesota Historical Society Press, 2004), 65.

27. Ford Risley, *Abolition and the Press: The Moral Struggle against Slavery* (Evanston, IL: Northwestern University Press, 2008), 156–57.

28. C. Peter Ripley et al., eds., *The Black Abolitionist Papers,* Vol. 5: *The United States, 1859–1865* (Chapel Hill: University of North Carolina Press, 1992), 98.

29. James M. McPherson, *The Negro's Civil War: How American Blacks Felt and Acted during the War for the Union* (New York: Vintage Books, 1991), 11–18.

30. Ripley et al., *The Black Abolitionist Papers*, 5:97–99.

31. Quoted in Current, *The History of Wisconsin*, 2:289.

32. Roy P. Basler, ed., *The Collected Works of Abraham Lincoln*, 9 vols. (New Brunswick, NJ: Rutgers University Press, 1953), 4:268.

33. Randall C. Jimerson, *The Private Civil War: Popular Thought During the Sectional Conflict* (Baton Rouge: Louisiana State University Press, 1988); George M. Fredrickson, *The Inner Civil War: Northern Intellectuals and the Crisis of the Union* (New York: Harper & Row, 1965), 54.

34. Leonard L. Richards, *Who Freed the Slaves? The Fight Over the Thirteenth Amendment* (Chicago: University of Chicago Press, 2015), 15.

35. Henry Steele Commager, ed., *The Civil War Archive: The History of the Civil War in Documents*, revised and expanded by Erik Bruun (New York: Tess Press, 2000), 43.

36. Oliver Otis Howard, *The Autobiography of Oliver Otis Howard, Major General United States Army*, 2 vols. (New York: Baker & Taylor Company, 1907), 1:104.

37. Michael A. Ross, *Justice of Shattered Dreams: Samuel Freeman Miller and the Supreme Court during the Civil War Era* (Baton Rouge: Louisiana State University Press, 2003), 60.

38. On Democratic concerns, see Russell McClintock, *Lincoln and the Decision for War: The Northern Response to Secession* (Chapel Hill: University of North Carolina Press, 2008), 95–99.

39. Ross, *Justice of Shattered Dreams*, 60.

40. "Forbearance Has Ceased to Be a Virtue," Columbus *Daily Ohio State Journal*, January 15, 1861, in Perkins, ed., *Northern Editorials on Secession*, 1:216.

41. Earl J. Hess, *Liberty, Virtue, and Progress: Northerners and Their War for the Union*, 2nd ed. (New York: Fordham University Press, 1997), 22.

42. Bacon and Howland, *My Heart toward Home*, 18.

43. Howard, *Autobiography*, 1: 100.

44. Maria Lydig Daly, *Diary of a Union Lady, 1861–1865*, ed. Harold Earl Hammond (Lincoln: University of Nebraska Press, 2000), 5.

45. For the role of Virginia and other Upper-South states in the crisis, see Daniel W. Crofts, *Reluctant Confederates: Upper South Unionists in the Secession Crisis* (Chapel Hill: University of North Carolina Press, 1989).

46. Bacon and Howland, *My Heart toward Home*, 18.

47. Richard F. Nation and Stephen E. Towne, eds., *Indiana's War: The Civil War in Documents* (Athens: Ohio University Press, 2009), 39–41.

48. Ross, *Justice of Shattered Dreams*, 60.

49. Jennifer L. Weber, *Copperheads: The Rise and Fall of Lincoln's Opponents in the North* (New York: Oxford University Press, 2006), 1–33; Jean H. Baker, *Affairs of Party: The Political Culture of Northern Democrats in the Mid-nineteenth Century* (New York: Fordham University Press, 1998), 327–30.

50. Baker, *Affairs of Party*, 329.

51. Weber, *Copperheads*, 28.

52. Nation and Towne, *Indiana's War*, 40–41.

53. Christine Dee, ed., *Ohio's War: The Civil War in Documents* (Athens: Ohio University Press, 2006), 49–50.

54. George Winston Smith and Charles Judah, *Life in the North during the Civil War: A Source History* (Albuquerque: University of New Mexico Press, 1966), 16.

55. Kenneth M. Stampp, *America in 1857: A Nation on the Brink* (New York: Oxford University Press, 1990), 219–38.

56. Russell L. Johnson, *Warriors into Workers: The Civil War and the Formation of Urban-Industrial Society in a Northern City* (New York: Fordham University Press, 2003), 60.

57. William Gillette, *Jersey Blue: Civil War Politics in New Jersey, 1854–1865* (New Brunswick, NJ: Rutgers University Press, 1995), 111.

58. Current, *The History of Wisconsin*, 2:302–4.

59. Bacon and Howland, *My Heart toward Home*, 18. It did become the policy of the Confederacy to have debtors pay what they owed their Northern creditors into state treasuries. See Stampp, *And the War Came*, 291.

60. George Templeton Strong, *Diary of the Civil War, 1860–1865*, ed. Allan Nevins (New York: Macmillan Co., 1962), 105.

61. On such worries, see, for example, the editorial on "The Free Navigation of the Mississippi," *Milwaukee Daily Sentinel*, March 4, 1861, reprinted in Perkins, ed., *Northern Editorials on Secession*, 2:559–60; and for a counterthreat that any such disruption of commerce by a Confederacy would cause Northerners to take their trade away from the river, see, for example, the editorial on "The Course of Western Commerce," *Cincinnati Daily Commercial*, February 20, 1861, in ibid., 2:592–96.

62. For a brief look at Buchanan and the sectional crisis, see Jean H. Baker, *James Buchanan* (New York: Times Books, Henry Holt and Company, 2004), 75–143.

63. Gillette, *Jersey Blue*, 129.

64. Green, *Freedom, Union, and Power*, 70–74.

65. Quoted in David W. Blight, *Frederick Douglass' Civil War: Keeping Faith in Jubilee* (Baton Rouge: Louisiana State University Press, 1989), 59.

66. Basler, *Collected Works of Abraham Lincoln*, 4:331–32.

67. Commager, *Civil War Archive*, 72.

CHAPTER THREE

1. Emil and Ruth Rosenblatt, eds., *Hard Marching Every Day: The Civil War Letters of Private Wilbur Fisk, 1861–1865* (Lawrence: University Press of Kansas, 1992), 356.

2. Rollin G. Osterweis, *Three Centuries of New Haven, 1638–1938* (New Haven, CT: Yale University Press, 1953), 319.

3. Anna Howard Shaw, *The Story of a Pioneer* (New York: Harper and Brothers, 1915), 51.

4. John Niven, *Connecticut for the Union: The Role of the State in the Civil War* (New Haven, CT: Yale University Press, 1965), 54; W. A. Croffut and John M. Morris, *The Military and Civil History of Connecticut during the War of 1861–1865* (New York: Ledyard Bill, 1869), 40.

5. Mary Livermore, *My Story of the War: A Woman's Narrative of Four Years Personal Experience* (New York: Da Capo Press, 1995), 88.

6. Ibid.

7. James H. Moorhead, *American Apocalypse: Yankee Protestants and the Civil War, 1860–1869* (New Haven, CT: Yale University Press, 1978), 36.

8. Edmund J. Raus Jr., *Banners South: A Northern Community at War* (Kent, OH: Kent State University Press, 2005), 10–11.

9. Quoted in David V. Mollenhoff, *Madison: A History of the Formative Years*, 2nd ed. (Madison: University of Wisconsin Press, 2013), 86.

10. George M. Fredrickson, "The Coming of the Lord: The Northern Protestant Clergy and the Civil War Crisis," in *Religion and the American Civil War*, ed. Randall M. Miller, Harry S. Stout, and Charles Reagan Wilson (New York: Oxford University Press, 1998), 118.

11. Edward J. Blum, "'The First Secessionist Was Satan': Secession and the Religious Politics of Evil in Civil War America," *Civil War History* 60 (September 2014): 234–69.

12. Livermore, *My Story of the War*, 86.

13. Duane E. Shaffer, *Men of Granite: New Hampshire's Soldiers in the Civil War* (Columbia: University of South Carolina Press, 2008), 18.

14. Henry Steele Commager, ed., *The Civil War Archive: The History of the Civil War in Documents*, revised and expanded by Erik Bruun (New York: Tess Press, 2000), 72.

15. Livermore, *My Story of the War*, 91–92.

16. Georgiana Woolsey Bacon and Eliza Woolsey Howland, *My Heart toward Home: Letters of a Family during the Civil War*, ed. Daniel John Hoisington (Roseville, MN: Edinborough Press, 2001), 37.

17. Henry Mayer, *All on Fire: William Lloyd Garrison and the Abolition of Slavery* (New York: W. W. Norton and Co., 1998), 518.

18. Livermore, *My Story of the War*, 90.

19. Kerry A. Trask, *Fire Within: A Civil War Narrative from Wisconsin* (Kent, OH: Kent State University Press, 1995), 42–43.

20. Jeffrey D. Marshall, ed., *A War of the People: Vermont Civil War Letters* (Hanover, NH: University Press of New England, 1999), 19.

21. Bacon and Howland, *My Heart toward Home*, 37.

22. Earl J. Hess, ed., *A German in the Yankee Fatherland: The Civil War Letters of Henry A. Kircher* (Kent, OH: Kent State University Press, 1983), 1.

23. *Appleton (Wisconsin) Crescent*, June 1, 7, 1861.

24. Marshall, *A War of the People*, 24.

25. Richard F. Miller, *Harvard's Civil War: A History of the Twentieth Massachusetts Volunteer Infantry* (Hanover, NH: University Press of New England, 2005), 16.

26. Francis B. Greene, *History of Boothbay, Southport and Boothbay Harbor, Maine, 1623–1905 with Family Genealogies* (Portland, ME: Loring, Short and Harmon, 1906), 423; William Schouler, *Massachusetts in the Civil War* (Boston: E. P. Dutton and Company, 1868), 51; Bacon and Howland, *My Heart toward Home*, 23, 25, 31; William Gillette, *Jersey Blue: Civil War Politics in New Jersey, 1854–1865* (New Brunswick, NJ: Rutgers University Press, 1995), 134.

27. Bacon and Howland, *My Heart toward Home*, 25.

28. Gillette, *Jersey Blue*, 134; Bacon and Howland, *My Heart toward Home*, 37.

29. Bacon and Howland, *My Heart toward Home*, 22.

30. "The Salutary Effects of the War," *New York Herald*, April 29, 1861, in Howard Cecil Perkins, ed., *Northern Editorials on Secession*, 2 vols. (Washington, DC: American Historical Association, 1942; Gloucester, MA: Peter Smith, 1964), 2:1071.

31. Ibid., 2:1072.

32. Roy P. Basler, ed., *The Collected Works of Abraham Lincoln*, 9 vols. (New Brunswick, NJ: Rutgers University Press, 1953), 4:249–71.

33. Marshall, *A War of the People*, 21.

34. Christine Dee, ed., *Ohio's War: The Civil War in Documents* (Athens: Ohio University Press, 2006), 51–52.

35. Kurt H. Hackemer, ed., *To Rescue My Native Land: The Civil War Letters of William T. Shepherd, First Illinois Light Artillery* (Knoxville: University of Tennessee Press, 2005), 7.

36. Ulysses S. Grant, *Personal Memoirs of U.S. Grant*, ed. James M. McPherson (New York: Penguin, 1999), 121.

37. Commager, *The Civil War Archive*, 73.

38. Moorhead, *American Apocalypse*, 36–37. For more on the slave power idea, see Leonard L. Richards, *The Slave Power: The Free North and Southern Domination, 1780–1860* (Baton Rouge: Louisiana State University Press, 2000).

39. "The War Begun—The Duty of American Citizens," *Pittsburgh Post*, April 15, 1861, in Perkins, ed., *Northern Editorials on Secession*, 2:739.

40. Gillette, *Jersey Blue*, 139–40.

41. White, *A Philadelphia Perspective*, 84.

42. Richard F. Nation and Stephen E. Towne, eds., *Indiana's War: The Civil War in Documents* (Athens: Ohio University Press, 2009), 48–49.

43. Trask, *Fire Within*, 41.

44. Handbill reproduced in Frank L. Klement, *Wisconsin in the Civil War: The Home Front and the Battle Front, 1861–1865* (Madison: State Historical Society of Wisconsin, 1997), 11.

45. Gillette, *Jersey Blue*, 135–36.

46. Rockland, Maine, *Democrat and Free Press*, April 24, May 22, 1861.

47. White, *A Philadelphia Perspective*, 85.

48. Nation and Towne, *Indiana's War*, 46.

49. Charles F. Herberger, ed., *A Yankee at Arms: The Diary of Lieutenant Augustus D. Ayling, 29th Massachusetts Volunteers* (Knoxville: University of Tennessee Press, 1999), 5.

50. "Chapter 1," *Buffalo Commercial Advertiser*, April 15, 1861, in Perkins, ed., *Northern Editorials on Secession*, 2:734–35.

51. "The People and the Issue!" *New York Times*, April 15, 1861, in ibid., 2:735–37.

52. Quoted in David D. Van Tassel with John Vacha, *"Behind Bayonets": The Civil War in Northern Ohio* (Kent, OH: Kent State University Press, 2006), 38.

53. "Stand by the Flag," *Boston Post*, April 16, 1861, in Perkins, ed., *Northern Editorials on Secession*, 2:739.

54. "The War Begun—The Duty of American Citizens," *Pittsburgh Post*, April 15, 1861, in ibid., 738–39.

55. Harold Adams Small, ed., *The Road to Richmond: The Civil War Memoirs of Major Abner R. Small of the Sixteenth Maine Volunteers* (Berkeley: University of California Press, 1939), 4.

56. Shaw, *The Story of a Pioneer*, 51.

57. Marshall, *A War of the People*, 19.

58. Hackemer, *To Rescue My Native Land*, 5.

59. Ibid., 6.

60. Noah Andre Trudeau, *Like Men of War: Black Troops in the Civil War 1862–1865* (Boston: Little, Brown and Company, 1998), 7.

61. James M. McPherson, *The Negro's Civil War: How American Blacks Felt and Acted during the War for the Union* (New York: Pantheon Books, 1965; New York: Vintage Books, 1991), 19–21.

62. Louis P. Masur, ed., *The Real War Will Never Get in the Books: Selections from Writers during the Civil War* (New York: Oxford University Press, 1993), 101–5.

63. Quoted in James Oakes, *The Radical and the Republican: Frederick Douglass, Abraham Lincoln, and the Triumph of Antislavery Politics* (New York: W. W. Norton and Co., 2007), 161.

64. C. Peter Ripley et al., eds., *The Black Abolitionist Papers*, Vol. 5: *The United States, 1859–1865* (Chapel Hill: University of North Carolina Press, 1992), 112.

65. Ibid., 114.

66. Versalle F. Washington, *Eagles on Their Buttons: A Black Infantry Regiment in the Civil War* (Columbia: University of Missouri Press, 1999), 2.

67. Trudeau, *Like Men of War*, 8; McPherson, *The Negro's Civil War*, 20–23.

68. C. Peter Ripley et al., eds., *The Black Abolitionist Papers*, Vol. 2: *Canada, 1830–1865* (Chapel Hill: University of North Carolina Press, 1986), 39.

69. McPherson, *The Negro's Civil War*, 22.

70. Ripley et al., *The Black Abolitionist Papers*, 5:112–13, 117.

71. Washington, *Eagles on Their Buttons*, 2.

CHAPTER FOUR

1. William B. Hesseltine, *Lincoln and the War Governors* (New York: Alfred A. Knopf, 1948), 74–91, 115–35. Also see William C. Harris, *Lincoln and the Union Governors* (Carbondale: Southern Illinois University Press, 2013).

2. Fred Albert Shannon, *The Organization and Administration of the Union Army, 1861–1865*, 2 vols. ([Cleveland, OH]: Arthur H. Clark Co., 1928; Gloucester, MA: Peter Smith, 1965), 1:29–20.

3. Marcus Cunliffe, *Soldiers and Civilians: The Martial Spirit in America* (Boston: Little, Brown and Company, 1968), 177–254.

4. John Niven, *Connecticut for the Union: The Role of the State in the Civil War* (New Haven, CT: Yale University Press, 1965), 125–26.

5. Duane E. Shaffer, *Men of Granite: New Hampshire's Soldiers in the Civil War* (Columbia: University of South Carolina Press, 2008), 20.

6. John K. Mahon, *History of the Militia and the National Guard* (New York: Macmillan, 1983), 98–99.

7. Richard N. Current, *The History of Wisconsin*, Vol. 2: *The Civil War Era, 1848–1873* (Madison: State Historical Society of Wisconsin, 1976), 2:302; Jack Dempsey, *Michigan and the Civil War: A Great and Bloody Sacrifice* (Charleston, SC: The History Press, 2011), 25–26; Shannon, *The Organization and Administration of the Union Army*, 1:22–24; Paul A.C. Koistinen, *Beating Plowshares into Swords: The Political Economy of American Warfare, 1606–1865* (Lawrence: University Press of Kansas, 1996), 113.

8. For the role of states and the creation of a federal army of volunteers, see Shannon, *The Organization and Administration of the Union Army*, 1:15–50; Mark R. Wilson, *The Business of Civil War: Military Mobilization and the State, 1861–1865* (Baltimore: Johns Hopkins University Press, 2006), 5–35; Koistinen, *Beating Plowshares into Swords*, 102–4, 106–17.

9. Koistinen, *Beating Plowshares into Swords*, 106–10.

10. W. A. Croffut and John M. Morris, *The Military and Civil History of Connecticut during the War of 1861–1865* (New York: Ledyard Bill, 1869), 48, 53.

11. David P. Krutz, *Distant Drums: Herkimer County in the War of the Rebellion* (Utica, NY: North Country Books, 1997), 3; Charles F. Herberger, ed., *A Yankee at Arms: The Diary of Lieutenant Augustus D. Ayling, 29th Massachusetts Volunteers* (Knoxville: University of Tennessee Press, 1999), 5; Shaffer, *Men of Granite*, 21; Shannon, *The Organization and Administration of the Union Army*, 1:24; Croffut and Morris, *The Military and Civil History of Connecticut during the War of 1861–1865*, 57; Thomas H. O'Connor, *Civil War Boston: Home Front and Battlefield* (Boston: Northeastern University Press, 1997), 53.

12. David V. Mollenhoff, *Madison: A History of the Formative Years*, 2nd ed. (Madison: University of Wisconsin Press, 2003), 86.

13. James I. Robertson Jr., ed., *The Civil War Letters of General Robert McAllister* (New Brunswick, NJ: Rutgers University Press, 1965; Baton Rouge: Louisiana State University Press, 1998), 28.

14. Croffut and Morris, *The Military and Civil History of Connecticut during the War of 1861–1865*, 56.

15. David D. Roe, ed., *A Civil War Soldier's Diary: Valentine C. Randolph, 39th Illinois Regiment*, with commentary and annotations by Stephen R. Wise (DeKalb: Northern Illinois University Press, 2006), 9; Croffut and Morris, *The Military and Civil History of Connecticut during the War of 1861–1865*, 46–53.

16. Jeffrey D. Marshall, ed., *A War of the People: Vermont Civil War Letters* (Hanover, NH: University Press of New England, 1999), 19.

17. Theodore J. Karamanski, *Rally 'Round the Flag: Chicago and the Civil War* (Chicago: Nelson-Hall Publishers, 1993), 72.

18. Michael H. Frisch, *Town Into City: Springfield, Massachusetts, and the Meaning of Community, 1840–1880* (Cambridge, MA: Harvard University Press, 1972), 61.

19. Shaffer, *Men of Granite*, 19.

20. Wilson, *The Business of Civil War*, 11–23.

21. Ibid., 23–71.

22. Hesseltine, *Lincoln and the War Governors*, 148–66.

23. Mark Hoffman, *"My Brave Mechanics": The First Michigan Engineers and Their Civil War* (Detroit: Wayne State University Press, 2007), 8.

24. Phillip Shaw Paludan, *"A People's Contest": The Union and Civil War*, 2nd ed. (Lawrence: University Press of Kansas, 1996) 18–19.

25. George Winston Smith and Charles Judah, *Life in the North during the Civil War: A Source History* (Albuquerque: University of New Mexico Press, 1966), 48–49.

26. Don Harrison Doyle, *The Social Order of a Frontier Community: Jacksonville, Illinois, 1825–70* (Urbana: University of Illinois Press, 1978), 233.

27. Richard Moe, *The Last Full Measure: The Life and Death of the First Minnesota Volunteers* (New York: Henry Holt and Company, 1993), 9–14.

28. David Herbert Donald, ed., *Gone for a Soldier: The Civil War Memoirs of Private Alfred Bellard* (Boston: Little, Brown and Company, 1975), 3.

29. Andrea R. Foroughi, *Go If You Think It Your Duty: A Minnesota Couple's Civil War Letters* (St. Paul: Minnesota Historical Society Press, 2008), 27.

30. Herberger, *A Yankee at Arms*, 4.

31. Victor Hicken, *Illinois in the Civil War*, 2nd ed. (Urbana: University of Illinois Press, 1966), 8.

32. Kerry A. Trask, *Fire Within: A Civil War Narrative from Wisconsin* (Kent, OH: Kent State University Press, 1995), 46–47.

33. Hicken, *Illinois in the Civil War*, 7.

34. Richard F. Nation and Stephen E. Towne, eds., *Indiana's War: The Civil War in Documents* (Athens: Ohio University Press, 2009), 47; Nina Silber and Mary Beth Sievens, eds., *Yankee Correspondence: Civil War Letters between New England Soldiers and the Home Front* (Charlottesville: University Press of Virginia, 1996), 130.

35. Mark A. Lause, *Free Labor: The Civil War and the Making of an American Working Class* (Urbana: University of Illinois Press, 2015), 42.

36. Hicken, *Illinois in the Civil War*, 7.

37. Lause, *Free Labor*, 43.

38. Adam Goodheart, *1861: The Civil War Awakening* (New York: Alfred A. Knopf, 2011), 47–48; Niven, *Connecticut for the Union*, 39.

39. Martin W. Öfele, *True Sons of the Republic: European Immigrants in the Union Army* (Westport, CT: Praeger, 2008), 19, 43.

40. Karamanski, *Rally 'Round the Flag*, 71–72, 77–78, 81.

41. Hicken, *Illinois in the Civil War*, 7.

42. Current, *History of Wisconsin*, 2:299; Niven, *Connecticut for the Union*, 48.

43. Current, *History of Wisconsin*, 2:299.

44. Nation and Towne, *Indiana's War*, 46–47.

45. Pearl T. Ponce, ed., *Kansas's War: The Civil War in Documents* (Athens: Ohio University Press, 2011), 74.

46. Marilyn Mayer Culpepper, ed., *Trials and Triumphs: The Women of the American Civil War* (East Lansing: Michigan State University Press, 1991), 26.

47. Marshall, *A War of the People*, 19.

48. Mary A. Livermore, *My Story of the War: The Civil War Memoirs of the Famous Nurse, Relief Organizer and Suffragette* (New York: Da Capo Press, 1995), 97.

49. Nina Silber, *Daughters of the Union: Northern Women Fight the Civil War* (Cambridge, MA: Harvard University Press, 2005), 21–22.

50. Quoted in Ethel Hurn, *Wisconsin Women in the War Between the States* ([Madison]: Wisconsin History Commission, 1911), 5.

51. Quoted in ibid., 1–2.

52. Andrew S. Coopersmith, *Fighting Words: An Illustrated History of Newspaper Accounts of the Civil War* (New York: The New Press, 2004), 9.

53. Hurn, *Wisconsin Women in the War Between the States*, 4.

54. David D. Van Tassel, with John Vacha, *"Behind Bayonets": The Civil War in Northern Ohio* (Kent, OH: Kent State University Press, 2006), 40–41.

55. Russell L. Johnson, *Warriors into Workers: The Civil War and the Formation of Urban-Industrial Society in a Northern City* (New York: Fordham University Press, 2003), 247.

56. Moe, *Last Full Measure*, 22.

57. Croffut and Morris, *The Military and Civil History of Connecticut during the War of 1861–1865*, 58–59.

58. Doyle, *The Social Order of a Frontier Community*, 232.

59. Charles F. Larimer, ed. *Love and Valor: Intimate Civil War Letters between Captain Jacob and Emeline Ritner* (Western Springs, IL: Sigourney Press, 2000), 26.

60. Silber, *Daughters of the Union*, 20.

61. Jeanie Attie, *Patriotic Toil: Northern Women and the American Civil War* (Ithaca, NY: Cornell University Press, 1998), 33.

62. Georgeanna Woolsey Bacon and Eliza Woolsey Howland, *My Heart toward Home: Letters of a Family during the Civil War*, ed. Daniel John Hoisington (Roseville, MN: Edinborough Press, 2001), 30.

63. Patricia L. Richard, *Busy Hands: Images of the Family in the Northern Civil War Effort* (New York: Fordham University Press, 2003), 194.

64. Moe, *The Last Full Measure*, 12.

65. Hoffman, *"My Brave Mechanics,"* 34.

66. Karamanski, *Rally 'Round the Flag*, 80; Maria Lydig Daly, *Diary of a Union Lady, 1861–1865*, ed. Harold Earl Hammond (Lincoln: University of Nebraska Press, 2000), 79.

67. Livermore, *My Story of the War*, 110.

68. Oliver Otis Howard, *Autobiography of Oliver Otis Howard, Major General United States Army*, 2 vols. (New York: Baker and Taylor Company, 1908), 1:121–132.

69. Donald, *Gone For a Soldier*, 4.

70. Christine Dee, ed., *Ohio's War: The Civil War in Documents* (Athens: Ohio University Press, 2006), 59.

71. Gilbert Claflin and Esther Claflin, *A Quiet Corner of the War: The Civil War Letters of Gilbert and Esther Claflin, Oconomowoc, Wisconsin, 1862–1863*, ed. Judy Cook (Madison: University of Wisconsin Press, 2013), 14.

72. James C. Mohr, ed., *The Cormany Diaries: A Northern Family in the Civil War* (Pittsburgh: University of Pittsburgh Press, 1982), 253.

73. Ibid., 253.

74. Charles F. Larimer, ed., *Love and Valor: Intimate Civil War Letters between Captain Jacob and Emeline Ritner* (Western Springs, IL: Sigourney Press, 2000), 18.

75. Marshall, *A War of the People*, 19.

CHAPTER FIVE

1. William Howard Russell, *My Diary North and South* (Boston: T.O.H.P. Burnham, 1863), 368–69.

2. Walter D. Kamphoefner and Wolfgang Helbich, eds., and Susan Carter Vogel, trans., *Germans in the Civil War: The Letters They Wrote Home* (Chapel Hill: University of North Carolina Press, 2006), 44.

3. Joan Silva Patrakis, *Andover in the Civil War: The Spirit and Sacrifice of a New England Town* (Charleston, SC: The History Press, 2008), 25–27, 33; Kerry A. Trask, *Fire Within: A Civil War Narrative from Wisconsin* (Kent, OH: Kent State University Press, 1995), 51; John Niven, *Connecticut for the Union: The Role of the State in the Civil War* (New Haven, CT: Yale University Press, 1965), 54; Thomas H. O'Connor, *Civil War Boston: Home Front and Battlefield* (Boston: Northeastern University Press, 1997), 58, 61.

4. David V. Mollenhoff, *Madison: A History of the Formative Years*, 2nd ed. (Madison: University of Wisconsin Press, 2003), 113.

5. Edward L. Ayers, *In the Presence of Mine Enemies: War in the Heart of America, 1859–1863* (New York: W. W. Norton and Co., 2003), 157.

6. Charles F. Herberger, ed., *A Yankee at Arms: The Diary of Lieutenant Augustus D. Ayling, 29th Massachusetts Volunteers* (Knoxville: University of Tennessee Press, 1999), 4; Robert Hunt Rhodes, ed., *All for the Union: The Civil War Diary and Letters of Elisha Hunt Rhodes* (New York: Vintage Civil War Library, 1992), 3–5; J. M. Favill, *Diary of a Young Army Officer Serving with the Armies of the United States during the War of the Rebellion* (Chicago: R. R. Donnelley and Sons Company, 1909), 11; Theodore J. Karamanski, *Rally 'Round the Flag: Chicago and the Civil War* (Chicago: Nelson-Hall, 1993), 72.

7. J. Matthew Gallman, *Mastering Wartime: A Social History of Philadelphia during the Civil War* (Cambridge, UK: Cambridge University Press, 1990), 11; Courtney MacLachlan, *The Amanda Letters: Civil War Days on the Coast of Maine* (Bowie, MD: Heritage Books, 2003), 38; Stuart Murray, *A Time of War: A Northern Chronicle of the Civil War* (Lee, MA: Berkshire House Publishers, 2001), 51; Russell L. Johnson, *Warriors into Workers: The Civil War and the Formation of Urban-Industrial Society in a Northern City* (New York: Fordham University Press, 2003), 61.

8. William Gillette, *Jersey Blue: Civil War Politics in New Jersey, 1854–1865* (New Brunswick, NJ: Rutgers University Press, 1995), 161.

9. Duane E. Shaffer, *Men of Granite: New Hampshire's Soldiers in the Civil War* (Columbia: University of South Carolina Press, 2008), 20.

10. Favill, *The Diary of a Young Officer*, 42.

11. Edward K. Spann, *Gotham at War: New York City, 1860–1865* (Wilmington, DE: SR Books, 2002), 58.

12. Karamanski, *Rally 'Round the Flag*, 71; Martin W. Öfele, *True Sons of the Republic: European Immigrants in the Union Army* (Westport, CT: Praeger, 2008), 43; Joseph R. Reinhart, ed.,

August Willich's Gallant Dutchmen: Civil War Letters from the 32nd Indiana Infantry (Kent, OH: Kent State University Press, 2006), 10, 22–23; Kamphoefner and Helbich, *Germans in the Civil War*, 487; James S. Pula, *The Sigel Regiment: A History of the 26th Wisconsin Volunteer Infantry, 1862–1865* (Campbell, CA: Savas Books, 1998), 25.

13. Robert Knox Sneden, *Eye of the Storm: A Civil War Odyssey*, ed. Charles F. Bryan and Nelson D. Lankford (New York: Free Press, 2000), xiii.

14. Niven, *Connecticut for the Union*, 49–50, 67.

15. Oliver Otis Howard, *Autobiography of Oliver Otis Howard, Major General United States Army*, 2 vols. (New York: Baker and Taylor Company, 1908), 1:116. Thomas W. Hyde, *Following the Greek Cross or Memories of the Sixth Army Corps* (Columbia: University of South Carolina Press, 2005), 13; Ruth Douglas Currie, ed., *Emma Spaulding Bryant: Civil War Bride, Carpetbagger's Wife, Ardent Feminist: Letters and Diaries, 1860–1900* (New York: Fordham University Press, 2004), 10–11; Shaffer, *Men of Granite*, 22.

16. "The Army's Century on Davids Island, Fort Slocum, New Rochelle, N.Y.," Westchester County, New York, Virtual Archives, http://davidsisland.westchesterarchives.com.

17. Marti Skipper and Jane Taylor, eds., *A Handful of Providence: The Civil War Letters of Lt. Richard Goldwaite, New Volunteers, and Ellen Goldwaite* (Jefferson, NC: McFarland and Company, 2004), 17; Spann, *Gotham at War*, 67.

18. Spann, *Gotham at War*, 67.

19. Roy Rosenzweig and Elizabeth Blackmar, *The Park and the People: A History of Central Park* (Ithaca, NY: Cornell University Press, 1992), 252.

20. Edmund J. Raus Jr., *Banners South: A Northern Community at War* (Kent, OH: Kent State University Press, 2005), 32; *Rockland (Maine) Gazette*, June 20, 1861.

21. John G. Gammons, *The Third Massachusetts Volunteer Militia in the War of the Rebellion, 1861–1868* (Providence, RI: Snow and Farnham Company, 1906), 19–20.

22. Bernard A. Olsen, *Upon the Tented Field: An Historical Account of the Civil War as Told by the Men Who Fought and Gave their Lives* (Red Bank, NJ: Historic Projects, Inc., 1993), 19; Barbara Pepe, *Freehold: A Hometown History* (Charleston, SC: Arcadia Publishing, 2003), 97.

23. David D. Van Tassell, with John Vacha, *"Behind Bayonets": The Civil War in Northern Ohio* (Kent, OH: Kent State University Press, 2006), 52.

24. Richard N. Current, *The History of Wisconsin*, Vol. 2: *The Civil War Era, 1848–1873* (Madison: State Historical Society of Wisconsin, 1976), 339–40.

25. George Worthington Adams, *Doctors in Blue: The Medical History of the Union Army in the Civil War* (Baton Rouge: Louisiana State University Press, 1952, 1996), 149.

26. Gallman, *Mastering Wartime*, 130.

27. Mollenhoff, *Madison*, 93; Ethel Hurn, *Wisconsin Women in the War between the States* ([Madison]: Wisconsin History Commission, 1911), 119–33.

28. Adams, *Doctors in Blue*, 151–58.

29. Ibid., 151–53.

30. Michael A. Ross, *Justice of Shattered Dreams: Samuel Freeman Miller and the Supreme Court during the Civil War Era* (Baton Rouge: Louisiana State University Press, 2003), 63; Donald C. Elder III, ed., *Love amid the Turmoil: The Civil War Letters of William and Mary Vermilion* (Iowa City: University of Iowa Press, 2003), 339 n.30; Gerald Kennedy, "U.S. Army Hospital: Keokuk, 1862–1865," *The Annals of Iowa*, 40 (Fall 1969): 118–36.

31. Eugene G. Stackhouse, *Germantown in the Civil War* (Charleston, SC: The History Press, 2010), 106–7.

32. Mollenhoff, *Madison*, 51, 93; Erika Janik, *Madison: History of a Model City* (Charleston, SC: The History Press, 2010), 49.

33. Frank L. Grzyb, *Rhode Island's Civil War Hospital: Life and Death at Portsmouth Grove, 1862–1865* (Jefferson, NC: McFarland and Company, 2012), 17, 28–29.

34. Nathaniel West, *History of the Satterlee U.S.A. Gen. Hospital, at West Philadelphia, Pa., from October 8, 1862 to October 3, 1863* ([Philadelphia, PA]: The Hospital Press, 1863; [Ithaca, NY]: Cornell University Library Digital Collections, n.d.), 6; Ira M. Rutkow, *Bleeding Blue and Gray: Civil War Surgery and the Evolution of American Medicine* (New York: Random House, 2005), 156–57; Stewart Brooks, *Civil War Medicine* (Springfield, IL: Charles C. Thomas, 1966), 43.

35. Brooks, *Civil War Medicine*, 43.

36. Paul A. Cimbala, "Soldiering on the Home Front: The Veteran Reserve Corps and the Northern People," in *Union Soldiers and the Northern Home Front: Wartime Experiences, Postwar Adjustments*, ed. Paul A. Cimbala and Randall M. Miller (New York: Fordham University Press, 2002), 210–12. Current, *The History of Wisconsin*, 2:341; Richard Moe, *The Last Full Measure: The Life and Death of the First Minnesota Volunteers* (New York: Henry Holt and Co., 1993), 21.

37. Barbara Butler Davis, ed., *Affectionately Yours: The Civil War Home-Front Letters of the Ovid Butler Family* (Indianapolis: Indiana Historical Society Press, 2004), 86.

38. Chapter Five, James M. Randall Diary, Primary Source Section, eHistory, Department of History, Ohio State University, Columbus, OH, http://ehistory.osu.edu/osu/sources/letters/randall/05.cfm (The James M. Randall Diary is divided into chapters with no specific reference dates or pagination).

39. Jonathan W. White, ed., *A Philadelphia Perspective: The Civil War Diary of Sidney George Fisher* (New York: Fordham University Press, 2007), 91.

40. William J. Miller, *Civil War City: Harrisburg, Pennsylvania, 1861–1865* (Shippensburg, PA: White Mane Publishing, 1990), 16–17.

41. Niven, *Connecticut for the Union*, 51.

42. Oliver Otis Howard, *Autobiography of Oliver Otis Howard*, 2 vols. (New York: Baker and Taylor Company, 1908), 1:117.

43. *Rockland (Maine) Gazette*, June 20, 1861.

44. Shaffer, *Men of Granite*, 26.

45. Diary entry for December 23, 1861, Anonymous Hartford, Connecticut Female Civilian Diary, Connecticut Historical Society, Hartford, CT.

46. J. E. A. Smith, *The History of Pittsfield, (Berkshire County,) Massachusetts, from the Year 1800 to the Year 1976*, 2 vols. (Springfield, MA: C. W. Bryan & Co., 1876), 2:620.

47. Current, *The History of Wisconsin*, 2:370–71.

48. Ann Gorman Condon, ed., *Architects of Our Fortunes: The Journal of Eliza A. W. Otis, 1860–1863, with Letters and Civil War Journal of Harrison Gray Otis* (San Marino, CA: Huntington Library, 2001), 130.

49. Winifred Gallagher, *How the Post Office Created America: A History* (New York: Penguin Press, 2016), 145.

50. Cimbala, "The Veteran Reserve Corps and the Northern People," 201.

51. Niven, *Connecticut for the Union*, 326.

52. Gerald F. Linderman, *Embattled Courage: The Experience of Combat in the American Civil War* (New York: The Free Press, 1987), 84.

53. Chapter Five, James M. Randall Diary.

54. Christine Dee, ed., *Ohio's War: The Civil War in Documents* (Athens: Ohio University Press, 2006), 90–91 (quotations); Eugene H. Roseboom, *The Civil War Era, 1850–1873*, Vol. 4 of *The History of the State of Ohio*, ed. Carl Wittke (Columbus: Ohio State Archaeological and Historical Society, 1944), 408, 410.

55. Niven, *Connecticut for the Union*, 327.

56. Patricia L. Richard, *Busy Hands: Images of Family in the Northern Civil War Effort* (New York: Fordham University Press, 2003), 63, 65.

57. Capt. G. W. Merrick to Commanding Officer, Invalid Company No. 17, October 20, 1863, Regimental Papers, 16th Veteran Reserve Corps, Adjutant Generals Office, Record Group 94, National Archives Building, Washington, D.C.

58. Ross, *Justice of Shattered Dreams*, 63.

59. Elder, *Love Amid the Turmoil*, 16–17.

60. Richard, *Busy Hands*, 71.

61. Don Harrison Doyle, *The Social Order of a Frontier Community: Jacksonville, Illinois, 1825–70* (Urbana: University of Illinois Press, 1978), 211.

62. *Hartford (Connecticut) Daily Courant*, January 19, February 25, 1865.

63. Capt. G. Nagle to Capt. J. W. De Forrest, October 17, 1865, Letters Received, Veteran Reserve Corps Records, Provost Marshal General's Department, Record Group 110, National Archives Building, Washington, DC; *Indianapolis Daily Journal*, December 29, 1864.

64. *Indianapolis Daily Journal*, December 24, 1864.

65. Joseph Williamson, *History of the City of Belfast in the State of Maine, From its First Settlement in 1770 to 1875* (Portland, ME: Loring, Short, and Harmon, 1877), 157.

66. Doyle, *The Social Order of Frontier Town*, 212.

CHAPTER SIX

1. James M. McPherson, *For Cause and Comrades: Why Men Fought in the Civil War* (New York: Oxford University Press, 1997), 182.

2. Jane Turner Censer, ed., *The Papers of Frederick Law Olmsted*, Vol. 4: *Defending the Union: The Civil War and the U.S. Sanitary Commission, 1861–1863* (Baltimore: Johns Hopkins University Press, 1986), 150–51, n.4, 230, n.5.

3. William Quentin Maxwell, *Lincoln's Fifth Wheel: The Political History of the United States Sanitary Commission* (New York: Longmans, Green and Co., 1956), 45–48; Bell Irvin Wiley, *The Life of Billy Yank: The Common Soldier of the Union* (Indianapolis: Bobbs-Merrill Co., 1952; Garden City, NY: Doubleday and Co., 1971), 371, n.22; John D. Billings, *Hardtack and Coffee: The Unwritten Story of Army Life* (Boston: George M. Smith and Co., 1887; Lincoln: University of Nebraska Press, 1993), 97–98.

4. Censer, *The Papers of Frederick Law Olmsted*, 4:150–51, n.4.

5. Peter Messent and Steve Courtney, eds., *The Civil War Letters of Joseph Hopkins Twichell* (Athens: University of Georgia Press, 2006), 66–67, 68, 169, 211.

6. William Gillette, *Jersey Blue: Civil War Politics in New Jersey, 1854–1865* (New Brunswick, NJ: Rutgers University Press, 1995), 186–87, 201; Michael A. Ross, *Justice of Shattered Dreams: Samuel Freeman Miller and the Supreme Court during the Civil War Era* (Baton Rouge: Louisiana State University Press, 2003), 62.

7. Judith Ann Giesberg, *Army at Home: Women and the Civil War on the Northern Home Front* (Chapel Hill: University of North Carolina Press, 2009), 31, 49; Robert H. Bremner, *The Public Good: Philanthropy and Welfare in the Civil War Era* (New York: Alfred A. Knopf, 1980), 75; Gillette, *Jersey Blue*, 176; J. Matthew Gallman, *Mastering Wartime: A Social History of Philadelphia during the Civil War* (Cambridge, UK: Cambridge University Press, 1990), 123–24; *Rockland (Maine) Gazette*, May 16, 1861; David P. Krutz, *Distant Drums: Herkimer County, New York in the War of the Rebellion* (Utica, NY: North Country Books, 1997), 3.

8. Bremner, *The Public Good*, 76.

9. *Rockland (Maine) Gazette*, June 13, 1861.

10. Giesberg, *Army at Home*, 33.

11. Bremner, *The Public Good*, 33, 76.

12. Ethel Hurn, *Wisconsin Women in the War between the States* ([Madison]: Wisconsin History Commission, 1911), 66; *Rockland (Maine) Gazette*, June 13, 1861.

13. William G. Andrews, *Civil War Brockport: A Canal Town and the Union Army* (Charleston, SC: The History Press, 2013), 65–67.

14. *Appleton (Wisconsin) Crescent*, September 13, 1862.

15. Richard N. Current, *The History of Wisconsin*, Vol. 2: *The Civil War Era, 1848–1873* (Madison: State Historical Society of Wisconsin, 1976), 394, 395, 397; Russell Johnson, *Warriors into Workers: The Civil War and the Formation of Urban-Industrial Society in a Northern City* (New York: Fordham University Press, 2003), 245–47; Giesberg, *Army at Home*, 56–63.

16. Giesberg, *Army at Home*, 30–32; Judith Ann Giesberg, "From Harvest Field to Battlefield: Rural Pennsylvania Women and the U.S. Civil War," *Pennsylvania History* 72: 2 (2005): 172–73.

17. Nicole Etcheson, "'No Fit Wife': Soldiers' Wives and Their In-Laws on the Indiana Home Front," in *Union Heartland: The Midwestern Home Front during the Civil War*, ed. Ginette Aley and J.L. Anderson (Carbondale: Southern Illinois University Press, 2013), 97–124.

18. Donald C. Elder III, ed., *Love amid the Turmoil: The Civil War Letters of William and Mary Vermilion* (Iowa City: University of Iowa Press, 2003), 25.

19. Ibid., 13.

20. Ibid., 17, 29–30, 32.

21. Ginette Aley, "Inescapable Realities: Rural Midwestern Women and Families during the Civil War," in Aley and Anderson, eds., *Union Heartland*, 128.

22. Current, *History of Wisconsin*, 2:126.

23. Paul W. Gates, *Agriculture and the Civil War* (New York: Alfred A. Knopf, 1965), 229.

24. Pearl T. Ponce, ed., *Kansas's War: The Civil War in Documents* (Athens: University of Ohio Press, 2011), 216–17.

25. Robert L. Bee, ed., *The Boys from Rockville: Civil War Narratives of Sgt. Benjamin Hirst, Company D, 14th Connecticut Volunteers* (Knoxville: University of Tennessee Press, 1998), 122.

26. Nicole Etcheson, *A Generation at War: The Civil War Era in a Northern Community* (Lawrence: University Press of Kansas, 2011), 138–39; Mary A. Livermore, *My Story of the War: A Woman's Narrative of Four Years Personal Experiences* (Hartford, CT: [A.D. Worthington], 1887; New York: Da Capo Press, 1995), 148.

27. Benjamin F. Gue, *History of Iowa from the Earliest Times to the Beginning of the Twentieth Century*, Vol. 2: *The Civil War* (New York: The Century History Company, 1903), 419.

28. Richard Bak, *A Distant Thunder: Michigan in the Civil War* (Ann Arbor, MI: Huron River Press, 2004), 90 (quotation as well).

29. Charles F. Larimer, ed., *Love and Valor: Intimate Civil War Letters between Captain Jacob and Emeline Ritner* (Western Springs, IL: Sigourney Press, 2000), 68–69.

30. Ibid., 164.

31. Hurn, *Wisconsin Women in the War between the States*, 78–80.

32. Livermore, *My Story of the War*, 148–49.

33. Ibid.

34. Elder, *Love amid the Turmoil*, 85.

35. David D. Van Tassel, with John Vacha, *"Behind Bayonets": The Civil War in Northern Ohio* (Kent, OH: Kent State University Press, 2006), 65–66.

36. Marilyn Mayer Culpepper, ed., *Trials and Triumphs: The Women of the American Civil War* (East Lansing: Michigan State University Press, 1991), 268.

37. Jennifer Cain Bohrnstedt, ed., *While Father Is Away: The Civil War Letters of William H. Bradbury* (Lexington: University Press of Kentucky, 2003), 3.

38. Gilbert Claflin and Esther Claflin, *A Quiet Corner of the War: The Civil War Letters of Gilbert and Esther Claflin, Oconomowoc, Wisconsin, 1862–1863*, ed. Judy Cook (Madison: University of Wisconsin Press, 2013), 98, 112.

39. Nina Silber, *Daughters of the Union: Northern Women Fight the Civil War* (Cambridge, MA: Harvard University Press, 2005), 41–86.

40. Rachel Filene Seidman, "A Monstrous Doctrine?: Northern Women on Dependency during the Civil War," in *An Uncommon Time: The Civil War and the Northern Home Front*, ed. Paul A. Cimbala and Randall M. Miller (New York: Fordham University Press, 2002), 170–88.

41. Claflin and Claflin, *A Quiet Corner of the War*, 21, 150.

42. Ibid., 40.

43. Ruth Douglas Currie, ed., *Emma Spaulding Bryant: Civil War Bride, Carpetbagger's Wife, Ardent Feminist: Letters and Diaries, 1860–1900* (New York: Fordham University Press, 2004), 68.

44. Andrea R. Foroughi, *Go If You Think It Your Duty: A Minnesota Couple's Civil War Letters* (St. Paul: Minnesota Historical Society Press, 2008), 187.

45. Bak, *A Distant Thunder*, 104.

46. Nina Silber and Mary Beth Sievens, eds., *Yankee Correspondence: Civil War Letters between New England Soldiers and the Home Front* (Charlottesville: University Press of Virginia, 1996), 143.

47. Marti Skipper and Jane Taylor, eds., *A Handful of Providence: The Civil War Letters of Lt. Richard Goldwaite, New York Volunteers and Ellen Goldwaite* (Jefferson, NC: McFarland and Company, 2004), 31, 32.

48. Paul A. Cimbala, *Veterans North and South: The Transition from Soldier to Civilian after the American Civil War* (Santa Barbara, CA: Praeger, 2016), 60, 61; Silber, *Daughters of the Union*, 110–15.

49. Currie, *Emma Spaulding Bryant*, 68.

50. Coralou Peel Lassen, ed., *Dear Sarah: Letters Home from a Soldier of the Iron Brigade* (Bloomington: Indiana University Press, 1999), 11.

51. Larimer, *Love and Valor*, 19. Jeffrey D. Marshall, ed., *"A War of the People": Vermont Civil War Letters* (Hanover, NH: University Press of New England, 1999), 62; Patricia L. Richard, *Busy Hands: Images of the Family in the Northern Civil War Effort* (New York: Fordham University Press, 2003), 40–78; Culpepper, *Trials and Triumphs*, 106.

52. Foroughi, *Go If You Think It Your Duty*, 243.

53. Ibid., 58.

54. Ibid., 182.

55. Silber and Sievens, *Yankee Correspondence*, 115.

56. Richard L. Kiper, ed., *Dear Catharine, Dear Taylor: The Civil War Letters of a Union Soldier and His Wife* (Lawrence: University Press of Kansas, 2002), 159–60, 196.

57. Goldwaite and Goldwaite, *A Handful of Providence*, 94.

58. Ibid., 133, 174, 179.

59. James C. Mohr, ed., *The Cormany Diaries: A Northern Family in the Civil War* (Pittsburgh: University of Pittsburgh Press, 1982), 284.

60. Ibid., 380.

61. Ibid., 253, 408.

62. Elder, *Love amid the Turmoil*, 260.

63. Claflin and Claflin, *A Quiet Corner of the War*, 78.

64. Ibid., 103.

65. Donald C. Manness and H. Jason Combs, eds., *Do They Miss Me At Home?: The Civil War Letters of William McKnight, Seventh Ohio Volunteer Cavalry* (Athens: Ohio University Press, 2010), 179.

66. Bee, *The Boys from Rockville*, 131.

67. Ibid., 30.

68. Ibid., 176.

69. Quoted in Current, *The History of Wisconsin*, 2:392.

70. Ibid.

71. Kiper, *Dear Catharine, Dear Taylor*, 93, 110.

72. James Goodnow to Sam [Goodnow], November 20, 1862, Charles Goodnow Letters, reel 39, *A People at War: Civil War Manuscripts from the Holdings of the Library of Congress*, ed. John R. Sellers, 60 reels (Alexandria, VA: Chadwyck-Healey, 1989–1990).

73. John Goodnow to Sam [Goodnow], February 20, 1863; April 6, 1863, ibid.

74. John Goodnow to Sam [Goodnow], December 29, 1863, ibid.

75. Silas W. Browning to Minnie Browning, March 4, [1863?], Silas W. Browning Papers, reel 6, *A People at War*.

76. Manness and Combs, eds. *Do They Miss Me At Home*, 45, 46.

77. James Goodnow to Sam [Goodnow], January 11, 1863, reel 39, *A People at War*.

78. Silber and Sievens, *Yankee Correspondence*, 60.

79. Claflin and Claflin, *A Quiet Corner of the War*, 25, 35, 103, 118, 161.

80. James Marten, *The Children's Civil War* (Chapel Hill: University of North Carolina Press, 1998), 173–74.

81. Claflin and Claflin, *A Quiet Corner of the War*, 104, 118, 211.

82. Ibid., 44, 91.

83. Anna Howard Shaw, *The Story of a Pioneer* (New York: Harper and Brothers, 1915), 27, 52–53.

84. Ibid., 27, 51, 53–54.

CHAPTER SEVEN

1. Nancy L. Rhodes and Lucy E. Bailey, eds., *Wanted Correspondence—Women's Letters to a Union Soldier* (Athens: Ohio University Press 2009), 118.

2. Ibid., 120.

3. Jonathan W. White, ed., *A Philadelphia Perspective: The Civil War Diary of Sidney George Fisher* (New York: Fordham University Press, 2007), 211; Gari Carter, *Troubled State: Civil War Journals of Franklin Archibald Dick* (Kirksville, MO: Truman State University Press, 2008), 181; George Winston Smith and Charles Judah, *Life in the North during the Civil War* (Albuquerque: University of New Mexico Press, 1966), 268–71; John Niven, *Connecticut for the Union: The Role of the State in the Civil War* (New Haven, CT: Yale University Press, 1965), 340–41.

4. William Gillette, *Jersey Blue: Civil War Politics in New Jersey, 1854–1865* (New Brunswick, NJ: Rutgers University Press, 1995), 178.

5. Walter D. Kamphoefner and Wolfgang Helbich, eds., and Susan Carter Vogel, trans., *Germans in the Civil War: The Letters They Wrote Home* (Chapel Hill: University of North Carolina Press, 2006), 139, 141 (quotation).

6. Judith A. Bailey and Robert I. Cottom, eds., *After Chancellorsville: Letters from the Heart: The Civil War Letters of Private Walter G. Dunn and Emma Randolph* (Baltimore: Maryland Historical Society, 1998), 95–96, 190, 202, 204; David V. Mollenhoff, *Madison: A History of the Formative Years*, 2nd ed. (Madison: University of Wisconsin Press, 2003), 112.

7. Bailey and Cottom, *After Chancellorsville*, 89, 91, 96–98, 152; Sheila M. Cumberworth and Daniel V. Biles, eds., *An Enduring Love: The Civil War Diaries of Benjamin Franklin Pierce (14th New Hampshire Vol. Inf.) and His Wife Harriett Jane Goodwin Pierce* (Gettysburg, PA: Thomas Publications, 1995), 45.

8. Dorothy Denneen Volo and Jame M. Volo, *Daily Life in Civil War America* (Westport, CT: Greenwood Press, 1998), 219; Barbara Butler Davis, ed., *Affectionately Yours: The Civil War Letters of the Ovid Butler Family* (Indianapolis: Indiana Historical Society Press, 2004), 62.

9. Bailey and Cottom, *After Chancellorsville*, 95, 152.

10. George B. Kirsch, *Baseball in Blue and Gray: The National Pastime during the Civil War* (Princeton, NJ: Princeton University Press, 2003), 1–27, 48–65, 70–71.

11. Bailey and Cottom, *After Chancellorsville*, 165.

12. Jeffrey D. Marshall, ed., *A War of the People: Vermont Civil War Letters* (Hanover, NH: University Press of New England, 1997), 124.

13. Bailey and Cottom, *After Chancellorsville*, 152–53.

14. Peter Josyph, ed., *The Wounded River: The Civil War Letters of John Vance Lauderdale, M.D.* (East Lansing: Michigan State University Press, 1993), 150.

15. Kerry A. Trask, *Fire Within: A Civil War Narrative from Wisconsin* (Kent, OH: Kent State University Press, 1995), 165–66.

16. J. Matthew Gallman, *Mastering Wartime: A Social History of Philadelphia during the Civil War* (Cambridge, UK: Cambridge University Press, 1990), 97–108; Don Harrison Doyle, *The Social Order of a Frontier Community: Jacksonville, Illinois, 1825–70* (Urbana: University of Illinois Press, 1978), 236.

17. Gallman, *Mastering Wartime*, 90–94, 97–108.

18. Joseph Williamson, *History of the City of Belfast in the State of Maine, From its First Settlement in 1770 to 1875* (Portland: Loring, Short, and Harmon, 1877), 472.

19. Thomas H. O'Connor, *Civil War Boston: Home Front and Battlefield* (Boston: Northeastern University Press, 1997), 99, 150–51.

20. Georgeanna Woolsey Bacon and Eliza Woolsey Howland, *My Heart toward Home: Letters of a Family during the Civil War*, ed. Daniel John Hoisington (Roseville, MN: Edinborough Press, 2001), 261.

21. Mary A. Livermore, *My Story of the War: A Woman's Narrative of Four Years Personal Experience* (New York: Arno Press, 1972; New York: Da Capo Press, 1995), 176–78.

22. Gallman, *Mastering Wartime*, 107.

23. Entries for July 6, [7], 1863, Anson Miles Case Diary, Connecticut Historical Society, Hartford, CT.

24. White, *A Philadelphia Perspective*, 213, 214.

25. Davis, *Affectionately Yours*, 47.

26. Patricia L. Richard, *Busy Hands: Images of the Family in the Northern Civil War Effort* (New York: Fordham University Press, 2003), 155.

27. Bacon and Howland, *My Heart toward Home*, 43.

28. Livermore, *My Story of the War*, 138.

29. Patricia L. Richard, "'Listen Ladies One and All': Union Soldiers Yearn for the Society of Their 'Fair Cousins of the North'," in *Union Soldiers and the Northern Home Front: Wartime Experiences, Postwar Adjustments*, ed. Paul A. Cimbala and Randall M. Miller (New York: Fordham University Press, 2002), 143–81; Richard, *Busy Hands*, 87–175; Livermore, *My Story of the War*, 138.

30. See Beverly Hayes Kallgren and James L. Crouthamel, *"Dear Friend Anna": The Civil War Letters of a Common Soldier from Maine* (Orono: University of Maine Press, 1992), and its companion volume, Beverly Hayes Kallgren, *Abial and Anna: The Life of a Civil War Veteran as Told in Family Letters* (Orono: University of Maine Press, 1996). See also Bailey and Cottom, *After Chancellorsville*.

31. James C. Mohr, ed., *The Cormany Diaries: A Northern Family in the Civil War* (Pittsburgh: University of Pittsburgh Press, 1982), 254.

32. Nina Silber and Mary Beth Sievens, eds., *Yankee Correspondence: Civil War Letters between New England Soldiers and the Home Front* (Charlottesville: University Press of Virginia, 1996), 145.

33. Davis, *Affectionately Yours*, 60.

34. Livermore, *My Story of the War*, 199–200.

35. Ronald J. Zboray and Mary Saracino Zboray, "Cannonballs and Books: Reading and the Disruption of Social Ties on the New England Home Front," in *The War Was You and Me: Civilians in the American Civil War*, ed. Joan E. Cashin (Princeton, NJ: Princeton University Press, 2002), 245.

36. White, *A Philadelphia Perspective*; Mary Lydig Daly, *Diary of a Union Lady, 1861–1865*, ed. Harold Earl Hammond (New York: Funk & Wagnalls Company, Inc., 1962); George Templeton Strong, *The Diary of George Templeton Strong: The Civil War, 1860–1865*, ed. Allan Nevins (New York: The Macmillan Company, 1962).

37. Judith Ann Giesberg, ed., *Emilie Davis's Civil War: The Diaries of a Free Black Woman in Philadelphia, 1863–1865* (University Park: Pennsylvania State University Press, 2014); Mohr, *The Cormany Diaries*.

38. David D. Van Tassel, with John Vacha, *"Behind Bayonets": The Civil War in Northern Ohio* (Kent, OH: Kent State University Press, 2006), 61–63.

39. J. Matthew Gallman, *America's Joan of Arc: The Life of Anna Elizabeth Dickinson* (New York: Oxford University Press, 2006), 19–43.

40. Brooks D. Simpson, ed., *The Civil War: The Third Year Told by Those Who Lived It* (New York: Library of America, 2013), 139, 143.

41. Smith and Judah, *Life in the North during the Civil War*, 298.

42. Ibid., 299.

43. Zboray and Zboray, "Cannonballs and Books," 237–61.

44. Niven, *Connecticut for the Union*, 342–43.

45. Donald C. Elder III, ed., *Love amid the Turmoil: The Civil War Letters of William and Mary Vermilion* (Iowa City: University of Iowa Press, 2003), 37, 85.

46. Niven, *Connecticut for the Union,* 342; Sarah Emma Edmonds, *Soldier, Nurse and Spy: A Woman's Adventures in the Union Army* (Hartford, CT: Williams, 1865; DeKalb: Northern Illinois University Press, 1999). Elizabeth D. Leonard's introduction and annotation make the new edition all the more worthwhile.

47. Louisa May Alcott, *Hospital Sketches*, ed. Alice Fahs (Boston: Bedford/St. Martin's, 2004); Henry Morford, *The Days of Shoddy: A Novel of the Great Rebellion in 1861* (Philadelphia: T. B. Peterson & Brothers, 1863); J. Matthew Gallman, *Defining Duty in the Civil War: Personal Choice, Popular Culture, and the Union Home Front* (Chapel Hill: University of North Carolina Press, 2015), 65–66, 82–86, 195–96.

48. Alice Fahs, "A Thrilling Northern War: Gender, Race, and Sensational Popular War Literature," in *An Uncommon Time: The Civil War and the Northern Home Front*, ed. Paul A. Cimbala and Randall M. Miller (New York: Fordham University Press, 2002), 27–60.

49. Smith and Judah, *Life in the North during the Civil War*, 297.

50. Gallman, *Defining Duty in the Civil War*, 29–64 and passim.

51. Rhodes and Bailey, *Wanted—Correspondence*, 155.

52. William G. Andrew, *Civil War Brockport: A Canal Town and the Union Army* (Charleston, SC: The History Press, 2013), 60.

53. Jeanie Attie, *Patriotic Toil: Northern Women and the American Civil War* (Ithaca, NY: Cornell University Press, 1998), 95.

54. Davis, *Affectionately Yours*, 50, 56.

55. For near-contemporary details about fairs held across the North, see Frank B. Goodrich, *The Tribute Book: A Record of the Munificence, Self-Sacrifice and Patriotism of the American People during the War for the Union* (New York: Derby & Miller, 1865). For the larger context of Civil War fund-raising fairs, see Beverly Gordon, *Bazaars and Fair Ladies: The History of the American Fundraising Fair* (Knoxville: University of Tennessee Press, 1998).

56. Mark Hubbard, ed., *Illinois's War: The Civil War in Documents* (Athens: Ohio University Press, 2013), 75–76.

57. Bacon and Howland, *My Heart toward Home*, 34.

58. Livermore, *My Story of the War*, 129.

59. George M. Fredrickson, *The Inner Civil War: Northern Intellectuals and the Crisis of the Union* (New York: Harper & Row, Publishers, 1965; Urbana: University of Illinois Press, 1993), 98–112.

60. David A. Raney, "In the Lord's Army: The United States Christian Commission, Soldiers, and the Union War Effort," in *Union Soldiers and the Northern Home Front: Wartime Experiences, Postwar Adjustments*, ed. Paul A. Cimbala and Randall M. Miller (New York: Fordham University Press, 2002), 263–92; Michael J. Bennett, "Saving Jack: Religion, Benevolent Organizations, and Union Sailors during the Civil War," in ibid., 253–62.

61. Phillip Shaw Paludan, *"A People's Contest": The Union and Civil War, 1861–1865* (New York: Harper and Row, 1988), 352–54; William Quentin Maxwell, *Lincoln's Fifth Wheel: The Political History of the United States Sanitary Commission* (New York: Longmans, Green & Co., 1956), 297.

62. Russell L. Johnson, *Warriors into Workers: The Civil War and the Formation of Urban-Industrial Society in a Northern City* (New York: Fordham University Press, 2003), 249.

63. Attie, *Patriotic Toil*, 95.

64. Marilyn Mayer Culpepper, ed., *Trials and Triumphs: The Women of the American Civil War* (East Lansing: Michigan State University Press, 1991), 252.

65. Livermore, *My Story of the War*, 144–45.

66. James Marten, *The Children's Civil War* (Chapel Hill: University of North Carolina Press, 1998), 180–85; Gordon, *Bazaars and Fair Ladies*, 98–99.

67. Attie, *Patriotic Toil*, 3.

68. Judith Ann Giesberg, *Civil War Sisterhood: The U.S. Sanitary Commission and Women's Politics in Transition* (Boston: Northeastern University Press, 2000), 71.

69. Gordon, *Bazaars and Fair Ladies*, 9–11.

70. Circular, January 6, 1864, Soldiers' Aid Society of Northern Ohio (quotations); H. M. Chapin, Mary G. Brayton and Ellent T. Terry to Mrs. Samuel Colt, January 29, 1864, Samuel Colt Papers, 1856–1864, Connecticut Historical Society, Hartford, CT.

71. Theodore J. Karamanski, *Rally 'Round the Flag: Chicago and the Civil War* (Chicago: Nelson-Hall, 1993), 127–32.

72. Gordon, *Bazaars and Fair Ladies*, 66–72 for estimates of amounts raised as well as the various aspects of the more important Civil War fund-raising fairs.

73. David D. Van Tassel, with John Vacha, *"Behind Bayonets": The Civil War in Northern Ohio* (Kent, OH: Kent State University Press, 2006), 74–78.

74. White, *A Philadelphia Perspective*, 224–25.

75. Ibid., 225.

76. Melinda Lawson, *Patriotic Fires: Forging a New American Nationalism in the Civil War North* (Lawrence: University Press of Kansas, 2002), 14–39.

77. Paul A. Cimbala, "Mary Ann Shadd Cary and Black Abolitionism," in *Against the Tide: Women Reformers in American Society*, ed. Paul A. Cimbala and Randall M. Miller (Westport, CT: Praeger, 1997), 34–36; Dorothy Sterling, ed., *We are Your Sisters: Black Women in the Nineteenth Century* (New York: W. W. Norton & Company, 1984), 250, 256–58.

78. Nina Silber, *Daughters of the Union: Northern Women Fight the Civil War* (Cambridge, MA: Harvard University Press, 2005), 143–60.

79. Elder, *Love amid the Turmoil*, 15, 184, 216.

80. Attie, *Patriotic Toil*, 94–194, 218–19; Silber, *Daughters of the Union*, 178–93.

81. Livermore, *My Story of the War*, 435–36.

82. Giesberg, *Civil War Sisterhood*, 53–84.

CHAPTER EIGHT

1. James I. Robertson Jr., ed., *The Civil War Letters of General Robert McAllister* (Baton Rouge: Louisiana State University Press, 1965, 1998), 257.

2. Jeffrey D. Marshall, ed., *A War of the People: Vermont Civil War Letters* (Hanover, NH: University Press of New England, 1999), 262, 267–70.

3. Quoted in Frank L. Klement, *Wisconsin in the Civil War: The Home Front and the Battle Front, 1861–1865* (Madison: State Historical Society of Wisconsin, 2001), 32.

4. Ibid., 31–34, 33 (quotation).

5. Kenneth Carley, *Minnesota in the Civil War: An Illustrated History* (Minneapolis: Ross & Haines, 1961; St. Paul: Minnesota Historical Society Press, 2000), 78–79. For campaigns of one regiment before being sent south to fight Confederates, see Michael A. Eggleston, *The Tenth Minnesota Volunteers, 1862–1865: A History of Action in the Sioux Uprising and the Civil War, with a Regimental Roster* (Jefferson, NC: McFarland and Company, 2012), 11–75.

6. A. Konstam, *American Civil War Fortifications (1): Coastal Brick and Stone Forts*, illustrated by D. Spedaliere and S. S. Spedaliere (Oxford, UK: Osprey Publishing, 2003), 21.

7. William Gillette, *Jersey Blue: Civil War Politics in New Jersey, 1854–1865* (New Brunswick, NJ: Rutgers University Press, 1995), 174–76, 232, 273; Joseph Williamson, *History of the City of Belfast in the State of Maine, From its First Settlement in 1770 to 1875* (Portland, ME: Loring, Short, and Harmon, 1877), 486; Thomas H. O'Connor, *Civil War Boston: Home Front and Battlefield* (Boston: Northeastern University Press, 1997), 64–65; William Schouler, *Massachusetts in the Civil War* (Boston: E. P. Dutton & Co., 1868; Scituate,

MA: Digital Scanning Inc., 2003), 491–95; Edward K. Spann, *Gotham at War: New York City, 1860–1865* (Wilmington, DE: SR Books, 2002), 158.

8. Pearl T. Ponce, ed., *Kansas's Civil War: The Civil War in Documents* (Athens: Ohio University Press, 2011), 62.

9. Daniel E. Sutherland, *A Savage Conflict: The Decisive Role of Guerrillas in the American Civil War* (Chapel Hill: University of North Carolina Press, 2009), 11–12, 16, 23–24, 193–94.

10. Ponce, *Kansas's Civil War*, 122, 123.

11. Sutherland, *A Savage Conflict*, 193; Albert Castel, *Civil War Kansas: Reaping the Whirlwind*, authorized edition (Lawrence: University Press of Kansas, 1997), 124–41; Silvana R. Siddali, ed., *Missouri's War: The Civil War in Documents* (Athens: Ohio University Press, 2009), passim.

12. Ponce, *Kansas's Civil War*, 127–30, 137–38.

13. Sutherland, *A Savage Conflict*, 193–204.

14. Maria Lydig Daly, *Diary of a Union Lady, 1861–1865*, ed., Harold Earl Hammond (New York: Funk and Wagnalls Co., 1962; Lincoln: University of Nebraska Press, 2000), 171; J.B. Jones, *A Rebel War Clerk's Diary: At the Confederate States Capital*, Vol. 1: *April 1861–July 1863*, ed. James I. Robertson Jr. (Lawrence: University Press of Kansas, 2015), 136.

15. Christine Dee, ed., *Ohio's War: The Civil War in Documents* (Athens: Ohio University Press, 2006), 86–87; Eugene H. Rosenboom, *Civil War Era, 1850–1873*, Vol. 4 in *The History of the State of Ohio*, ed. Carl Wittke (Columbus: Ohio State Archaeological and Historical Society, 1944), 398–99.

16. Steven E. Woodworth, *Decision in the Heartland: The Civil War in the West* (Westport, CT: Praeger, 2008), 37–40.

17. Stephen W. Sears, *Landscape Turned Red: The Battle of Antietam* (New Haven, CT: Ticknor & Fields, 1983).

18. For a complete but compact treatment of the Gettysburg campaign, see Steven E. Woodworth, *Beneath a Northern Sky: A Short History of the Gettysburg Campaign* (Wilmington, DE: SR Books, 2003).

19. William J. Miller, *Civil War City: Harrisburg, Pennsylvania, 1861–1865* (Shippensburg, PA: White Mane Publishing, 1990), 77, 111–12, 115–16, 185–86 (quotation on p. 112). See the front material of this book for a map of Pennsylvania with Harrisburg as the hub through which railroads connected Pittsburgh and Philadelphia as well northward to Scranton in northeastern Pennsylvania and to Elmira across the border in New York.

20. Mark A. Snell, "'If They Would Know What I Know It Would Be Pretty Hard to Raise One Company in York': Recruiting, the Draft, and Society's Response in York County, Pennsylvania, 1861–1865," in *Union Soldiers and the Northern Home Front: Wartime Experiences, Postwar Adjustments*, ed. Paul A. Cimbala and Randall M. Miller (New York: Fordham University Press, 2002), 95–97; Stephen W. Sears, *Gettysburg* (New York: Houghton Mifflin Company, 2003), 113–14. Entry for June 14, 1863, William Heyser Diary, The Valley of the Shadow, University of Virginia Library, Charlottesville, VA, http://valley.lib.virginia.edu/papers/FD1004.

21. Entry for June 14, 1863, William Heyser Diary, The Valley of the Shadow, University of Virginia Library, Charlottesville, VA, http://valley.lib.virginia.edu/papers/FD1004.

22. Sears, *Gettysburg*, 112–16; James C. Mohr, ed., *The Cormany Diaries: A Northern Family in the Civil War* (Pittsburgh: University of Pittsburgh Press, 1982), 328–41; Entry for June 24, 1863, William Heyser Diary, The Valley of the Shadow, University of Virginia Library, Charlottesville, VA, http://valley.lib.virginia.edu/papers/FD1004.

23. Kent Masterson Brown, *Retreat from Gettysburg: Lee, Logistics, and the Pennsylvania Campaign* (Chapel Hill: University of North Carolina Press, 2005), 387–90.

24. Margaret S. Creighton, *The Colors of Courage: Gettysburg's Forgotten History: Immigrants, Women, and African Americans in the Civil War's Defining Battle* (New York: Perseus Books Group, 2005), 129–41; Snell, "'If They Would Know What I Know It Would Be Pretty Hard to Raise One Company in York'," 96–97; J. Matthew Gallman with Susan Baker, "Gettysburg's Gettysburg: What the Battle Did to the Borough," in *The Gettysburg Nobody Knows*, ed. Gabor S. Boritt (New York: Oxford University Press, 1997), 144–45; John R. Neff, *Honoring the Civil War Dead: Commemoration and the Problem of Reconciliation* (Lawrence: University Press of Kansas, 2005), 42; Entry for July 7, 1863, William Heyser Diary, The Valley of the Shadow, University of Virginia Library, Charlottesville, VA, http://valley.lib.virginia.edu/papers/FD1004.

25. Creighton, *The Colors of Courage*, 145–62; Gabor Boritt, *The Gettysburg Gospel: The Lincoln Speech that Nobody Knows* (New York: Simon & Schuster, 2006), 32–35.

26. John H. Brinton, *Personal Memoirs of John H. Brinton, Civil War Surgeon, 1861–1865* (Carbondale: Southern Illinois University Press, 1996), 243–45.

27. Mohr, *The Cormany Diaries*, 328–29, 330.

28. Creighton, *The Colors of Courage*, 126–41; Sears, *Gettysburg*, 111–12, 114–15.

29. Creighton, *The Colors of Courage*, 155.

30. For a brief history of the cemetery's development, its dedication, and Lincoln's place in the event, see Gary Wills, *Lincoln at Gettysburg: The Words That Remade America* (New York: Simon and Schuster, 1992), 21–37.

31. Jonathan W. White, ed., *A Philadelphia Perspective: The Civil War Diary of Sidney George Fisher* (New York: Fordham University Press, 2007), 208–9.

32. Hans L. Trefousse, *"First among Equals": Abraham Lincoln's Reputation during His Administration* (New York: Fordham University Press, 2005), 80–81.

33. See Wills, *Lincoln at Gettysburg*, 148–75 for the president's unique rhetorical style. For the significance of Lincoln's address with its connection to the Declaration of Independence and Lincoln's expansive view of liberty, see Boritt, *The Gettysburg Gospel*, 113–23.

34. B. F. Cooling, *Jubal Early's Raid on Washington, 1864* (Baltimore: Nautical & Aviation Publishing Company of America, 1989), 216–20.

35. Thomas Barnhart, George W. Brewer, and H.S. Stoner to members of the Grand and Subordinate Lodges of Pennsylvania, September 15, 1864, The Valley of the Shadow, University of Virginia Library, Charlottesville, VA, http://valley.lib.virginia.edu/papers/F6069.

36. Sutherland, *A Savage Conflict*, 168–70; Roseboom, *The Civil War Era, 1850–1873*, 423–26.

37. Barbara Butler Davis, ed., *Affectionately Yours: The Civil War Home-Front Letters of the Ovid Butler Family* (Indianapolis: Indiana Historical Society Press, 2004), 9–10; Richard F. Nation and Stephen E. Towne, eds., *Indiana's War: The Civil War in Documents* (Athens: Ohio University Press, 2009), 146–48, 152; Emma Lou Thornbrough, *Indiana in the Civil War Era, 1850–1880* (Indianapolis: Indiana Historical Society, 1965, 1995), 203–4; Roseboom, *The Civil War Era*, 423–26; Sutherland, *A Savage Conflict*, 169–70.

38. Henry Steele Commager, ed., *The Civil War Archive: The History of the Civil War in Documents*, rev. and expanded by Erik Bruun ([Indianapolis]: Bobbs-Merrill Co., 1950, 1973; New York: Black Dog and Leventhal Publishers, 2000), 507–10; Eleanor Jones Harvey, *The Civil War and American Art* (Washington, DC: Smithsonian American Art Museum and New Haven, CT: Yale University Press, [2012]), 74–94.

39. Walter D. Kamphoefner and Wolfgang Helbich, eds., and Susan Carter Vogel, trans., *Germans in the Civil War: The Letters They Wrote Home* (Chapel Hill: University of North Carolina Press, 2006), 68.

40. Richard Moe, *The Last Full Measure: The Life and Death of the First Minnesota Volunteers* (New York: Avon Books, 1993), 31.

41. There are numerous volumes of published letters written by soldiers, but for suggestions of what is available, see Paul A. Cimbala, *Soldiers North and South: The Everyday Experiences of the Men Who Fought America's Civil War* (New York: Fordham University Press, 2010), 239–48.

42. Joan Silva Patrakis, *Andover in the Civil War: The Spirit and Sacrifice of a New England Town* (Charleston, SC: The History Press, 2008), 63.

43. White, *A Philadelphia Perspective*, 171–72.

44. Ellen C. Collier, ed., *Letters of a Civil War Soldier: Chandler B. Gillam, 28th New York Volunteers, with Diary of W. L. Hicks* ([—]: Xlibris Corp., 2005), 291; Christian G. Samito, *Commanding Boston's Irish Ninth* (New York: Fordham University Press, 1998), 250–51; Doris Lake Cooper and Wayne L. Cooper, eds., *I Take My Pen in Hand: Civil War Letters of Two Soldiers and Friends: Sidney Lake and Conrad Litt, 100th N.Y. Volunteers, Cp. "C," Buffalo, N.Y.* (Bloomington, IN: AuthorHouse, 2008), 155; James A. Wright, *No More Gallant a Deed: A Civil War Memoir of the First Minnesota Volunteers*, ed. Steven J. Keillor (St. Paul: Minnesota Historical Society Press, 2001), 415–16; W. A. Croffut and John M. Morris, *The Military and Civil History of Connecticut during the War of 1861–65* (New York: Ledyard Bill, 1868), 520–21.

45. O'Connor, *Civil War Boston*, 203.

46. Thomas McManus, "The Battle of Irish Bend," in *The Twenty-fifth Regiment, Connecticut Volunteers in the War of the Rebellion* by George P. Bissell et al. (Rockville, CT: Press of the Rockville Journal, 1913; [Gloucester, UK]: Dodo Press, [2009]), 51.

47. Wright, *No More Gallant a Deed*, 412, 417.

48. Gallman, *Mastering Wartime*, 130; Michael H. Frisch, *Town into City: Springfield, Massachusetts, and the Meaning of Community, 1840–1880* (Cambridge, MA: Harvard University Press, 1972), 58; Theodore J. Karamanski, *Rally 'Round the Flag: Chicago and the Civil War* (Chicago: Nelson-Hall Publishers, 1993), 232; Andrea R. Foroughi, *Go If You Think it Your Duty: A Minnesota Couple's Civil War Letters* (St. Paul: Minnesota Historical Society Press, 2008), 199.

49. Donald C. Elder III, ed., *Love amid the Turmoil: The Civil War Letters of William and Mary Vermilion* (Iowa City: University of Iowa Press, 2003), 134–36, 310–11, 318.

50. John C. Mitchell, *Grand Traverse: The Civil War Era* (Suttons Bay, MI: Suttons Bay Publications, 2011), 313.

51. Charles F. Larimer, ed., *Love and Valor: Intimate Civil War Letters between Captain Jacob and Emeline Ritner* (Western Springs, IL: Sigourney Press, 2000), 294.

52. John Shaw, ed., *Crete and James: Personal Letters of Lucretia and James Garfield* (East Lansing: Michigan State University Press, 1994), 134.

53. *Trenton (New Jersey) Daily State Gazette*, June 6, 1864; *Indianapolis Daily Journal*, September 21, 1864; Stuart Murray, *A Time of War: A Northern Chronicle of the Civil War* (Lee, MA: Berkshire House Publishers, 2001), 277.

54. Robert Garth Scott, ed., *Fallen Leaves: The Civil War Letters of Major Henry Livermore Abbott* (Kent, OH: Kent State University Press, 1991), 254–55.

55. Marshall, *A War of the People*, 277.

56. Gary Laderman, *The Sacred Remains: American Attitudes toward Death, 1799–1883* (New Haven, CT: Yale University Press, 1996), 101.

57. Mohr, *The Cormany Diaries*, 256.

58. Laderman, *The Sacred Remains*, 22–85; John R. Neff, *Honoring the Civil War Dead: Commemoration and the Problem of Reconciliation* (Lawrence: University Press of Kansas, 2005), 22–53. For a complete treatment of death in the Civil War, see Drew Gilpin Faust, *This Republic of Suffering: Death and the American Civil War* (New York: Alfred A. Knopf, 2008).

59. Faust, *This Republic of Suffering*, 17–18; Neff, *Honoring the Civil War Dead*, 51–52.

60. Julie Holcomb, ed., *Southern Sons, Northern Soldiers: The Civil War Letters of the Remley Brothers, 22nd Iowa Infantry* (DeKalb: Northern Illinois University Press, 2004), 74–75.

61. Ibid., 80.

62. Ibid., 161.

63. Laderman, *The Sacred Remains*, 110–12; Neff, *Honoring the Civil War Dead*, 44, 50.

64. Murray, *A Time of War*, 277; Laderman, *The Sacred Remains*, 96–116.

65. Holcomb, *Southern Sons, Northern Soldiers*, 163–64.

66. Ibid., 82.

67. Elder, *Love amid the Turmoil*, 297.

68. Marshall, *A War of the People*, 239.

69. Ibid., 297.

CHAPTER NINE

1. Jennifer L. Weber, *Copperheads: The Rise and Fall of Lincoln's Opponents in the North* (New York: Oxford University Press, 2006), 36–37; Emma Lou Thornbrough, *Indiana in the Civil War Era, 1850–1880* (Indianapolis: Indiana Historical Society, 1977, 1995), 195–96 (quotation).

2. Jeffrey D. Marshall, ed., *A War of the People: Vermont Civil War Letters* (Hanover, NH: University Press of New England, 1999), 155.

3. Ibid., 254–55.

4. Judith Ann Giesberg, "From Harvest to Battlefield: Rural Pennsylvania Women and the U.S. Civil War," *Pennsylvania History*, 72, no. 2 (2005): 169.

5. Quoted in Rachel Filene Seidman, "A Monstrous Doctrine?: Northern Women on Dependency during the Civil War," in *An Uncommon Time: The Civil War and the Northern Home Front*, ed. Paul A. Cimbala and Randall M. Miller (New York: Fordham University Press, 2002), 184–85.

6. Walter D. Kamphoefner and Wolfgang Helbich, eds., and Susan Carter Vogel, trans., *Germans in the Civil War: The Letters They Wrote Home* (Chapel Hill: University of North Carolina Press, 2006), 63.

7. Ibid., 72.

8. R. Douglas Hurt, *Food and Agriculture during the Civil War* (Santa Barbara, CA: Praeger, 2016), 8; Heather Cox Richardson, *The Greatest Nation of the Earth: Republican Economic Policies during the Civil War* (Cambridge, MA: Harvard University Press, 1997), 46–47.

9. James M. McPherson, *Battle Cry of Freedom: The Civil War* (New York: Oxford University Press, 1998), 443.

10. David Ames Wells, *Our Burden and Our Strength, or, A Comprehensive and Popular Examination of the Debt and Resources of Our Country, Present and Prospective (Loyal Publication Society No. 54)*, New York, 1864, in Frank Freidel, ed., *Union Pamphlets of the Civil War, 1861–1865*, 2 vols. (Cambridge, MA: Belknap Press of Harvard University Press, 1967), 2:940–74, 973 (quotation).

11. Kamphoefner and Helbich, *Germans in the Civil War*, 238.

12. Richardson's *The Greatest Nation of the Earth* provides the best recent study of the Republican government's fiscal and monetary policies.

13. Bray Hammond, *Sovereignty and an Empty Purse: Banks and Politics in the Civil War* (Princeton, NJ: Princeton University Press, 1970), 359.

14. F.W. Taussig, *The Tariff History of the United States* (1931, New York: Capricorn Books, 1964), 158–70; and especially Richardson, *The Greatest Nation of the Earth*, 103–38. On Union tariff policy, see also Jane Flaherty, *The Revenue Imperative* (New York: Pickering and Chatto, 2009).

15. Sidney Ratner, *Taxation and Democracy in America* (New York: Wiley, 1967), 78, 88–89; Emerson D. Fite, *Social and Industrial Conditions in the North during the Civil War* (New York: Macmillan Co., 1910; New York: Peter Smith, 1930), 158; Phillip Shaw Paludan, *"A People's Contest": The Union and Civil War, 1861–1865*, 2nd ed. (Lawrence: University Press of Kansas, 1996), 121; Richardson, *Greatest Nation of the Earth*, 122–26, 136–38.

16. On various taxes, see Ratner, *Taxation and Democracy in America*, 61–64 and passim; Robert Franklin Bensel, *Yankee Leviathan: The Origins of Central State Authority in America, 1859–1877* (Cambridge, UK: Cambridge University Press, 1990), 168; Leonard P. Curry, *Blueprint for Modern America: Nonmilitary Legislation of the First Civil War Congress* (Nashville: Vanderbilt University Press, 1968), 149–80; Paludan, *"A People's Contest,"* 117–21; Steven R. Weisman, *The Great Tax Wars: Lincoln to Wilson—The Fierce Battles over Money and Power that Transformed the Nation* (New York: Simon and Schuster, 2002), 84–91 (quotation on p. 84). The income tax was repealed in 1872, and most of the excise taxes were eliminated after the war.

17. Hubert H. Wubben, *Civil War Iowa and the Copperhead Movement* (Ames: Iowa State University Press, 1980), 188–89 (quotation on p. 189).

18. Weisman, *The Great Tax Wars*, 91.

19. Melinda Lawson, "Let the Nation Be Your Bank: The Civil War Bond Drives and the Construction of National Patriotism," in Cimbala and Miller, *An Uncommon Time*, 90–119.

20. Mark Thornton and Robert B. Ekelund Jr., *Tariffs, Blockades, and Inflation: The Economics of the Civil War* (Wilmington, DE: SR Books, 2004), 60–65.

21. Curry, *Blueprint for Modern America*, 181–206; Paludan, *"A People's Contest,"* 111; and Jane Flaherty, "'The Exhausted Condition of the Treasury' on the Eve of the Civil War," *Civil War History* 55 (June 2009): 244–77.

22. Quoted in Gabor S. Boritt, *Lincoln and the Economics of the American Dream* (Urbana: University of Illinois Press, 1978, 1994), 208.

23. Bray Hammond, *Banks and Politics in America: From the Revolution to the Civil War* (Princeton, NJ: Princeton University Press, 1957), 727–32; Richardson, *The Greatest Nation of the Earth*, 66–102. On the connections between money and people's trust, see Stephen Mihm, *A Nation of Counterfeiters: Capitalists, Con Men, and the Making of the United States* (Cambridge, MA: Harvard University Press, 2007).

24. Roy P. Basler, ed., *The Collected Works of Abraham Lincoln*, 9 vols. (New Brunswick, NJ: Rutgers University Press, 1953), 5:522.

25. Ray Allen Billington, *Westward Expansion: A History of the Western Frontier*, 4th ed. (New York: Macmillan, 1974), 538–39; Richardson, *Greatest Nation of the Earth*, 193–95; telegram from the governor of Colorado to Abraham Lincoln, October 1863, quoted in ibid., 194.

26. Richardson, *Greatest Nation of the Earth*, 195–208.

27. Richard N. Current, *The History of Wisconsin*, Vol. 2: *The Civil War Era, 1848–1873* (Madison: State Historical Society of Wisconsin, 1976), 296–97.

28. Marshall, *A War of the People*, 155, n.2.

29. William Gillette, *Jersey Blue: Civil War Politics in New Jersey, 1854–1865* (New Brunswick, NJ: Rutgers University Press, 1995), 232, 254.

30. John Niven, *Connecticut for the Union: The Role of the State in the Civil War* (New Haven, CT: Yale University Press, 1965), 408–26.

31. Robin L. Einhorn, "The Civil War and Municipal Government in Chicago," in *Toward a Social History of the American Civil War: Exploratory Essays*, ed. Maris A. Vinovskis (Cambridge, UK: Cambridge University Press, 1990), 128–29.

32. Susan Sessions Rugh, *Our Common Country: Family Farming, Culture, and Community in the Nineteenth-Century Midwest* (Bloomington: Indiana University Press, 2001), 113.

33. Paul J. Ledman, *A Maine Town Responds: Cape Elizabeth and South Portland in the Civil War* (Cape Elizabeth, ME: Next Steps Publishing, 2003), 191.

34. Ibid., 195; Don Harrison Doyle, *The Social Order of a Frontier Community: Jacksonville, Illinois, 1825–70* (Urbana: University of Illinois Press, 1978), 211.

35. Ledman, *A Maine Town Responds*, 197–98.

36. Earl F. Mulderink III, *New Bedford's Civil War* (New York: Fordham University Press, 2012), 167–68, 172–73. Mulderink provides arguably the most detailed account of how the war influenced spending and government choices in one municipality.

37. David V. Mollenhoff, *Madison: A History of the Formative Years*, 2nd ed. (Madison: University of Wisconsin Press, 2003), 106.

38. Current, *The History of Wisconsin*, 2:397.

39. Michael H. Frisch, *Town into City: Springfield, Massachusetts, and the Meaning of Community, 1840–1880* (Cambridge, MA: Harvard University Press, 1972), 109–12.

40. Mulderink, *New Bedford's Civil War*, 179–80.

41. Kyle S. Sinisi, *Sacred Debts: State Civil War Claims and American Federalism, 1861–1880* (New York: Fordham University Press, 2003).

42. James E. Brown, "Guns and Butter: How Connecticut Financed the Civil War," in *Inside Connecticut and the Civil War: Essays on One State's Struggles*, ed. Matthew Warshauer (Middletown, CT: Wesleyan University Press, 2014), 27.

43. Mulderink, *New Bedford's Civil War*, 181–82 (quotation on p. 182).

44. Christine Dee, ed., *Ohio's War: The Civil War in Documents* (Athens: Ohio University Press, 2006), 184–85.

45. Grace Palladino, *Another Civil War: Labor, Capital, and the State in the Anthracite Regions of Pennsylvania, 1840–1868* (Urbana: University of Illinois Press, 1990), 88.

46. "The Home of the American Citizen after the Tax Bill Has Passed," *Frank Leslie's Illustrated Newspaper*, July 19, 1862, p. 272 (https://archive.org/stream/franklesliesilluv1314lesl#page/272/mode/2up).

47. Timothy Shay Arthur, *Growler's Income Tax. (Loyal Publication Society, No. 57)*, New York, 1864, in Freidel, ed., *Union Pamphlets of the Civil War, 1861–1865*, 2:975–80.

48. George Templeton Strong, *Diary of the Civil War, 1860–1865*, ed. Allan Nevins (New York: The Macmillan Company, 1962), 201.

49. Nina Silber and Mary Beth Sievens, eds. *Yankee Correspondence: Civil War Letters between New England Soldiers and the Home Front* (Charlottesville: University Press of Virginia, 1996), 59.

50. Strong, *Diary of the Civil War*, 201.

51. George Winston Smith and Charles Judah, *Life in the North during the Civil War: A Source History* (Albuquerque: University of New Mexico Press, 1966), 198–99.

52. Robert F. Engs and Corey M. Brooks, eds., *Their Patriotic Duty: The Civil War Letters of the Evans Family of Brown County, Ohio* (New York: Fordham University Press, 2007), 121.

53. Hammond, *Sovereignty and an Empty Purse*, 307.

54. Donald C. Elder III, ed., *Love amid the Turmoil: The Civil War Letters of William and Mary Vermilion* (Iowa City: University of Iowa Press, 2003), 119.

55. Thornton and Ekelund, *Tariffs, Blockades, and Inflation*, 68–72; McPherson, *Battle Cry of Freedom*, 447.

56. Throughout his book *Lincoln and the Economics of the American Dream*, Gabor S. Boritt describes Lincoln's continued beliefs in the Whig principles of an active government in service of the people's needs.

57. See the speech of Richard Yates made at a Republican meeting in June 1860 reprinted in Mark Hubbard, ed., *Illinois's War: The Civil War in Documents* (Athens: Ohio University Press, 2013), 50–52.

58. Winifred Gallagher, *How the Post Office Created America: A History* (New York: Penguin, 2016), 150–51.

59. Justin Martin, *Genius of Place: The Life of Frederick Law Olmsted* (Boston: Da Capo Press, 2011, 2012), 232–53; Adam Wesley Dean, *An Agrarian Republic: Farming, Antislavery Politics, and Nature Parks in the Civil War Era* (Chapel Hill: University of North Carolina Press, 2015), 108–32.

60. Jocelyn Wills, *Boosters, Hustlers, and Speculators: Entrepreneurial Culture and the Rise of Minneapolis and St. Paul, 1849–1883* (St. Paul: Minnesota Historical Society Press, 2005), 108–109.

61. Dean, *An Agrarian Republic*, 99.

62. Ray Allen Billington and Martin Ridge, *Westward Expansion: A History of the American Frontier*, 6th ed., abridged (Albuquerque: University of New Mexico Press, 2001), 350.

63. Current, *The History of Wisconsin*, 2:436.

64. Paul W. Gates, *Agriculture and the Civil War* (New York: Alfred A. Knopf, 1965), 284–94.

65. Boritt, *Lincoln and the Economics of the American Dream*, 217.

66. Hurt, *Food and Agriculture during the Civil War*, 55; Richardson, *The Greatest Nation of the Earth*, 139–49; Michael S. Green, *Freedom, Union, and Power: Lincoln and His Party during the Civil War* (New York: Fordham University Press, 2004), 308–309 (quotation).

67. Phillip Shaw Paludan, *The Presidency of Abraham Lincoln* (Lawrence: University Press of Kansas, 1994), 135.

68. Allan Nevins, *The War for the Union*, Vol. 2: *War Becomes Revolution* (New York: Charles Scribner's Sons, 1960), 207; Richardson, *The Greatest Nation of the Earth*, 154–60. States with no or little federal public lands received scrip to be sold. The act also provided for distributions to future states, which later allowed Southern states to benefit from the Union wartime measure. Postwar sale of the scrip proved to be a disappointment, as speculators purchased it at discounted rates. See Paludan, *"A People's Contest,"* 131–32; Emma Lou Thornbrough, *Indiana in the Civil War Era, 1850–1880* (Indianapolis: Indiana Historical Society, 1965, 1995), 526–27.

69. Curry, *Blueprint for Modern America*, 116–36. For the quotation from the *American Railroad Journal*, June 28, 1862, see Richardson, *Greatest Nation of the Earth*, 187.

70. For additional discussion of the transcontinental railroad legislation and policy, see Richardson, *Greatest Nation of the Earth*, 170–208; John F. Stover, *American Railroads* (Chicago: University of Chicago Press, 1961), 67–73.

CHAPTER TEN

1. William Gillette, *Jersey Blue: Civil War Politics in New Jersey, 1854–1865* (New Brunswick, NJ: Rutgers University Press, 1995), 176.

2. R. Douglas Hurt, "The Agricultural Power of the Midwest during the Civil War," in *Union Heartland: The Midwestern Home Front during the Civil War*, ed. Ginette Aley and J.L. Anderson (Carbondale: Southern Illinois University Press, 2013), 70, 74.

3. J. Matthew Gallman, *Mastering Wartime: A Social History of Philadelphia during the Civil War* (Cambridge, UK: Cambridge University Press, 1990), 225.

4. George Winston Smith and Charles Judah, *Life in the North during the Civil War: A Source History* (Albuquerque: University of New Mexico Press, 1966), 170–71.

5. Gillette, *Jersey Blue*, 172.

6. Gallman, *Mastering Wartime*, 224.

7. Edward K. Spann, *Gotham at War: New York City 1860–1865* (Wilmington, DE: SR Books, 2002), 137.

8. Christian Wolmar, *The Great Railroad Revolution: The History of Trains in America* (New York: Public Affairs, 2012), 121–22.

9. Walter D. Kamphoefner and Wolfgang Helbich, eds., and Susan Carter Vogel, trans., *Germans in the Civil War: The Letters They Wrote Home* (Chapel Hill: University of North Carolina Press, 2006), 69, 70.

10. Richard L. Kiper, ed., *Dear Catharine, Dear Taylor: The Civil War Letters of a Union Soldier and His Wife* (Lawrence: University Press of Kansas, 2002), 92.

11. Ibid.

12. Kamphoefner and Helbich, *Germans in the Civil War*, 69.

13. James M. McPherson, *Battle Cry of Freedom: The Civil War Era* (New York: Oxford University Press, 1988), 447.

14. *American Railroad Journal* 37 (October 8, 1864), 989; Smith and Judah, *Life in the North during the Civil War*, 211.

15. Phillip Shaw Paludan, *The Presidency of Abraham Lincoln* (Lawrence: University Press of Kansas, 1994), 216; Wolmar, *The Great Railroad Revolution*, 122.

16. Roy P. Basler, ed., *The Collected Works of Abraham Lincoln*, 9 vols. (New Brunswick, NJ: Rutgers University Press, 1953), 8:151.

17. Kenneth N. Metcalf and Lewis Beeson, *Effects of the Civil War on Manufacturing in Michigan* (Lansing: Michigan Civil War Centennial Observance Commission, 1966), 5.

18. Richard N. Current, *The History of Wisconsin*, Vol. 2: *The Civil War Era, 1848–1873* (Madison: State Historical Society of Wisconsin, 1976), 376.

19. Paul W. Gates, *Agriculture and the Civil War* (New York: Alfred A. Knopf, 1965), 224–27. On the uncertainty of the diplomatic impact of Northern agricultural products and European powers, see R. Douglas Hurt, *Food and Agriculture during the Civil War* (Santa Barbara, CA: Praeger, 2016), 19.

20. For a general view of agriculture in the North during the war years, see appropriate chapters in Gates, *Agriculture and the Civil War*; Hurt, *Food and Agriculture during the Civil War*; and Fred A. Shannon, *The Farmer's Last Frontier: Agriculture, 1860–1897* (New York: Farrar and Rinehart, 1945; Armonk, NY: M.E. Sharpe, 1973).

21. Jonathan W. White, ed., *A Philadelphia Perspective: The Civil War Diary of Sidney George Fisher* (New York: Fordham University Press, 2007), 174.

22. Mary A. Livermore, *My Story of the War: A Woman's Narrative of Four Years Personal Experience* (Hartford, CT: A.D. Worthington and Co., 1887; New York: Da Capo Press, 1995), 145–46.

23. Richard F. Nation and Stephen E. Towne, eds., *Indiana's Civil War: The Civil War in Documents* (Athens: Ohio University Press, 2009), 95.

24. Robert F. Harris and John Niflot, eds., *Dear Sister: The Civil War Letters of the Brothers Gould* (Westport, CT: Praeger, 1998), xiii–xv.

25. Robert F. Engs and Corey M. Brooks, eds., *Their Patriotic Duty; The Civil War Letters of the Evans Family of Brown County, Ohio* (New York: Fordham University Press, 2007), xxii, 227, 233.

26. Richard F. Nation, *At Home in the Hoosier Hills: Agriculture, Politics, and Religion in Southern Indiana, 1810–1870* (Bloomington: Indiana University Press, 2005), 105.

27. Anna Howard Shaw, *The Story of a Pioneer* (New York: Harper and Brothers, 1915), 27, 31, 53.

28. Ibid., 27, 51, 52–54.

29. Quoted in Scott Nelson and Carol Sheriff, *A People at War: Civilians and Soldiers in America's Civil War* (New York: Oxford University Press, 2007), 231–32.

30. Hurt, *Food and Agriculture during Civil War*, 120–21.

31. Gates, *Agriculture and the Civil War*, 229.

32. Gillette, *Jersey Blue*, 161.

33. Pearl T. Ponce, ed., *Kansas's War: The Civil War in Documents* (Athens: Ohio University Press, 2011), 217.

34. Kamphoefner and Helbich, *Germans in the Civil War*, 283.

35. Ponce, *Kansas's War*, 217.

36. Gates, *Agriculture and the Civil War*, 241–42; Phillip Shaw Paludan, *"A People's Contest": The Union and the Civil War*, 2nd ed. (Lawrence: University Press of Kansas, 1996), 162; Hurt, *Food and Agriculture during the Civil War*, 157.

37. Kamphoefner and Helbich, *Germans in the Civil War*, 67.

38. Susanna Ural Bruce, *The Harp and the Eagle: Irish-American Volunteers and the Union Army, 1861–1865* (New York: New York University Press, 2006), 197–201.

39. Gates, *Agriculture and the Civil War*, 241.

40. Kamphoefner and Helbich, *Germans in the Civil War*, 283.

41. Paludan, *"A People's Contest,"* 156.

42. Smith and Judah, *Life in the North during the Civil War*, 167.

43. Hurt, *Food and Agriculture during the Civil War*, 51.

44. Quoted in Gates, *Agriculture and the Civil War*, 234.

45. Smith and Judah, *Life in the North during the Civil War*, 168.

46. Gates, *Agriculture and the Civil War*, 239.

47. Hurt, *Food and Agriculture during the Civil War*, 85.

48. Livermore, *My Story of the War*, 148–49.

49. Ibid., 149.

50. Gates, *Agriculture and the Civil War*, 242–43.

51. Susan Sessions Rugh, *Our Common Country: Family Farming, Culture, and Community in the Nineteenth-Century Midwest* (Bloomington: Indiana University Press, 2001), 114 (quotation); Hurt, *Food and Agriculture during the Civil War*, 87.

52. For the illustration, see Hurt, *Food and Agriculture during the Civil War*, 87.

53. Barbara Butler Davis, ed., *Affectionately Yours: The Civil War Home-Front Letters of the Ovid Butler Family* (Indianapolis: Indiana Historical Society Press, 2004), 106, 175.

54. Gates, *Agriculture and the Civil War*, 228.

55. Hurt, *Food and Agriculture during the Civil War*, 121–22; Gates, *Agriculture and the Civil War*, 233.

56. Paludan, *"A People's Contest,"* 170–81.

57. Paludan, *The Presidency of Abraham Lincoln*, 211.

58. Nina Silber and Mary Beth Sievens, eds., *Yankee Correspondence: Civil War Letters between New England Soldiers and the Home Front* (Charlottesville: University Press of Virginia, 1996), 139.

59. Mark A. Lause, *Free Labor: The Civil War and the Making of an American Working Class* (Urbana: University of Illinois Press, 2015), 42–43.

60. David Montgomery, *Beyond Equality: Labor and the Radical Republicans, 1862–1872* (New York: Random House, Vintage ed., 1967), 93; Lause, *Free Labor*, 48–51.

61. Grace Palladino, *Another Civil War: Labor, Capital, and the State in the Anthracite Regions of Pennsylvania, 1840–68* (Urbana: University of Illinois Press, 1990), 85–86.

62. Walter Licht, *Working for the Railroad: The Organization of Work in the Nineteenth Century* (Princeton, NJ: Princeton University Press, 1983), 69–70, 128, 145.

63. Gillette, *Jersey Blue*, 177.

64. Kamphoefner and Helbich, *Germans in the Civil War*, 67.

65. James M. McPherson, *Ordeal by Fire: The Civil War and Reconstruction*, 3rd ed. (Boston: McGraw Hill, 2001), 406.

66. Nina Silber, *Daughters of the Union: Northern Women Fight the Civil War* (Cambridge, MA: Harvard University Press, 2005), 78–79.

67. Kamphoefner and Helbich, *Germans in the Civil War*, 304.

68. Russell L. Johnson, *Warriors into Workers: The Civil War and the Formation of Urban-Industrial Society in a Northern City* (New York: Fordham University Press, 2003), 95–96.

69. Theodore J. Karamanski and Eileen M. McMahon, eds., *Civil War Chicago: Eyewitness to History* (Athens: Ohio University Press, 2014), 188.

70. Johnson, *Warriors into Workers*, 95–96.

71. Lause, *Free Labor*, 82–84; Judith Ann Giesberg, *Army at Home: Women and the Civil War on the Northern Home Front* (Chapel Hill: University of North Carolina Press, 2009), 68–91.

72. Giesberg, *Army at Home*, 68–72, 78, 89–91, passim; Brian Dirck, "A Succession of Horrors: The Washington Arsenal Fire of June 17, 1864," *Civil War Monitor* 2 (Winter 2012), 47–55 and 76–77.

73. Giesberg, *Army at Home*, 79–89.

74. "The Sewing Women," from *Fincher's Trades' Review*, March 18, 1865, in *A Documentary History of American Industrial Society*, ed. John R. Commons, 10 vols. (Cleveland: Arthur Clarke, 1910), 9:72–73; Mark R. Wilson, *The Business of Civil War: Military Mobilization and the State, 1861–1865* (Baltimore: Johns Hopkins University Press, 2006), 94–98.

75. Lause, *Free Labor*, 86–89.

76. For labor militancy during 1863, see Lause, *Free Labor*, 96–105. On labor unrest, also see Daniel T. Rodgers, *The Work Ethic in Industrial America, 1850–1920* (Chicago: University of Chicago Press, 1978), 30–32; Montgomery, *Beyond Equality*, 90–134.

77. Robert M. Sandow, *Deserter Country: Civil War Opposition in the Pennsylvania Appalachians* (New York: Fordham University Press, 2009), 61–145; Palladino, *Another Civil War,* 95–165; Spann, *Gotham at War,* 150–51.

78. Thomas Weber, *The Northern Railroads in the Civil War, 1861–1865* (New York: Columbia University Press, 1952), 7–17, 152–53, 199–204, 228–32; Allan Nevins, *The War for the Union.* Vol. III: *The Organized War* (New York: Charles Scribner's Sons, 1971), 300–2; Paludan, *"A People's Contest,"* 139–43.

79. Alfred D. Chandler, *The Visible Hand: The Managerial Revolution in American Business* (Cambridge, MA: The Belknap Press of Harvard University Press, 1977), 212, 215–20; Thomas C. Cochran and William Miller, *A Social History of Industrial America,* rev. ed. (New York: Harper & Row, 1961), 115–16. On the use of the telegraph for military and political purposes, see Tom Wheeler, *Mr. Lincoln's T-Mails: How Abraham Lincoln Used the Telegraph to Win the Civil War* (New York: HarperCollins, 2008).

80. Basler, *Collected Works of Abraham Lincoln,* 5:527.

81. Brian R. Harden, et al., *Shore Village Story: An Informal History of Rockland, Maine* (Rockland, ME: Shore Village Historical Society, 1989), 345.

82. Rockland, Maine, *Democrat and Free Press,* November 13, 1861.

83. On the interactions of transportation and communications in developing exchanges, and the centrality of Chicago in that process, see William Cronon, *Nature's Metropolis: Chicago and the Great West* (New York: W.W. Norton & Company, 1991), especially chapters 2–4; and Donald L. Miller, *City of the Century: The Epic of Chicago and the Making of America* (New York: Simon & Schuster, 1996), 91–92, 109–14.

84. Robin L. Einhorn, *Property Rules: Political Economy in Chicago, 1833–1872* (Chicago: University of Chicago Press, 1991), 209–15.

85. Glenn Porter and Harold Livesay, *Merchants and Manufacturers: Studies in the Changing Structure of 19th-Century Manufacturing* (Baltimore: Johns Hopkins University Press, 1971), 116–21.

86. Wilson, *The Business of Civil War,* 5–126.

87. Smith and Judah, *Life in the North during the Civil War,* 195.

88. Jocelyn Wills, *Boosters, Hustlers, and Speculators: Entrepreneurial Culture and the Rise of Minneapolis and St. Paul, 1849–1883* (St. Paul: Minnesota Historical Society Press, 2005), 100–108.

89. Wilson, *The Business of Civil War,* 1.

90. Emerson D. Fite, *Social and Industrial Conditions in the North during the Civil War* (New York: Macmillan Co., 1910; New York: Frederick Ungar Publishing, 1963), 99–104.

91. Joe B. Frantz, *Gail Borden: Dairyman to a Nation* (Norman: University of Oklahoma Press, 1951), 258–61.

92. Quoted in Maury Klein, *The Flowering of the Third America: The Making of an Organizational Society, 1850–1920* (Chicago: Ivan R. Dee, 1993), 37.

93. David McCullough, *Mornings on Horseback* (New York: Simon and Schuster, 1981), 57.

94. On the fear of corruption, see Michael Thomas Smith, *The Enemy Within: Fear of Corruption in the Civil War North* (Charlottesville: University of Virginia Press, 2011).

95. Ibid., 15–17. For the popular perceptions and representations of this problem, see J. Matthew Gallman, *Defining Duty in the Civil War: Personal Choice, Popular Culture, and the Union Home Front* (Chapel Hill: University of North Carolina Press, 2015), 91–122.

96. Smith and Judah, *Life in the North during the Civil War*, 232.

97. Kamphoefner and Helbich, *Germans in the Civil War*, 68.

98. Ibid., 114.

99. White, *A Philadelphia Perspective*, 111.

100. Julie A. Doyle, John David Smith, and Richard M. McMurry, eds., *This Wilderness of War: The Civil War Letters of George W. Squier, Hoosier Volunteer* (Knoxville: University of Tennessee Press, 1998), 20.

101. Julie Holcomb, ed., *Southern Sons, Northern Soldiers: The Civil War Letters of the Remley Brothers, 22nd Iowa Infantry* (DeKalb: Northern Illinois University Press, 2004), 14.

CHAPTER ELEVEN

1. *New York Times*, July 7, 1861.

2. Jean H. Baker, *Affairs of Party: The Political Culture of Northern Democrats in the Mid-Nineteenth Century* (Ithaca, NY: Cornell University Press, 1983; New York: Fordham University Press, 1998), 336–37, 337 (quotation).

3. Jerome Mushkat, *Fernando Wood: A Political Biography* (Kent, OH: Kent State University Press, 1990), 117; Jennifer L. Weber, *Copperheads: The Rise and Fall of Lincoln's Opponents in the North* (New York: Oxford University Press, 2006), 15–16.

4. Richard F. Nation and Stephen E. Towne, eds., *Indiana's War: The Civil War in Documents* (Athens: Ohio University Press, 2009), 128–29.

5. Melinda Lawson, *Patriot Fires: Forging a New American Nationalism in the Civil War North* (Lawrence: University Press of Kansas, 2002), 74–76.

6. Nation and Towne, *Indiana's War*, 130.

7. Mark Hubbard, ed., *Illinois's War: The Civil War in Documents* (Athens: Ohio University Press, 2013), 60; Lawson, *Patriot Fires*, 73.

8. Stephen E. Towne, *Surveillance and Spies in the Civil War: Exposing Confederate Conspiracies in America's Heartland* (Athens: Ohio University Press, 2015), 11–23.

9. Nina Silber and Mary Beth Sievens, eds., *Yankee Correspondence: Civil War Letters between New England Soldiers and the Home Front* (Charlottesville: University Press of Virginia, 1996), 132.

10. Ibid., 113.

11. Quoted in Susannah Ural Bruce, *The Harp and the Eagle: Irish-American Volunteers and the Union Army, 1861–1865* (New York: New York University Press, 2006), 141.

12. Jeffrey D. Marshall, ed., *A War of the People: Vermont Civil War Letters* (Hanover, NH: University Press of New England, 1999), 124.

13. William C. Harris, *Lincoln and the Union Governors* (Carbondale: Southern Illinois University Press, 2013), 87; Weber, *Copperheads*, 68–76.

14. Weber, *Copperheads*, 69; Allen C. Guelzo, *Lincoln's Emancipation Proclamation: The End of Slavery in America* (New York: Simon & Schuster, 2004), 167.

15. William Gillette, *Jersey Blue: Civil War Politics in New Jersey, 1854–1865* (New Brunswick, NJ: Rutgers University Press, 1995), 215–16.

16. Quoted in Michael S. Green, *Freedom, Union, and Power: Lincoln and His Party during the Civil War* (New York: Fordham University Press, 2004), 252.

17. C. Peter Ripley et al., eds., *The Black Abolitionist Papers*, Vol. 5: *The United States, 1859–1865* (Chapel Hill: University of North Carolina Press, 1992), 306.

18. Green, *Freedom, Union, and Power*, 254–55.

19. David Herbert Donald, *Lincoln* (New York: Simon and Schuster, 1995), 502–3; Phillip Shaw Paludan, *The Presidency of Abraham Lincoln* (Lawrence: University Press of Kansas, 1994), 270–71.

20. Donald, *Lincoln*, 505–6.

21. Weber, *Copperheads*, 184–86.

22. Christine Dee, ed., *Ohio's War: The Civil War in Documents* (Athens: Ohio University Press, 2006), 184–85.

23. Joel H. Silbey, *A Respectable Minority: The Democratic Party in the Civil War Era, 1860–1868* (New York: W. W. Norton & Company, Inc., 1977), 137–39.

24. Weber, *Copperheads*, 190–91; Green, *Liberty, Union, and Power*, 261–89.

25. On the election of 1864, see John C. Waugh, *Reelecting Lincoln: The Battle for the 1864 Presidency* (New York: Crown, 1997) and David E. Long, *The Jewel of Liberty: Abraham Lincoln's Re-election and the End of Slavery* (New York: Da Capo, 1997).

26. George Templeton Strong, *Diary of the Civil War, 1860–1865*, ed. Allan Nevins (New York: Macmillan Co., 1962), 511.

27. Maria Lydig Daly, *Diary of a Union Lady, 1861–1865*, ed. Harold Earl Hammond (New York: Funk & Wagnalls Company, 1962), 312.

28. Walter D. Kamphoefner and Wolfgang Helbich, eds., and Susan Carter Vogel, trans., *Germans in the Civil War: The Letters They Wrote Home* (Chapel Hill: University of North Carolina Press, 2006), 278–79.

29. Glenn C. Altschuler and Stuart M. Blumin, *Rude Republic: Americans and Their Politics in the Nineteenth Century* (Princeton, NJ: Princeton University Press, 2000), 47–86; James A. Rawley, *The Politics of Union: Northern Politics during the Civil War* (Lincoln: University of Nebraska Press, 1974); Phillip Shaw Paludan, "War Is the Health of the Party: Republicans in the American Civil War," in *The Birth of the Grand Old Party: The Republicans' First Generation*, ed. Robert F. Engs and Randall M. Miller (Philadelphia: University of Pennsylvania Press, 2002), 60–80; Jon Grinspan, *The Virgin Vote: How Young Americans Made Democracy Social, Politics Personal, and Voting Popular in the Nineteenth Century* (Chapel Hill: University of North Carolina Press, 2016).

30. Gillette, *Jersey Blue*, 284–85.

31. Kamphoefner and Helbich, *Germans in the Civil War*, 278–79.

32. George Winston Smith and Charles Judah, *Life in the North during the Civil War: A Source History* (Albuquerque: University of New Mexico Press, 1966), 112–13.

33. Andrea R. Foroughi, *Go If You Think It Your Duty: A Minnesota Couple's Civil War Letters* (St. Paul: Minnesota Historical Society Press, 2008), 271.

34. For examples of Civil War fare and paraphernalia, see the John McAllister Collection at the Library Company of Philadelphia.

35. James Marten, *The Children's Civil War* (Chapel Hill: University of North Carolina Press, 1998), 153; James Marten, *Children for the Union: The War Spirit on the Northern Home Front* (Chicago: Ivan R. Dee, 2004), 86.

36. Frank L. Byrne, ed., *Uncommon Soldiers: Harvey Reid and the 22nd Wisconsin March with Sherman* (Knoxville: University of Tennessee Press, 2001), 86–87, 90–92.

37. Steven R. Boyd, *Patriotic Envelopes of the Civil War: The Iconography of Union and Confederate Covers* (Baton Rouge: Louisiana State University Press, 2010).

38. Sarah Burns and Daniel Greene, "The Home at War, the War at Home: The Visual Culture of the Northern Home Front," in *Home Front: Daily Life in the Civil War North*, ed. Peter John Brownlee et al. (Chicago: University of Chicago Press, 2013), 1–11.

39. Baker, *Affairs of Party*, 261–316.

40. Gillette, *Jersey Blue*, 235.

41. Bridget Ford, *Bonds of Union: Religion, Race, and Politics in a Civil War Borderland* (Chapel Hill: University of North Carolina Press, 2016), 285–86.

42. Altschuler and Blumin, *Rude Republic*, 173.

43. Jonathan W. White, ed., *A Philadelphia Perspective: The Civil War Diary of Sidney George Fisher* (New York: Fordham University Press, 2007), 179, 185–86.

44. Daniel R. Biddle and Murray Dubin, *Tasting Freedom: Octavius Catto and the Battle for Equality in Civil War America* (Philadelphia: Temple University Press, 2010), 281.

45. Lawson, *Patriot Fires*, 98–116.

46. Frank Freidel, ed., *Union Pamphlets of the Civil War, 1861–1865*, 2 vols. (Cambridge, MA: Belknap Press of Harvard University Press, 1967), 1:5.

47. Ibid.

48. Barbara J. Mitnick, "The Union League and the War to Preserve the Union," in *The Union League of Philadelphia: The First One Hundred and Fifty Years*, ed. Barbara J. Mitnick (Philadelphia: The Abraham Lincoln Foundation of the Union League of Philadelphia, 2012), 61–67.

49. Hubbard, *Illinois's War*, 110–11, 111 (quotation); Karamanski, *Rally 'Round the Flag*, 208; Weber, *Copperheads*, 184–85.

50. Gillette, *Jersey Blue*, 286.

51. Towne, *Surveillance and Spies in the Civil War*, 14–15.

52. Weber, *Copperheads*, 24–27, 49, 54–55, 80–81, 92–93, 94 (quotation), 128–30.

53. Nation and Towne, *Indiana's War*, 157–59.

54. Ibid., 145.

55. Emma Lou Thornbrough, *Indiana in the Civil War Era, 1850–1880* (Indianapolis: Indiana Historical Society, 1965, 1995), 117–19, 117–18 (quotations).

56. Brett Barker, "Limiting Dissent in the Midwest: Ohio Republicans' Attacks on the Democratic Press," in *Union Heartland: The Midwestern Home Front during the Civil War*, ed. Ginette Aley and J.L. Anderson (Carbondale: Southern Illinois University Press, 2013), 169–187; Dee, *Ohio's War*, 90.

57. Michael J. Connolly, "'Irresistible Outbreaks against Tories and Traitors': The Suppression of New England Antiwar Sentiment in 1861," in *The Battlefield and Beyond: Essays*

on the American Civil War, ed. Clayton E. Jewett (Baton Rouge: Louisiana State University Press, 2012), 173–95.

58. Thornbrough, *Indiana in the Civil War Era*, 117–19, 117–18 (quotations).

59. Donald C. Elder III, ed., *Love amid the Turmoil: The Civil War Letters of William and Mary Vermilion* (Iowa City: University of Iowa Press, 2005), 142.

60. Towne, *Spies and Surveillance*, 15.

61. Robert F. Engs and Corey M. Brooks, eds., *Their Patriotic Duty: The Civil War Letters of the Evans Family of Brown County, Ohio* (New York: Fordham University Press, 2007), xviii–xix, 287–89, 294, 298, 389–91.

62. Marten, *The Children's Civil War*, 153.

63. Nation and Towne, *Indiana's War*, 161–62.

64. Towne, *Surveillance and Spies in the Civil War*, 15–19.

65. Silber and Sievens, *Yankee Correspondence*, 155.

66. Charles F. Larimer, ed., *Love and Valor: Intimate Civil War Letters between Captain Jacob and Emeline Ritner* (Western Springs, IL: Sigourney Press, 2000), 294.

67. Niven, *Connecticut for the Union*, 301.

68. Nation and Towne, *Indiana's War*, 159.

69. Ibid.

70. On the interrelationship of politics and religion, see George C. Rable, *God's Almost Chosen Peoples: A Religious History of the American Civil War* (Chapel Hill: University of North Carolina Press, 2010); Timothy L. Wesley, *The Politics of Faith during the Civil War* (Baton Rouge: Louisiana State University Press, 2013); and Sean A. Scott, *A Visitation of God: Northern Civilians Interpret the Civil War* (New York: Oxford University Press, 2011).

71. Gillette, *Jersey Blue*, 135 (and quotation).

72. Hubert H. Wubben, *Civil War Iowa and the Copperhead Movement* (Ames: Iowa State University Press, 1980), 176; William B. Kurtz, *Excommunicated from the Union: How the Civil War Created a Separate Catholic America* (New York: Fordham University Press, 2016), 27–128; Bruce, *The Harp and the Eagle*, 136–40.

73. Kurtz, *Excommunicated from the Union*, 108–28.

74. Scott, *A Visitation of God*, 100.

75. Wubben, *Civil War Iowa and the Copperhead Movement*, 176.

76. Dee, *Ohio's War*, 51.

77. On African Americans and their churches before the war, see Leon F. Litwack, *North of Slavery: The Negro in the Free States, 1790–1860* (Chicago: University of Chicago Press, 1961, 1965), 188–213.

78. Robert J. Miller, *Both Prayed to the Same God: Religion and Faith in the American Civil War* (Lanham, MD: Lexington Books, 2007), 78; Matthew Warshauer, *Connecticut in the American Civil War: Slavery, Sacrifice, and Survival* (Middletown, CT: Wesleyan University Press, 2011), 103; Ripley et al., *The Black Abolitionist Papers*, 5:304.

79. Hubbard, *Illinois's War*, 92.

80. Quoted in Rable, *God's Almost Chosen Peoples*, 295.

81. Gillette, *Jersey Blue*, 210.

82. Quoted in William A. Blair, *With Malice toward Some: Treason and Loyalty in the Civil War Era* (Chapel Hill: University of North Carolina Press, 2014), 63.

83. Quoted in William Warren Sweet, *Methodism in American History* (New York: Abington Press, 1961), 120–21.

84. James Moorhead, *American Apocalypse: Yankee Protestants and the Civil War 1860–1869* (New Haven, CT: Yale University Press, 1978), 152–53.

85. Scott, *A Visitation from God*, 110.

86. Quoted in Wubben, *Civil War Iowa and the Copperhead Movement*, 177.

87. Wesley, *The Politics of Faith during the Civil War*, 38–40, 39 (quotation).

88. Ibid., 43–59.

89. Bryon C. Andreasen, "Civil War Church Trials: Repressing Dissent on the Northern Home Front," in *An Uncommon Time: The Civil War and the Northern Home Front*, ed. Paul A. Cimbala and Randall M. Miller (New York: Fordham University Press, 2002), 235–36.

90. Ibid., 214–42. Andreasen discusses Blundell's case on pp. 222–24.

91. Quoted in Wesley, *The Politics of Faith during the Civil War*, 73.

92. Ibid., 64–92.

93. Quoted in Gillette, *Jersey Blue*, 286.

94. Scott, *A Visitation from God*, 110 (and quotation).

95. Gillette, *Jersey Blue*, 287.

96. Quoted in Scott, *A Visitation from God*, 111.

97. Wubben, *Civil War Iowa and the Copperhead Movement*, 177.

98. Ibid., 177, 214–15.

99. Harry S. Stout, *Upon the Altar of the Nation: A Moral History of the Civil War* (New York: Viking, 2006), 248–51; Niven, *Connecticut for the Union*, 270–71, 275–76, 276 (quotation).

CHAPTER TWELVE

1. David W. Blight, *Frederick Douglass' Civil War: Keeping Faith in Jubilee* (Baton Rouge: Louisiana State University Press, 1989), 106; Matthew Warshauer, *Connecticut in the American Civil War: Slavery, Sacrifice, and Survival* (Middletown, CT: Wesleyan University Press, 2011), 103. Allen C. Guelzo, *Lincoln's Emancipation Proclamation: The End of Slavery in America* (New York: Simon and Schuster, 2004), 183–85. Also see Harold Holzer's effort to remind readers of the complexity of the situation in which Lincoln issued the proclamation in *Emancipating Lincoln: The Proclamation, in Text, Context, and Memory* (Cambridge, MA: Harvard University Press, 2012).

2. Quoted in William Gillette, *Jersey Blue: Civil War Politics in New Jersey, 1854–1865* (New Brunswick, NJ: Rutgers University Press, 1995), 206.

3. James M. McPherson, *The Negro's Civil War: How American Blacks Felt and Acted during the War for the Union* (New York: Vintage Books, 1965, 1993), 51–52.

4. C. Peter Ripley et al., eds., *The Black Abolitionist Papers*, Vol. 5: *The United States, 1859–1865* (Chapel Hill: University of North Carolina Press, 1992), 175–77. For Edward Bates's quotation, see this volume, p. 177, n.4.

5. Quoted in Michael S. Green, *Freedom, Union, and Power: Lincoln and His Party during the Civil War* (New York: Fordham University Press, 2004), 158.

6. Gillette, *Jersey Blue*, 197.

7. Quoted in John Niven, *Connecticut for the Union: The Role of the State in the Civil War* (New Haven, CT: Yale University Press, 1965), 282.

8. Theodore J. Karamanski and Eileen M. McMahon, eds., *Civil War Chicago: Eyewitness to History* (Athens: Ohio University Press, 2014), 126–27.

9. Carol Reardon, "We are All in This War: The 148th Pennsylvania and Home Front Dissension in Centre County during the Civil War," in *Union Soldiers and the Northern Home Front: Wartime Experiences, Postwar Adjustments*, ed. Paul A. Cimbala and Randall M. Miller (New York: Fordham University Press, 2002), 13.

10. Gillette, *Jersey Blue*, 197–98, 204.

11. Guelzo, *Lincoln's Emancipation Proclamation*, 187.

12. Quoted in Thomas H. O'Connor, *Civil War Boston: Home Front and Battlefield* (Boston: Northeastern University Press, 1997), 119.

13. Eugene C. Murdock, *One Million Men: The Civil War Draft in the North* (Westport, CT: Greenwood Press, 1971), 6.

14. Jennifer L. Weber, *Copperheads: The Rise and Fall of Lincoln's Opponents in the North* (New York: Oxford University Press, 2006), 63–66; Mark E. Neely Jr., *The Fate of Liberty: Abraham Lincoln and Civil Liberties* (New York: Oxford University Press, 1991), 52–53.

15. Mark Hubbard, ed., *Illinois's War: The Civil War in Documents* (Athens: Ohio University Press, 2013), 96–97.

16. Quoted in Richard N. Current, *The History of Wisconsin*, Vol. 2: *The Civil War Era, 1848–1873* (Madison: State Historical Society of Wisconsin, 1976), 314.

17. Susannah Ural Bruce, *The Harp and the Eagle: Irish-American Volunteers and the Union Army, 1861–1865* (New York: New York University Press, 2006), 136–40.

18. Karamanski and McMahon, *Civil War Chicago*, 210–12.

19. Quoted in Bruce, *The Harp and the Eagle*, 137.

20. Christian G. Samito, *Becoming American Under Fire: Irish Americans, African Americans, and the Politics of Citizenship during the Civil War Era* (Ithaca, NY: Cornell University Press, 2009), 127.

21. Gillette, *Jersey Blue*, 239–40.

22. Jonathan W. White, ed., *A Philadelphia Perspective: The Civil War Diary of Sidney George Fisher* (New York: Fordham University Press, 2007), 198.

23. Ripley et al., *Black Abolitionist Papers*, 5:305.

24. Hubbard, *Illinois's War*, 145.

25. Quoted in Blight, *Frederick Douglass' Civil War*, 163.

26. James M. McPherson, *The Struggle for Equality: Abolitionists and the Negro in the Civil War and Reconstruction* (Princeton, NJ: Princeton University Press, 1964), 192–220; Dudley Taylor Cornish, *The Sable Arm: Black Troops in the Union Army, 1861–1865* (New York: Longmans, Green, 1956; Lawrence: University Press of Kansas, 1987), 288.

27. James W. Geary, *We Need Men: The Union Draft in the Civil War* (DeKalb: Northern Illinois University Press, 1991), 34, 35.

28. Bruce, *The Harp and the Eagle*, 147.

29. Geary, *We Need Men*, 65–86, 140–50.

30. James C. Mohr, ed., *The Cormany Diaries: A Northern Family in the Civil War* (Pittsburgh: University of Pittsburgh Press, 1982), 229.

31. Russell L. Johnson, *Warriors into Workers: The Civil War and the Formation of Urban-Industrial Society in a Northern City* (New York: Fordham University Press, 2003), 74–77.

32. Gillette, *Jersey Blue*, 159.

33. Michael H. Frisch, *Town into City: Springfield, Massachusetts, and the Meaning of Community, 1840–1880* (Cambridge, MA: Harvard University Press, 1972), 62–63.

34. Geary, *We Need Men*, 47.

35. Ibid., 114–15, 145–46; Richard F. Nation and Stephen E. Towne, eds., *Indiana's War: The Civil War in Documents* (Athens: Ohio University Press, 2009), 61.

36. Gillette, *Jersey Blue*, 158–59.

37. Hubbard, *Illinois's War*, 111.

38. Murdock, *One Million Men*, 198.

39. Nina Silber and Mary Beth Sievens, eds., *Yankee Correspondence: Civil War Letters between New England Soldiers and the Home Front* (Charlottesville: University Press of Virginia, 1996), 162.

40. Ibid., 110.

41. Geary, *We Need Men*, 145, 154, 168.

42. Christine Dee, ed., *Ohio's War: The Civil War in Documents* (Athens: Ohio University Press, 2006), 146–48.

43. William Blair, "We Are Coming, Father Abraham—Eventually: The Problem of Northern Nationalism in the Pennsylvania Recruiting Drives of 1862," in *The War Was You and Me: Civilians in the American Civil War*, ed. Joan E. Cashin (Princeton, NJ: Princeton University Press, 2002), 187–88.

44. Geary, *We Need Men*, 39.

45. Dee, *Ohio's War*, 146–48.

46. Thomas F. Curran, *Soldiers of Peace: Civil War Pacifism and the Postwar Radical Peace Movement* (New York: Fordham University Press, 2003), xiii, 65–67.

47. Quoted in Johnson, *Warriors Into Workers*, 89–90.

48. Walter D. Kamphoefner and Wolfgang Helbich, eds., and Susan Carter Vogel, trans, *Germans in the Civil War: The Letters They Wrote Home* (Chapel Hill: University of North Carolina Press, 2006), 63.

49. Jean H. Baker, *Affairs of Party: The Political Culture of Northern Democrats in the Mid-Nineteenth Century* (New York: Fordham University Press, 1999), 156, 338.

50. Hubert H. Wubben, *Civil War Iowa and the Copperhead Movement* (Ames: Iowa State University Press, 1980), 63.

51. Grace Palladino, *Another Civil War: Labor, Capital, and the State in the Anthracite Regions of Pennsylvania, 1840–68* (Urbana: University of Illinois Press, 1990), 99–103.

52. Paul A. Cimbala, "Union Corps of Honor," *Columbiad* 3 (Winter 2000): 75–76; Palladino, *Another Civil War*, 104–17; George Winston Smith and Charles Judah, *Life in the North during the Civil War: A Source History* (Albuquerque: University of New Mexico Press, 1966), 57–58.

53. Current, *History of Wisconsin*, 2:315.

54. Kamphoefner and Helbich, *Germans in the Civil War*, 6–7.

55. Theodore J. Karamanski, *Rally 'Round the Flag: Chicago and the Civil War* (Chicago: Nelson-Hall Publishers, 1993), 198; Karamanski and McMahon, *Civil War Chicago*, 114–15, 128, 129, 133–34.

56. Adrian Cook, *The Armies of the Streets: The New York City Draft Riots of 1863* (Lexington: University Press of Kentucky, 1974), 52.

57. Kamphoefner and Helbich, *Germans in the Civil War*, 66.

58. Cook, *The Armies of the Streets*, 194, 213–18; Edward K. Spann, *Gotham at War: New York City, 1860–1865* (Wilmington, DE: SR Books, 2002), 95–101.

59. White, *A Philadelphia Perspective*, 198.

60. O'Connor, *Civil War Boston*, 140–41.

61. Silber and Sievens, *Yankee Correspondence*, 121–22.

62. Palladino, *Another Civil War*, 104–17.

63. Wubben, *Civil War Iowa and the Copperhead Movement*, 123.

64. Kenneth H. Wheeler, "Local Autonomy and Civil War Draft Resistance: Holmes County, Ohio," *Civil War History* 45 (June 1999): 147–59.

65. Geary, *We Need Men*, 110–11.

66. Joan E. Cashin, "Deserters, Civilians, and Draft Resistance in the North," in Cashin, ed., *The War Was You and Me*, 262–85.

67. Cimbala, "Union Corps of Honor," 76–77.

68. Stephen E. Towne, *Surveillance and Spies in the Civil War: Exposing Confederate Conspiracies in America's Heartland* (Athens: Ohio University Press, 2015), 89–115.

69. Gillette, *Jersey Blue*, 158.

70. Wubben, *Civil War Iowa and the Copperhead Movement*, 127.

71. Weber, *Copperheads*, 103.

72. White, *Philadelphia Perspective*, 108.

73. Harold Melvin Hyman, *Era of the Oath: Northern Loyalty Tests during the Civil War and Reconstruction* (Philadelphia: University of Pennsylvania Press, 1954), 1–20.

74. Phillip Shaw Paludan, *The Presidency of Abraham Lincoln* (Lawrence: University Press of Kansas, 1994), 73.

75. White, *A Philadelphia Perspective*, 108.

76. Quotations in Reardon, "We Are All in This War," 14.

77. Current, *History of Wisconsin*, 2:315.

78. White, *A Philadelphia Perspective*, 190.

79. Karamanski, *Rally 'Round the Flag*, 188–97, 188 (first quotation); Ford Risley, *Civil War Journalism* (Santa Barbara, CA: Praeger, 2012); Karamanski and McMahon, *Civil War Chicago*, 139–43, 141 (second quotation).

80. Risley, *Civil War Journalism*, 85, 88, 95; Emmet Crozier, *Yankee Reporters, 1861–1865* (New York: Oxford University Press, 1956; Westport, CT: Greenwood Press, 1973), 134–35, 379–80.

81. Risley, *Civil War Journalism*, 87.

82. Paul Starr, *The Creation of the Media: Political Origins of Mass Communications* (New York: Basic Books, 2004), 186–87.

83. Mark E. Neely Jr., *The Fate of Liberty: Abraham Lincoln and Civil Liberties* (New York: Oxford University Press, 1991), 161, 124–33; Paludan, *The Presidency of Abraham Lincoln*, 191 (and quotation).

84. Quoted in Niven, *Connecticut for the Union*, 276. For the development of government policy concerning disloyalty and treason, see William A. Blair, *With Malice toward Some: Treason and Loyalty in the Civil War Era* (Chapel Hill: University of North Carolina Press, 2014), 36–65.

85. Dee, *Ohio's War*, 136–37.

86. Weber, *Copperheads*, 96–98.

87. Karamanski, *Rally 'Round the Flag*, 185–223, 276, n.59; Karamanski and McMahon, *Civil War Chicago*, 149–55, 109 (quotation).

CHAPTER THIRTEEN

1. Quoted in William Schouler, *Massachusetts in the Civil War* (Boston: E. P. Dutton & Co., 1868; Scituate, MA: Digital Scanning, Inc., 2003), 610.

2. Ibid., 623–26; Thomas H. O'Connor, *Civil War Boston: Home Front and Battlefield* (Boston: Northeastern University Press, 1997), 226–27.

3. Georgeanna Woolsey Bacon and Eliza Woolsey Howland, *My Heart toward Home: Letters of a Family during the Civil War*, ed. Daniel John Hoisington (Roseville, MN: Edinborough Press, 2001), 385.

4. Quoted in Stuart Murray, *A Time of War: A Northern Chronicle of the Civil War* (Lee, MA: Berkshire House, 2001), 292.

5. George Templeton Strong, *Diary of the Civil War, 1860–1865*, ed. Allan Nevins (New York: Macmillan Co., 1962), 576–81.

6. Richard F. Nation and Stephen E. Towne, eds., *Indiana's War: The Civil War in Documents* (Athens: Ohio University Press, 2009), 192.

7. Robert F. Engs and Corey M. Brooks, eds., *Their Patriotic Duty: The Civil War Letters of the Evans Family of Brown County, Ohio* (New York: Fordham University Press, 2007), 351.

8. Christine Dee, ed., *Ohio's War: The Civil War in Documents* (Athens: Ohio University Press, 2006), 193.

9. Amy Reynolds and Debra Reddin van Tuyll, eds., *The Greenwood Library of American War Reporting*, Vol. 3: *The Civil War, North and South* (Westport, CT: Greenwood Press, 2005), 276.

10. Ibid., 275.

11. David W. Blight, *Frederick Douglass' Civil War: Keeping Faith in Jubilee* (Baton Rouge: Louisiana State University Press, 1989), 163.

12. Christian G. Samito, *Becoming American under Fire, Irish Americans, African Americans, and the Politics of Citizenship during the Civil War Era* (Ithaca, NY: Cornell University Press, 2009), 40–76.

13. Mark Hubbard, ed., *Illinois's War: The Civil War in Documents* (Athens: Ohio University Press, 2013), 182.

14. Samito, *Becoming American under Fire*, 140; John David Smith, "Let Us All Be Grateful That We Have Colored Troops That Will Fight," in *Black Soldiers in Blue: African American Troops in the Civil War Era*, ed. John David Smith (Chapel Hill: University of North Carolina Press, 2002), 63.

15. Quoted in Samito, *Becoming American under Fire*, 140.

16. James M. McPherson, *The Negro's Civil War: How American Black Felt and Acted during the War for the Union* (New York: Vintage Civil War Library, 2003), 51–52.

17. Martha Hodes, *Mourning Lincoln* (New Haven, CT: Yale University Press, 2015), 35.

18. Dee, *Ohio's War*, 194.

19. Mary A. Livermore, *My Story of the War: A Woman's Narrative of Four Years Personal Experience* (Hartford, CT: [—], 1887; New York: Da Capo Press, 1995), 471.

20. Bacon and Howland, *My Heart toward Home*, 390.

21. Quoted in James Oakes, *The Radical and the Republican: Frederick Douglass, Abraham Lincoln, and the Triumph of Antislavery Politics* (New York: W. W. Norton & Company, 2007), 141.

22. Hodes, *Mourning Lincoln*, 97–98.

23. Nina Silber and Mary Beth Sievens, eds., *Yankee Correspondence: Civil War Letters between New England Soldiers and the Home Front* (Charlottesville: University Press of Virginia, 1996), 127.

24. Jeffrey D. Marshall, ed., *A War of the People: Vermont Civil War Letters* (Hanover, NH: University Press of New England, 1999), 305.

25. Strong, *Diary of the Civil War*, 580.

26. The quotation is from the *Cincinnati Commercial*, as quoted by Hans Trefousse. Trefousse makes the case that Northerners considered Lincoln to be second only to Washington among their presidents and that his good reputation was quite secure before his assassination. Hans L. Trefousse, *"First among Equals": Abraham Lincoln's Reputation during His Administration* (New York: Fordham University Press, 2005), 134–35, 135 (quotation).

27. Marshall, *A War of the People*, 301.

28. Jonathan W. White, ed., *A Philadelphia Perspective: The Civil War Diary of Sidney George Fisher* (New York: Fordham University Press, 2006), 252.

29. Pearl T. Ponce, ed., *Kansas's War: The Civil War in Documents* (Athens: Ohio University Press, 2011), 179.

30. Strong, *Diary of the Civil War*, 579–81; William Gillette, *Jersey Blue: Civil War Politics in New Jersey, 1854–1865* (New Brunswick, NJ: Rutgers University Press, 1995), 306.

31. Strong, *Diary of the Civil War*, 583–86; Nation and Towne, *Indiana's War*, 194–95. Thomas Reed Turner describes the willingness to forgive now that peace was upon the land and how it turned into something harsher in the wake of the assassination in *Beware the People Weeping: Public Opinion and the Assassination of Abraham Lincoln* (Baton Rouge: Louisiana state University Press, 1982), 18–52.

32. Nation and Towne, *Indiana's War*, 195.

33. Hodes, *Mourning Lincoln*, 251.

34. Paul A. Cimbala, *Veterans North and South: The Transition from Soldier to Civilian after the American Civil War* (Santa Barbara, CA: Praeger, 2015), 3.

35. Judith A. Bailey and Robert I. Cottom, eds., *After Chancellorsville: Letters from the Heart: The Civil War Letters of Private Walter G. Dunn and Emma Randolph* (Baltimore: Maryland Historical Society, 1998), 213.

36. Kamphoefner and Helbich, *Germans in the Civil War*, 244.

37. White, *A Philadelphia Perspective*, 253.

38. Turner, *Beware the People Weeping*, 26–27.

39. Ibid., 27.

40. Nation and Towne, *Indiana's War*, 197; Mary Lydig Daly, *Diary of a Union Lady, 1861–1865*, ed. Harold Earl Hammond (Lincoln: University of Nebraska Press, 2000), 357.

41. Quoted in David D. Van Tassel, with John Vacha, *"Behind Bayonets": The Civil War in Northern Ohio* (Kent, OH: Kent State University Press, 2006), 100.

42. Ibid., 103.

43. Margaret Leech, *Reveille in Washington, 1860–1865* (New York: Harper & Brothers, Publishers, 1941), 399; Allen C. Guelzo, *Abraham Lincoln: Redeemer President* (Grand Rapids, MI: William B. Eerdmans Publishing Company, 1999), 439–40; White, *A Philadelphia Perspective*, 255–57; Merrill D. Peterson, *Lincoln in American Memory* (New York: Oxford University Press, 1995), 6–7; Hodes, *Mourning Lincoln*, 85–90.

44. Turner, *Beware the People Weeping*, 28.

45. Ernest B. Ferguson, *Freedom Rising: Washington in the Civil War* (New York: Alfred A. Knopf, 2004), 392–94.

46. Kerry A. Trask, *Fire Within: A Civil War Narrative from Wisconsin* (Kent, OH: Kent State University Press, 1995), 235–36; Peterson, *Lincoln in American Memory*, 14–21; Bailey and Cottom, *After Chancellorsville*, 213; Marshall, *A War of the People*, 305; Franny Nudelman, *John's Brown Body: Slavery, Violence, and the Culture of War* (Chapel Hill: University of North Carolina Press, 2004), 88–89; Van Tassel with Vacha, *"Behind Bayonets,"* 104–9; Gillette, *Jersey Blue*, 307.

47. Eugene H. Roseboom, *The Civil War Era, 1850–1873*, Vol. 4 of *The History of the State of Ohio*, ed. Carl Wittke (Columbus: Ohio State Archaeological and Historical Society, 1944), 437; Peterson, *Lincoln in American Memory*, 7–8; James H. Moorhead, *American Apocalypse: Yankee Protestants and the Civil War, 1860–1869* (New Haven, CT: Yale University Press, 1978), 174–76; Melinda Lawson, *Patriot Fires: Forging a New American Nationalism in the Civil War North* (Lawrence: University Press of Kansas, 2002), 173–78; Turner, *Beware the People Weeping*, 80. Scott D. Trostel, *The Lincoln Funeral Train: The Final Journey and National Funeral for Abraham Lincoln* (Fletcher, OH: Cam-Tech Publishing, 2002) describes the funeral route of the train that brought Lincoln to Springfield, Illinois; see pp. 198–99 for the crowds in Springfield.

48. Fred C. Ainsworth and Joseph W. Kirkley, compilers, *The War of the Rebellion: A Compilation of the Official Records of the Union and Confederate Armies*, Series 3, Vol. 5 (Washington, DC: Government Printing Office, 1900), 61 [hereinafter cited as *Official Records*].

49. Paul A. Cimbala, *Soldiers North and South: The Everyday Experiences of the Men Who Fought America's Civil War* (New York: Fordham University Press, 2010), 204–13.

50. Lois Bryan Adams, *Letters from Washington, 1863–1865*, ed. Evelyn Lasher (Detroit: Wayne State University Press, 1999), 263–68; Leech, *Reveille in Washington*, 415–17; Paul A. Cimbala, "The Veteran Reserve Corps and the Northern People," in *Union Soldiers and the Northern Home Front: Wartime Experiences, Postwar Adjustments*, ed. Paul A. Cimbala and Randall M. Miller (New York: Fordham University Press, 2002), 202–3.

51. James C. Mohr, ed., *The Cormany Diaries: A Northern Family in the Civil War* (Pittsburgh: University of Pittsburgh Press, 1982), 576.

52. Ibid., 578, 579; Edward K. Spann, *Gotham at War: New York City, 1860–1865* (Wilmington, DE: SR Books, 2002), 190.

53. Mohr, *The Cormany Diaries*, 582.

54. For the problems of readjustment, see Cimbala, *Veterans North and South*.

55. Gillette, *Jersey Blue*, 312.

56. *Official Records*, Series 3, Vol. 5, 211.

57. John Niven, *Connecticut for the Union: The Role of the State in the Civil War* (New Haven, CT: Yale University Press, 1965), 429–30.

58. Cimbala, *Veterans North and South*, 20.

59. *Official Records*, Series 3, Vol. 5, 1031.

60. Office of the Chief of Military History, Department of the Army, *History of Military Mobilization in the United States Army, 1775–1945*, Washington, DC: Department of the Army Pamphlet No. 20–212, November 1955: 141.

61. *Official Records*, Series 3, Vol. 5, 1031; John C. Sparrow, *History of Personnel Demobilization in the United States Army*, Washington, DC: Department of the Army Pamphlet No. 20-210, July 1952: 299; Mark R. Wilson, *The Business of Civil War: Military Mobilization and the State, 1861–1865* (Baltimore: Johns Hopkins University Press, 2006), 204–5.

62. For the distribution of soldiers in the former Confederacy during Reconstruction, see James E. Sefton, *The United States Army and Reconstruction, 1865–1877* (Baton Rouge: Louisiana State University Press, 1967), 261–62.

63. *Official Records*, Series 3, Vol. 5, 352–53.

64. Wilson, *The Business of Civil War*, 202–3.

65. Spann, *Gotham at War*, 188.

66. Hattie Lou Winslow and Joseph R. H. Moore, *Camp Morton, 1861–1865: Indianapolis Prison Camp* (Indianapolis: Indiana Historical Society, 1940, 1995), 139–40.

67. David V. Mollenhoff, *Madison: A History of the Formative Years*, 2nd ed. (Madison: University of Wisconsin Press, 2003), 114.

68. Michael P. Gray, *The Business of Captivity: Elmira and Its Civil War Prison* (Kent, OH: Kent State University Press, 2001), 148–51.

69. Roger Pickenpaugh, *Camp Chase and the Evolution of Union Prison Policy* (Tuscaloosa: University of Alabama Press, 2007), 145–46.

70. George Levy, *To Die in Chicago: Confederate Prisoners at Camp Douglas, 1862–1865* (Gretna, LA: Pelican Publishing Co., 1999), 341; David Keller, *The Story of Camp Douglas: Chicago's Forgotten Civil War Prison* (Charleston, SC: The History Press, 2015), 216.

71. George Worthington Adams, *Doctors in Blue: The Medical History of the Union Army in the Civil War* (Baton Rouge: Louisiana State University Press, 1952, 1996), 172.

72. Alfred Jay Bollett, *Civil War Medicine: Challenges and Triumphs* (Tucson, AZ: Galen Press, 2002), 221.

73. Margaret Humphreys, *Marrow of Tragedy: The Health Crisis of the American Civil War* (Baltimore: Johns Hopkins University Press, 2013), 181.

74. R. J. Bickel, "The Estes House," *The Annals of Iowa*, 40 (fall 1970): 437 (http://ir.uiowa.edu/annals-of-iowa/vol40/iss6/4).

75. Richard N. Current, *The History of Wisconsin*, Vol. 2: *The Civil War Era* (Madison: State Historical Society of Wisconsin, 1976), 515–16.

76. *Official Records*, Series 3, Vol. 5, 1032.

77. Spann, *Gotham at War*, 188.

78. Wilson, *The Business of Civil War*, 57, 194–95.

79. Cindy Sondik Aron, *Ladies and Gentlemen of the Civil Service: Middle-Class Workers in Victorian America* (New York: Oxford University Press, 1987), 3, 5.

80. Wilson, *The Business of Civil War*, 208–12.

81. Ibid., 194.

82. Kamphoefner and Helbich, *Germans in the Civil War*, 244–45.

83. Ibid.; Wilson, *The Business of Civil War*, 194.

84. Kamphoefner and Helbich, *Germans in the Civil War*, 244–45.

85. Spann, *Gotham at War*, 188.

86. Michael H. Frisch, *Town into City: Springfield, Massachusetts, and the Meaning of Community, 1840–1880* (Cambridge, MA: Harvard University Press, 1972), 117.

87. *Official Records*, Series 3, Vol. 5, 143, 1042.

88. Ibid., 141.

89. Spann, *Gotham at War*, 191–92; Frances Clarke, "'Honorable Scars': Northern Amputees and the Meaning of Civil War Injuries," in Cimbala and Miller, eds., *Union Soldiers and the Northern Home Front*, 361–94.

90. Current, *History of Wisconsin*, Vol. 2: *The Civil War*, 370–71.

91. Richard L. Kiper, ed., *Dear Catharine, Dear Taylor: The Civil War Letters of a Union Soldier and His Wife* (Lawrence: University Press of Kansas, 2002), 18, 414.

92. For the transition of veterans to civilian life, see Cimbala, *Veterans North and South*, 59–87.

93. Heather Cox Richardson, *West from Appomattox: The Reconstruction of America after the Civil War* (New Haven, CT: Yale University Press, 2007), 31–77, and passim.

94. Wilson, *The Business of Civil War*, 193–94.

95. Niven, *Connecticut for the Union*, 429–38.

96. Jacqueline T. Lynch, *The Ames Manufacturing Company of Chicopee Massachusetts: A Northern Factory Town's Perspective on the Civil War* ([—]: Jacqueline T. Lynch, 2013), 11, 27, 46–47.

97. Reuel Robinson, *History of Camden and Rockport, Maine* (Camden, ME: Camden Publishing Co., 1907), 393.

98. Wilson, *The Business of Civil War*, 194; Frisch, *Town Into City*, 117–23.

99. Earl F. Mulderink III, *New Bedford's Civil War* (New York: Fordham University Press, 2012), 191–93.

100. Niven, *Connecticut for the Union*, 442–45.

101. For example, see Theodore J. Karamanski, *Rally 'Round the Flag: Chicago and the Civil War* (Chicago: Nelson Hall, 1993), 242. Van Tassel, with Vacha, *"Behind Bayonets,"* 98; Robert L. Bee, ed., *The Boys from Rockville: Civil War Narratives of Sgt. Benjamin Hirst, Company D, 14th Connecticut Volunteers* (Knoxville: University of Tennessee Press, 1998), 176; Lary Lankton, *Beyond the Boundaries: Life and Landscape at the Lake Superior Copper Mines, 1840–1875* (New York: Oxford University Press, 1997), 171.

102. Russell L. Johnson, *Warriors into Workers: The Civil War and the Formation of Urban-Industrial Society in a Northern City* (New York: Fordham University Press, 2003), 286.

103. Jocelyn Wills, *Boosters, Hustlers, and Speculators: Entrepreneurial Culture and the Rise of Minneapolis and St. Paul, 1849–1883* (St. Paul: Minnesota Historical Society Press, 2005), 114–48.

104. Jeanie Attie, *Patriotic Toil: Northern Women and the American Civil War* (Ithaca: Cornell University Press, 1998), 240.

105. Ibid., 240–41; Spann, *Gotham at War*, 188.

106. Karamanski, *Rally 'Round the Flag*, 236; Beverly Gordon, *Bazaars and Fair Ladies: The History of the American Fundraising Fair* (Knoxville: University of Tennessee Press, 1998), 90–91; quotation in Frank B. Goodrich, *The Tribute Book: A Record of the Munificence, Self Sacrifice and Patriotism of the American People during the War for the Union* (New York: Derby and Miller, 1865), 288.

107. Goodrich, *The Tribute Book*, 288.

108. Ibid., 290–91.

109. Ibid., 291; Current, *History of Wisconsin*, Vol. 2: *The Civil War*, 370.

110. Spann, *Gotham at War*, 188; William Quentin Maxwell, *Lincoln's Fifth Wheel: The Political History of the United States Sanitary Commission* (New York: Longmans, Green and Co., 1956), 288.

111. David A. Raney, "In the Lord's Army: The United States Christian Commission, Soldiers, and the Union War Effort," in Cimbala and Miller, eds., *Union Soldiers and the Northern Home Front*, 263–92.

112. Maxwell, *Lincoln's Fifth Wheel*, 287–88.

113. Biographical/Historical Information, Collection Overview, United States Sanitary Commission Records, 1861–1879, Archives and Manuscripts, The New York Public Library, MssCol 3101, http://archives.nypl.org/mss/3101.

114. Bacon and Howland, *My Heart toward Home*, 419.

115. Ibid., 420–21.

116. Carol Faulkner, *Women's Radical Reconstruction: The Freedmen's Aid Movement* (Philadelphia: University of Pennsylvania Press, 2004); Ronald E. Butchart, *Northern Schools, Southern Blacks, and Reconstruction: Freedmen's Education, 1862–1875* (Westport, CT: Greenwood Press, 1980), 115–34.

117. Attie, *Patriotic Toil*, 268–69; Eric Foner, *Reconstruction: America's Unfinished Revolution, 1863–1877* (New York: Harper & Row, Publishers, 1988), 472–73.

118. Henry Mayer, *All on Fire: William Lloyd Garrison and the Abolition of Slavery* (New York: W. W. Norton, 1998), 587–88.

119. Quoted in James M. McPherson, *The Struggle for Equality: Abolitionists and the Negro in the Civil War and Reconstruction* (Princeton, NJ: Princeton University Press, 1964), 304.

120. Mayer, *All on Fire*, 589–94, 597–601, 613; McPherson, *The Struggle for Equality*, 304–5, 429.

121. McPherson, *The Struggle for Equality*, 304.

122. Ibid., 287–432.

123. C. Peter Ripley et al., eds., *The Black Abolitionist Papers*, Vol. 5: *The United States, 1859–1865* (Chapel Hill: University of North Carolina Press, 1992), 321–23.

124. Glenn M. Linden, *Voices from the Reconstruction Years, 1865–1877* (Fort Worth, TX: Harcourt Brace College Publishers, 1999), 72–73.

125. David W. Blight, *Frederick Douglass' Civil War: Keeping Faith in Jubilee* (Baton Rouge: Louisiana State University Press, 1989), 208–9; Samito, *Becoming American under Fire*, 141–42.

126. Nation and Towne, *Indiana's War*, 204–6.

127. Gillette, *Jersey Blue*, 318–20.

128. Foner, *Reconstruction*, 470–80; Leslie A. Schwalm, *Emancipation's Diaspora: Race and Reconstruction in the Upper Midwest* (Chapel Hill: University of North Carolina Press, 2009), 175–217.

BIBLIOGRAPHIC ESSAY

The best place to start studying the Northern home front experience is with the words of those individuals who lived it. Home-front correspondents, who sent their efforts to men in the army, remain underrepresented in the volumes of published letters. Soldiers' letters dominate those publications because the home folks had safely preserved and passed them on through the generations, whereas it was more likely that soldiers would lose letters from home because of the circumstances of camp life, the march, and battle. Nevertheless, there are some published family collections that provide a good starting point. Among the best are Georgeanna Woolsey Bacon and Eliza Woolsey Howland, *My Heart toward Home: Letters of a Family during the Civil War*, ed. Daniel John Hoisington (Roseville, MN: Edinborough Press, 2001); Judith A. Bailey and Robert I. Cottom, eds., *After Chancellorsville: Letters from the Heart, The Civil War Letters of Private Walter G. Dunn and Emma Randolph* (Baltimore: Maryland Historical Society, 1998); Judy Cook, ed., *A Quiet Corner of the War: The Civil War Letters of Gilbert and Esther Claflin, Oconomowoc, Wisconsin 1862–1863* (Madison: University of Wisconsin Press, 2013); Barbara Butler Davis, ed., *Affectionately Yours: The Civil War Home-Front Letters of the Ovid Butler Family* (Indianapolis: Indiana Historical Society Press, 2004); Donald C. Elder III, ed., *Love amid the Turmoil: The Civil War Letters of William and Mary Vermilion* (Iowa City: University of Iowa Press, 2003); Robert F. Engs and Corey

M. Brooks, eds., *Their Patriotic Duty: The Civil War Letters of the Evans Family of Brown County, Ohio* (New York: Fordham University Press, 2007); Andrea R. Foroughi, *Go If You Think It Your Duty: A Minnesota Couple's Civil War Letters* (St. Paul: Minnesota Historical Society Press, 2008); Richard L. Kiper, ed., *Dear Catharine, Dear Taylor: The Civil War Letters of a Union Soldier and His Wife* (Lawrence: University Press of Kansas, 2002); Charles F. Larimer, ed., *Love and Valor: Intimate Civil War Letters between Captain Jacob and Emeline Ritner* (Western Springs, IL: Sigourney Press, 2000); and Marti Skipper and Jane Taylor, eds., *A Handful of Providence: The Civil War Letters of Lt. Richard Goldwaite, New York Volunteers, and Ellen Goldwaite* (Jefferson, NC: McFarland & Company, 2004). Arguably the best collection of letters written by immigrant soldiers and civilians to their families is Walter D. Kamphoefner and Wolfgang Helbich, eds., and Susan Carter Vogel, trans. *Germans in the Civil War: The Letters They Wrote Home* (Chapel Hill: University of North Carolina Press, 2006). For an Irish Catholic perspective, see Lawrence F. Kohl and Margaret C. Richard, eds., *Irish Green and Union Blue: The Civil War Letters of Peter Welsh, Color Sergeant 28th Regiment Massachusetts Volunteers* (New York: Fordham University Press, 1986).

For an unusual collection that is especially revealing about the lives of women on the home front, see Nancy L. Rhodes and Lucy E. Bailey, eds., *Wanted— Correspondence: Women's Letters to a Union Soldier* (Athens: Ohio University Press, 2009). Ruth Douglas Currie, ed., *Emma Spaulding Bryant: Civil War Bride, Carpetbagger's Wife, Ardent Feminist, Letters and Diaries, 1860–1900* (New York: Fordham University Press, 2004) devotes only a short section to the war, but it is worth reading for the intelligent writing of Emma Bryant on a number of topics. Julie Holcomb, ed., *Southern Sons, Northern Soldiers: The Civil War Letters of the Remley Brothers, 22nd Iowa Infantry* (DeKalb: Northern Illinois University Press, 2004) is primarily a collection of thoughtful soldiers' letters that illustrate what the home folks were learning of the war from their soldiers in the field, but it also contains some correspondence from family members at home. A good example of what soldiers told their children about their experiences and how they tried to maintain paternal involvement with their lives is Anita Palladino's *Diary of a Yankee Engineer: The Civil War Story of John H. Westervelt, Engineer, 1st New York Volunteer Engineer Corps* (New York: Fordham University Press, 1997), which consists of letters written in diary form and sent to Westervelt's son. Nina Silber and Mary Beth Sievens, eds., *Yankee Correspondence: Civil War Letters between New England Soldiers and the Home Front* (Charlottesville: University Press of Virginia 1996) is an excellent example of the kind of home-front material, scattered through a wide range of manuscript collections, that is available to the diligent researcher. So, too, is Jeffrey D. Marshall's collection of Vermont correspondence, *A War of the People: Vermont Civil War Letters* (Hanover, NH: University Press of New England, 1999).

Ohio University Press, Athens, Ohio, is publishing a series of books, *The Civil War in the Great Interior*, which deals with the oft-neglected Midwest. Volumes now available are Christine Dee, ed., *Ohio's War: The Civil War in Documents* (2006), Mark Hubbard, ed., *Illinois's War: The Civil War in Documents* (2013), Richard F. Nation and Stephen E. Towne, eds., *Indiana's War: The Civil War in Documents* (2009), Pearl T. Ponce, ed., *Kansas's War: The Civil War in Documents* (2011), and Silvana R. Siddali, ed., *Missouri's War: The Civil War in Documents* (2009), all excellent compilations that range over the spectrum of wartime and home-front topics. The press plans similar volumes for Michigan and Wisconsin.

Northerners not only kept up with the war through letters received from their loved ones at the front, they could also read letters by soldiers published in their local newspapers, some of which are now available in book form. For example, see Stephen W. Sears, ed., *Mr. Dunn Browne's Experiences in the Army: The Civil War Letters of Samuel W. Fiske* (New York: Fordham University Press, 1998), from the Springfield, Massachusetts, *Republican*; and Emil and Ruth Rosenblatt, eds., *Hard Marching Every Day: The Civil War Letters of Private Wilbur Fisk, 1861–1865* (Lawrence: University Press of Kansas, 1992), from the Montpelier, Vermont, *Green Mountain Freeman*. The African American community heard from one of its own in letters from Corporal James H. Gooding of the 54th Massachusetts Volunteer Infantry Regiment, printed in the New Bedford, Massachusetts, *Mercury*, now available in Virginia M. Adams, ed., *On the Altar of Freedom: A Black Soldier's Civil War Letters from the Front* (Amherst: University of Massachusetts Press, 1991).

Diaries and memoirs also help bring immediacy to the Northern home-front experience. Revealing diaries include Jennifer Cain Bohrnstedt, ed., *Views from My Schoolroom Window: The Diary of Schoolteacher Mary Laurentine Martin* (Bloomington, IN: AuthorHouse, 2006); Harold Earl Hammond, ed., *Diary of a Union Lady, 1861–1865* (New York: Funk & Wagnalls Company, 1962); James C. Mohr, ed., *The Cormany Diaries: A Northern Family in the Civil War* (Pittsburgh: University of Pittsburgh Press, 1982); George Templeton Strong, *Diary of the Civil War, 1860–1865*, ed. by Allan Nevins (New York: Macmillan Company, 1962); Jonathan W. White, ed., *A Philadelphia Perspective: The Civil War Diary of Sidney George Fisher* (New York: Fordham University Press, 2006). For a different Philadelphia perspective in diary form, see Judith Ann Giesberg, ed., *Emilie Davis's Civil War: The Diaries of a Free Black Woman in Philadelphia, 1863–1865* (University Park: Pennsylvania State University Press, 2014).

For memoirs, see, for example, Mary A. Livermore, *My Story of the War: A Woman's Narrative of Four Years Personal Experience* (1887; Williamstown, MA: Corner House Publisher, 1978); and Sarah Emma Edmonds, *Memoirs of a Soldier Nurse and Spy: A Woman's Adventures in the Union Army*, ed. by Elizabeth D. Leonard (DeKalb: Northern Illinois University Press, 1999). Also see Louisa May Alcott,

Hospital Sketches, ed. by Alice Fahs (Boston: Bedford/St. Martins, 2004), a fictionalized rendering of the author's experience as a nurse. James Marten provides samples of what children on both sides read in *Lessons of War: The Civil War in Children's Magazines* (Wilmington, DE: SR Books, 1999).

There are several miscellaneous collections of original Civil War writings that supplement those volumes noted above. The best among them is Louis P. Masur, ed., *The Real War Will Never Get in the Books: Selections from Writers during the Civil War* (New York: Oxford University Press, 1993), which contains a good sampling of revealing journal entries, letters, and other writings by Northern authors. For an excellent collection of Walt Whitman's writings, see Walter Lowenfels, *Walt Whitman's Civil War* (New York: Alfred A. Knopf, 1961; New York: Da Capo Press, 1989); and for Herman Melville's poetry, see *Battle-Pieces and Aspects of the War*, with a new introduction by Lee Rust Brown (New York: Da Capo Press, 1995). George Winston Smith and Charles Judah, *Life in the North during the Civil War: A Source History* (Albuquerque: University of New Mexico Press, 1966) contains a range of primary material touching on all aspects of the Northern war experience. Marilyn Mayer Culpepper, *Trials and Triumphs: The Women of the American Civil War* (East Lansing: Michigan State University Press, 1991) uses narrative to weave together excerpts from the writings of Northern and Southern women.

For the first-hand documentation of the African American experience, the best starting place remains James M. McPherson's *The Negro's Civil War: How American Blacks Felt and Acted during the War for the Union* (New York: Vintage Civil War Library, 1991), supplemented with Donald Yacavone, ed., *Freedom's Journey: African American Voices of the Civil War* (Chicago: Lawrence Hill Books, 2004). Any deeper understanding of the African American experience in the North must also rely on C. Peter Ripley et al., eds., *The Black Abolitionist Papers*, Vol. 5: *The United States, 1859–1865* (Chapel Hill: University of North Carolina Press, 1992).

There are a number of general studies on everyday life and leisure and thought on the home front that cover both the North and the South, including Randall C. Jimerson's *The Private Civil War: Popular Thought during the Sectional Conflict* (Baton Rouge: Louisiana State University Press, 1988); Anne C. Rose's *Victorian America and the Civil War* (Cambridge, UK: Cambridge University Press, 1992); Joan E. Cashin, ed., *The War Was You and Me: Civilians in the American Civil War* (Princeton, NJ: Princeton University Press, 2002); and Susannah J. Ural, ed., *Civil War Citizens: Race, Ethnicity, and Identity in America's Bloodiest Conflict* (New York: New York University Press, 2010). On the importance of baseball in the North and South, see George B. Kirsch, *Baseball in Blue and Gray: The National Pastime during the Civil War* (Princeton, NJ: Princeton University Press, 2003).

For an expansive coverage and analysis of the Northern home front, see Phillip Shaw Paludan, *"A People's Contest": The Union and Civil War, 1861–1865*, 2nd ed.

(Lawrence: University Press of Kansas, 1996); and for a more compact treatment, J. Matthew Gallman, *The North Fights the Civil War: The Home Front* (Chicago: Ivan R. Dee, 1994). Gallman has also written one of the most innovative recent books concerning the Civil War North: *Defining Duty in the Civil War: Personal Choice, Popular Culture, and the Union Home Front* (Chapel Hill: University of North Carolina Press, 2015). An important study that uses topics such as fairs and war bond drives to come to an understanding of the development of nationalism in the North during the war is Melinda Lawson's *Patriot Fires: Forging a New American Nationalism in the Civil War North* (Lawrence: University Press of Kansas, 2002).

Several essay collections advance our understanding of the Civil War North, including recent volumes that suggest that there remains much room for new approaches in the field. See Maris A. Vinovskis, ed., *Toward a Social History of the American Civil War: Exploratory Essays* (Cambridge, UK: Cambridge University Press, 1990); Paul A. Cimbala and Randall M. Miller, eds., *An Uncommon Time: The Civil War and the Northern Home Front* (New York: Fordham University Press, 2002); and Andrew L. Slap and Michael Thomas Smith, eds., *This Distracted and Anarchical People: New Answers for Old Questions about the Civil War-Era North* (New York: Fordham University Press, 2013).

For how soldiers and veterans viewed and interacted with the Northern home front, see Reid Mitchell, *The Vacant Chair: The Northern Soldier Leaves Home* (New York: Oxford University Press, 1993); Gerald F. Linderman, *Embattled Courage: The Experience of Combat in the American Civil War* (New York: The Free Press, 1987); Steven J. Ramold, *Across the Divide: Union Soldiers View the Northern Home Front* (New York: New York University Press, 2013); and Paul A. Cimbala and Randall M. Miller, eds., *Union Soldiers and the Northern Home Front: Wartime Experiences, Postwar Adjustments* (New York: Fordham University Press, 2002). Edmund J. Raus Jr., *Banners South: A Northern Community at War* (Kent, OH: Kent State University Press, 2005), which follows the 23rd New York Volunteer Infantry, is a unique approach to a regimental history in connecting the soldiers' experience with the home front of at Cortland, New York. On the persistence of Union as the fulcrum of soldiers' and civilians' support for the war, see Gary W. Gallagher, *The Union War* (Cambridge, MA: Harvard University Press, 2011); and for the ways soldiers understood and argued for emancipation, and their effects on civilian thinking, see the chapters in Chandra Manning, *What This Cruel War Was Over: Soldiers, Slavery and the Civil War* (New York: Alfred A. Knopf, 2007).

There still is a serious need for more local studies that consider how the war influenced life in Northern communities. Some studies that are available approach the war's impact on Northern towns, cities, and regions as part of the larger social and economic development of those communities over a longer period of time, while others focus explicitly on the communities at war and their men in the field. Both Grace

Palladino, *Another Civil War: Labor, Capital, and the State in the Anthracite Regions of Pennsylvania 1840–68* (Urbana: University of Illinois Press, 1990), and Robert M. Sandow, *Deserter Country: Civil War Opposition in the Pennsylvania Appalachians* (New York: Fordham University Press, 2009), look at dissent in working-class communities. Don Harrison Doyle, *The Social Order of a Frontier Community, Jacksonville, Illinois, 1825–70* (Urbana: University of Illinois Press, 1978), and Michael H. Frisch, *Town into City: Springfield, Massachusetts, and the Meaning of Community, 1840–1880* (Cambridge, MA: Harvard University Press, 1972) are excellent examples of community studies with large historical scope. For a similar approach but with a regional perspective, see Richard F. Nation, *At Home in the Hoosier Hills: Agriculture, Politics, and Religion in Southern Indiana, 1810–1870* (Bloomington: Indiana University Press, 2005). See Alvin M. Josephy Jr., *The Civil War in the American West* (New York: Alfred A. Knopf, 1991), for an overview of the understudied West. For studies of communities at war, see Nicole Etcheson, *A Generation at War: The Civil War in a Northern Community* (Lawrence: University Press of Kansas, 2011); J. Matthew Gallman, *Mastering Wartime: A Social History of Philadelphia during the Civil War* (Cambridge, UK: Cambridge University Press, 1990); Theodore Karamanski, *Rally 'Round the Flag: Chicago and the Civil War* (Chicago: Nelson-Hall Publishers, 1993); Thomas H. O'Connor, *Civil War Boston: Home Front and Battlefield* (Boston: Northeastern University Press, 1997); Edward K. Spann, *Gotham at War: New York, 1860–1865* (Wilmington, DE: SR Books, 2002); David D. Van Tassel, with John Vacha, *"Behind Bayonets": The Civil War in Northern Ohio* (Kent, OH: Kent State University Press, 2006); and Kerry A. Trask, *Fire Within: A Civil War Narrative from Wisconsin* (Kent, OH: Kent State University Press, 1995). Michael P. Gray, *The Business of Captivity: Elmira and Its Civil War* (Kent, OH: Kent State University Press, 2001) is a model study of a community reshaped by the war, while Margaret S. Creighton, *The Colors of Courage: Gettysburg's Forgotten History, Immigrants, Women, and African Americans in the Civil War's Defining Battle* (New York: Basic Books, 2005) is a unique study of that famous town and its moment in Civil War history. Russell L. Johnson, *Warriors into Workers: The Civil War and the Formation of Urban-Industrial Society in a Northern City* (New York: Fordham University Press, 2003), about Dubuque, Iowa, is an innovative look at how war affected a community. Stuart Murray's *A Time of War: A Northern Chronicle of the Civil War* (Lee, MA: Berkshire House Publishers, 2001) looks at the people of Berkshire County in Massachusetts and their soldiers. David P. Krutz's *Distant Drums: Herkimer County, New York in the War of the Rebellion* (Utica, NY: North Country Books, 1997) similarly explores the contribution of a New York county and the impact of the war on the people there. Edward L. Ayers, *In the Presence of Mine Enemies: War in the Heart of America, 1859–1863* (New York: W.W. Norton & Company, 2003), insightfully compares Franklin County, Pennsylvania, and Augusta County, Virginia, as the first volume of an extended study. Also, in the above-mentioned essay collections, there are several chapters that deal with specific issues influencing individual communities. Some chronologically larger studies of towns and cities also have sections on the Civil War era worth attention.

The war also had an impact on white Northern communities that were united by their ethnicity. For the Germans in the North, see Christian B. Keller, *Chancellorsville and the Germans: Nativism, Ethnicity, and Civil War Memory* (New York: Fordham University Press, 2007); for the Irish, see Susannah Ural Bruce, *The Harp and the Eagle: Irish-American Volunteers and the Union Army, 1861–1865* (New York: New York University Press, 2006). For recruitment of German, Irish, and other immigrants and their communities, see William L. Burton, *Melting Pot Soldiers: The Union's Ethnic Regiments* (New York: Fordham University Press, 1998). The newest study of immigrants and ethnic groups in the Union army is Martin W. Öfele's *True Sons of the Republic: European Immigrants in the Union Army* (Westport, CT: Praeger, 2008).

There remains a need for new state studies, a genre that too many historians believe to be old fashioned, but one that could provide historians with a manageable way to explore in depth the important issues of the war on the home front. For political studies of Northern states in the Civil War era, see Kenneth M. Stampp, *Indiana Politics during the Civil War* (Bloomington: Indiana University Press, 1949, 1978); and Lex Renda, *Running on the Record: Civil War-Era Politics in New Hampshire* (Charlottesville: University Press of Virginia, 1997). William Gillette, *Jersey Blue: Civil War Politics in New Jersey, 1854–1865* (New Brunswick, NJ: Rutgers University Press, 1995) is a detailed examination of the political history of the state, but also includes much information concerning all aspects of the war's impact there. It serves as an example for future studies. For a supplement to Gillette's work, see the later chapters in James J. Gigantino II, *The Ragged Road to Abolition: Slavery and Freedom in New Jersey, 1775–1865* (Philadelphia: University of Pennsylvania Press, 2015); and William J. Jackson, *New Jerseyans in the Civil War: For Union and Liberty* (New Brunswick, NJ: Rutgers University Press, 2000). John Niven's *Connecticut for the Union: The Role of the State in the Civil War* (New Haven, CT: Yale University Press, 1965) remains satisfying for its detail and analysis. So too do Richard N. Current, *The History of Wisconsin*, Vol. 2: *The Civil War Era, 1848–1873* (Madison: State Historical Society of Wisconsin, 1976); and Emma Lou Thornbrough, *Indiana in the Civil War Era, 1850–1880* (Indianapolis: Indiana Historical Society 1965, 1995). For a newer exploration of Connecticut and the war, see Matthew Warshauer, *Connecticut in the American Civil War: Slavery, Sacrifice, and Survival* (Middletown, CT: Wesleyan University Press, 2011). Several essays in William Blair and William A. Pencak, eds., *Making and Remaking Pennsylvania's Civil War* (University Park: Pennsylvania State University Press, 2001) suggest the diverse ways communities in one state responded to war, as do those in Matthew Mason, Katheryn P. Viens, and Conrad Edick Wright, eds., *Massachusetts and the Civil War: The Commonwealth and National Disunion* (Amherst: University of Massachusetts Press, 2015). Also see Albert Castel's classic *Civil War Kansas: Reaping the Whirlwind* (Lawrence: University Press of Kansas, 1997). Ginette Aley and J. L. Anderson, eds., *Union Heartland: The Midwestern Home Front during the Civil War* (Carbondale: Southern Illinois University Press, 2013) reminds readers of the significance of the Midwest during the war and just how rural the Northern states remained at the time of the conflict. It is a good preview of new scholarship that should soon see its way into several book-length studies that will revive interest in the role of the Midwest in the Northern war effort. Glenna Matthews, *The Golden State in the Civil War: Thomas Starr King, the Republican Party, and the Birth of Modern California* (Cambridge, UK: Cambridge University Press, 2012), points the way for studies of Western states.

For the popular literature available to Northern readers and the relationship between the publishing industry, books, and Northern nationalism, see Alice Fahs, *The Imagined Civil War: Popular Literature of the North and the South, 1861–1865* (Chapel Hill: University of North Carolina Press, 2001). Lyde Cullen Sizer explores the significance of women writers in *The Political Work of Northern Women Writers and the Civil War, 1850–1872* (Chapel Hill: University of North Carolina Press, 2000); and Randall Fuller, *From Battlefields Rising: How the Civil War Transformed American Literature* (New York: Oxford University Press, 2011) assesses the effects of war on writing. For newspapers and the Civil War, the starting point is J. Cutler Andrews's *The North Reports the Civil War* (Pittsburgh: University of Pittsburgh Press, 1955). For an update on the topic, see Ford Risley's survey *Civil War Journalism* (Santa Barbara, CA: Praeger, 2012). It is also worthwhile to read Risley's *Abolition and the Press: The Moral Struggle against Slavery* (Evanston, IL: Northwestern University Press, 2008).

For how Northern intellectuals interpreted the war, see George M. Fredrickson, *The Inner Civil War: Northern Intellectuals and the Crisis of the Union* (Urbana: University of Illinois Press, 1993). For new interpretations of this topic, see the essays in Lorien Foote and Kanisorn Wongsrichanalai, eds., *So Conceived and So Dedicated: Intellectual Life in the Civil War-Era North* (New York: Fordham University Press, 2015).

For Northern economics, see Mark Thornton and Robert B. Ekelund Jr., *Tariffs, Blockades, and Inflation: The Economics of the Civil War* (Wilmington, DE: SR Books, 2004), a brief study that looks at both sections, but in doing so illuminates the Northern home-front experience. For Northern financial matters, see also Jane Flaherty, *The Revenue Imperative* (London, UK: Pickering & Chatto, 2009). For Republican economic ideas and policy, see Emerson David Fite, *Social and Industrial Conditions in the North during the Civil War* (New York: Macmillan, 1910; New York: Frederick Unger Publishing Co., 1963); Leonard P. Curry, *Blueprint for*

Modern America: Nonmilitary Legislation of the First Civil War Congress (Nashville: Vanderbilt University Press, 1968); Bray Hammond, *Sovereignty and an Empty Purse: Banks and Politics in the Civil War* (Princeton, NJ: Princeton University Press, 1970); Gabor S. Boritt, *Lincoln and the Economics of the American Dream* (Urbana: University of Illinois Press, 1978); and Heather Cox Richardson, *The Greatest Nation of the Earth: Republican Economic Policies during the Civil War* (Cambridge, MA: Harvard University Press, 1997). Also see Kyle S. Sinisi, *Sacred Debts: State Civil War Claims and American Federalism, 1861–1880* (New York: Fordham University Press, 2003); and Melinda Lawson's *Patriot Fires,* noted above. For economic developments and other aspects of the expansion of the federal government under the Republicans, see Richard Franklin Bensel, *Yankee Leviathan: The Origins of Central State Authority in America, 1859–1877* (New York: Cambridge University Press, 1990). Mark R. Wilson's *The Business of Civil War: Military Mobilization and the State, 1861–1865* (Baltimore: Johns Hopkins University Press, 2006) is an important exploration of the politics and economics of the North's efforts to raise and maintain its armies as well as the process of demobilization at the war's end.

For Republicans and labor, see David Montgomery, *Beyond Equality: Labor and the Radical Republicans, 1862–1872* (Urbana: University of Illinois Press, 1967). More recently, Mark A. Lause, *Free Labor: The Civil War and the Making of an American Working Class* (Urbana: University of Illinois Press, 2015), argues that the war remade the labor movement. For an understanding of the work ethic that influenced free-labor ideology, see Daniel T. Rodgers, *The Work Ethic in Industrial America, 1850–1920* (Chicago: University of Chicago Press, 1978). Robert L. Bee's introduction to *The Boys from Rockville: Civil War Narratives of Sgt. Benjamin Hirst, Company D, 14th Connecticut Volunteers* (Knoxville: University of Tennessee Press, 1998) is an excellent summary description of the life and work of New England mill operatives who entered the U.S. volunteer army.

For farm labor and the Northern agricultural economy around the time of the Civil War, see Fred A. Shannon, *The Farmer's Last Frontier: Agriculture, 1860–1897* (New York: Farrar & Rinehart, 1945; Armonk, NY: M. E. Sharpe, Inc., 1977); David E. Schob, *Hired Hands and Plowboys: Farm Labor in the Midwest, 1815–1860* (Urbana: University of Illinois Press, 1975); Paul W. Gates, *The Farmer's Age: Agriculture, 1815–1860* (New York: Holt, Rinehart and Winston, 1960); and Paul W. Gates, *Agriculture and the Civil War* (New York: Alfred A. Knopf, 1965). For a new survey of Northern and Southern Civil War era agriculture, see R. Douglas Hurt, *Food and Agriculture during the Civil War* (Santa Barbara, CA: Praeger, 2016).

Randall M. Miller, Harry S. Stout and Charles Reagan Wilson, eds., *Religion and the American Civil War* (New York: Oxford University Press, 1998) provides readers with a collection of innovative essays on religion North and South during the Civil War. George C. Rable, *God's Almost Chosen Peoples: A Religious History of the American Civil War* (Chapel Hill: University of North Carolina Press, 2010) is a copious and considered examination of religion during the Civil War era. On politics, national identity, and religion, see Timothy L. Wesley, *The Politics of Faith during the Civil War* (Baton Rouge: Louisiana State University, 2013); and Sean A. Scott, *A Visitation of God: Northern Civilians Interpret the Civil War* (New York: Oxford University Press, 2011). For a still influential look at Baptists, Congregationalists, Methodists, and Presbyterians in the North, see James H. Moorhead, *American Apocalypse: Yankee Protestants and the Civil War* (New Haven, CT: Yale University Press, 1978). For Catholics and the war, see William B. Kurtz, *Excommunicated from the Union: How the Civil War Created a Separate Catholic America* (New York: Fordham University Press, 2016). For an example of the role of churches in one community, see Doyle, *The Social Order of a Frontier Community*, noted above. For a general overview, see Robert J. Miller's recent synthesis of the religious aspects of the sectional crisis, *Both Prayed to the Same God: Religion and Faith in the American Civil War* (Lanham, MD: Lexington Books, 2007).

On the draft, see James W. Geary, *We Need Men: The Union Draft and the Civil War* (DeKalb: Northern Illinois University Press, 1991); Eugene C. Murdock, *One Million Men: The Civil War Draft in the North* (Madison: State Historical Society of Wisconsin, 1971). Grace Palladino, in *Another Civil War*, and Robert Sandow, in *Deserter Country*, both noted above, also suggest that draft resistance was a complicated matter that went beyond simple opposition to the war, as do various essays in Paul Cimbala and Randall Miller, eds., *Union Soldiers and the Northern Home Front*, noted above.

For a detailed account of the draft riot in New York City, see Adrian Cook, *The Armies of the Streets: The New York City Draft Riots of 1863* (Lexington: University Press of Kentucky, 1974); for a more analytical exploration of the riots, see Iver Bernstein, *The New York City Draft Riots: Their Significance for American Society and Politics in the Age of the Civil War* (New York: Oxford University Press, 1990).

Frank L. Klement believes that pro-Southern conspiracies were never a real threat to the Union war effort. See his *Dark Lanterns: Secret Political Societies, Conspiracies, and Treason Trials in the Civil War* (Baton Rouge: Louisiana State University Press, 1984), and *The Limits of Dissent: Clement L. Vallandigham and the Civil War* (New York: Fordham University Press, 1998). For a work that takes seriously the threat, see Stephen E. Towne, *Surveillance and Spies in the Civil War: Exposing Confederate Conspiracies in America's Heartland* (Athens: Ohio University Press, 2015). For another modern interpretation that sees Copperhead threats as real and pervasive, see Jennifer L. Weber, *Copperheads: The Rise and Fall of Lincoln's Opponents in the North* (New York: Oxford University Press, 2006). Also for state studies of dissent, see Hubert H. Wubben, *Civil War Iowa and the Copperhead Movement* (Ames: Iowa State University Press, 1980); and Arnold M. Shankman, *The Pennsylvania Antiwar Movement,*

1861–1865 (Rutherford, NJ: Fairleigh Dickinson University Press, 1980); as well as Frank L. Klement, *The Copperhead's of the Middle West* (Chicago: University of Chicago Press, 1960). One of the best recent studies of antiwar activity at the local level is Robert M. Sandow, *Deserter Country*, noted above. For how the Lincoln administration dealt with dissent, see Mark E. Neely Jr., *The Fate of Liberty: Abraham Lincoln and Civil Liberties* (New York: Oxford University Press, 1991). Not all dissent was political and pro-Southern; on this, see Thomas F. Curran, *Soldiers of Peace: Civil War Pacifism and the Postwar Radical Peace Movement* (New York: Fordham University Press, 2003). Also see Philip E. Webber's *Zoar in the Civil War* (Kent, OH: Kent State University Press, 2007), which explores the tension of conscientious objection to the war and support for the war in a German separatist community.

Despite the dramatic exceptions, Democrats generally worked within the political system. See Joel H. Silbey, *A Respectable Minority: The Democratic Party in the Civil War Era, 1860–1868* (New York: W. W. Norton & Company, 1977). For a broader study of the ideas and the people attracted by them into the Democratic Party, see Jean H. Baker, *Affairs of Party: The Political Culture of Northern Democrats in the Mid-Nineteenth Century* (Ithaca, NY: Cornell University Press, 1983; New York: Fordham University Press, 1998). Eric Foner's *Free Soil, Free Labor, Free Men: The Ideology of the Republican Party before the Civil War* (New York: Oxford University Press, 1970) remains the essential study for understanding the ideas that shaped the Republican Party during its formative years. For how the war years influenced the party's ideology, see Richardson *The Greatest Nation of the Earth*, noted above; Allan G. Bogue, *The Earnest Men: Republicans in the Civil War Senate* (Ithaca: Cornell University Press, 1981); Michael S. Green, *Freedom, Union, and Power: Lincoln and His Party during the Civil War* (New York: Fordham University Press, 2004); and John Syrett, *The Civil War Confiscation Acts: Failing to Reconstruct the South* (New York: Fordham University Press, 2005). By exploring cultural aspects of American life, Mark E. Neely Jr., in *The Boundaries of American Political Culture in the Civil War Era* (Chapel Hill: University of North Carolina Press, 2005), reminds readers of the centrality of politics in the Civil War era. Also see his *The Union Divided: Party Conflict in the Civil War North* (Cambridge, MA: Harvard University Press, 2002), which challenges the old interpretation of the positive influence of the two-party system on the Northern war effort. For a collection of essays on the character of the Republican Party during the Civil War era, see Robert F. Engs and Randall M. Miller, eds., *The Birth of the Grand Old Party: The Republicans' First Generation* (Philadelphia: University of Pennsylvania Press, 2002). For a concise yet essential treatment of the values that propelled Northerners to fight secession, see Earl J. Hess, *Liberty, Virtue, and Progress: Northerners and Their War for the Union* (New York: Fordham University Press, 1997); James M. McPherson, *For Cause & Comrades: Why Men Fought in the Civil War* (New York: Oxford University Press, 1997); and Gary Gallagher,

The Union War, noted above. An excellent new study of first-time voters during the 19th century is Jon Grinspan, *The Virgin Vote: How Young Americans Made Democracy Social, Politics Personal, and Voting Popular in the Nineteenth Century* (Chapel Hill: University of North Carolina Press, 2016).

Kanisorn Wongsrichanalai adds to our understanding of Northern thought, masculinity, concepts of honor, and the Yankee character in his *Northern Character: College-educated New Englanders, Honor, Nationalism, and Leadership in the Civil War Era* (New York: Fordham University Press, 2016). For Northern and Southern perceptions of the war, see Randall C. Jimerson, *The Private Civil War: Popular Thought during the Sectional Conflict* (Baton Rouge: Louisiana State University, 1988).

Many important new works dealing with Northern women and the war effort are available. Nina Silber, *Daughters of the Union: Northern Women Fight the Civil War* (Cambridge, MA: Harvard University Press, 2005) provides a suggestive recent study that especially considers women's relationship with the government. For Anna Dickinson's role in the war effort, see J. Matthew Gallman, *America's Joan of Arc: The Life of Anna Elizabeth Dickinson: The Story of a Remarkable Woman, the Civil War, and the Struggle for Women's Rights* (New York: Oxford University Press, 2006). Judith Ann Giesberg, *Army at Home: Women and the Civil War on the Northern Home Front* (Chapel Hill: University of North Carolina Press, 2009), adds an important dimension to women's wartime experiences by going beyond historians' emphasis on middle-class women to explore the impact of the war on working-class and "marginal" women. For an innovative look at women and family in the North, including the impact of correspondence between unacquainted women and soldiers and its impact on courtship, see Patricia L. Richard, *Busy Hands: Images of the Family in the Northern Civil War Effort* (New York: Fordham University Press, 2003). Three significant studies deal with Northern women's involvement with benevolence and its consequences: Judith Ann Giesberg, *Civil War Sisterhood: The U.S. Sanitary Commission and Women's Politics in Transition* (Boston: Northeastern University Press, 2000); Jeanie Attie, *Patriotic Toil: Northern Women and the American Civil War* (Ithaca, NY: Cornell University Press, 1998); and Lori D. Ginzberg, *Women and the Work of Benevolence* (New Haven, CT: Yale University Press, 1990). Also see Nancy Scripture Garrison, *With Courage and Delicacy: Civil War on the Peninsula, Women and the U.S. Sanitary Commission* (Cambridge, MA: Da Capo Press, 2003); Elizabeth D. Leonard, *Yankee Women: Gender Battles in the Civil War Era* (New York: W. W. Norton & Company, 1994); Wendy Hamand Venet, *Neither Ballots nor Bullets: Women Abolitionists and the Civil War* (Charlottesville: University Press of Virginia, 1991); and Jane E. Schultz, *Women at the Front: Hospital Workers in Civil War America* (Chapel Hill: University of North Carolina Press, 2004). For the larger context of the sanitary fairs that women organized to raise money for the war effort, see Beverly Gordon, *Bazaars and Fair Ladies: The History of the American Fundraising Fair* (Knoxville: University of Tennessee Press, 1998).

For the beginning of the involvement of women with the effort to educate the freedpeople, see Willie Lee Rose, *Rehearsal for Reconstruction: The Port Royal Experiment* (Indianapolis: Bobbs-Merrill Company, 1964); Joe M. Richardson, *Christian Reconstruction: The American Missionary Association and Southern Blacks, 1861–1890* (Athens: University of Georgia Press, 1986); and Patricia C. Click, *Time Full of Trial: The Roanoke Island Freedmen's Colony, 1862–1867* (Chapel Hill: University of North Carolina Press, 2001). For women and postwar educational efforts among the freedpeople, see Jacqueline Jones, *Soldiers of Light and Love: Northern Teachers and Georgia Blacks, 1865–1873* (Chapel Hill: University of North Carolina Press, 1980).

For the continuation of the efforts of Northern abolitionists and philanthropists to assist the ex-slaves, see James M. McPherson's two books, *The Struggle for Equality: Abolitionists and the Negro in the Civil War and Reconstruction* (Princeton, NJ: Princeton University Press, 1964), and *The Abolitionist Legacy: From Reconstruction to the NAACP* (Princeton, NJ: Princeton University Press, 1975). For further insight, see Carol Faulkner, *Women's Radical Reconstruction: The Freedmen's Aid Movement* (Philadelphia: University of Pennsylvania Press, 2004). For the larger context of philanthropy during the Civil War era, including the efforts to deal with the needs of women and children, see Robert H. Bremner, *The Public Good: Philanthropy and Welfare in the Civil War Era* (New York: Alfred A. Knopf, 1980).

James Marten's groundbreaking work *The Children's Civil War* (Chapel Hill: University of North Carolina Press, 1998) remains the best place to start for an understanding of the war's impact on the lives of children, but for the Northern home front in particular, see his *Children for the Union: The War Spirit on the Northern Home Front* (Chicago: Ivan R. Dee, 2004).

Drew Gilpin Faust, *This Republic of Suffering: Death and the American Civil War* (New York: Alfred A. Knopf, 2008), deals with the significance of the way soldiers died and families understood and memorialized death. On that subject, see also Gary Laderman, *The Sacred Remains: American Attitudes toward Death, 1799–1883* (New Haven, CT: Yale University Press, 1996). Also instructive is John R. Neff in *Honoring the Civil War Dead: Commemoration and the Problem of Reconciliation* (Lawrence: University Press of Kansas, 2005). Neff devotes a chapter to Lincoln's assassination, but also see Thomas Reed Turner, *Beware the People Weeping: Public Opinion and the Assassination of Abraham Lincoln* (Baton Rouge: Louisiana State University Press, 1982), and Martha Hodes, *Mourning Lincoln* (New Haven, CT: Yale University Press, 2015). For the handling of those involved in the assassination conspiracy and an exploration of related larger issues, see Elizabeth D. Leonard, *Lincoln's Avengers: Justice, Revenge, and Reunion after the Civil War* (New York: W. W. Norton & Company, 2004). For Northerners' positive view of Lincoln in spite of the opposition, see Hans L. Trefousse, *"First among Equals": Abraham Lincoln's Reputation during his Administration* (New York: Fordham University Press, 2005). For a treatment of the earliest constructions of Lincoln's postassassination image and how it developed through the years, see Merrill D. Peterson, *Lincoln in American Memory* (New York: Oxford University Press, 1994).

For the prejudicial treatment Northern blacks encountered before the war, see Leon F. Litwack, *North of Slavery: The Negro in the Free States, 1790–1860* (Chicago: University of Chicago Press, 1961); and Leslie M. Harris, *In the Shadow of Slavery: African Americans in New York City, 1626–1863* (Chicago: University of Chicago Press, 2003). For the Civil War era, see David W. Blight, *Frederick Douglass' Civil War: Keeping Faith in Jubilee* (Baton Rouge: Louisiana State University Press, 1989); James M. McPherson, *The Struggle for Equality*, noted above; and Margaret Creighton, *The Colors of Courage*, noted above. Much more work remains to be done on African American life during the war years, but in addition to the studies noted above, see the appropriate chapters in David A. Gerber, *Black Ohio and the Color Line, 1860–1915* (Urbana: University of Illinois Press, 1976); Graham Russell Hodges, *Root and Branch: African Americans in New York and East Jersey, 1613–1863* (Chapel Hill: University of North Carolina Press, 1999); and Daniel R. Biddle and Murray Dubin, *Tasting Freedom: Octavius Catto and the Battle for Equality in Civil War America* (Philadelphia: Temple University Press, 2010), which also includes telling descriptions of blacks' involvement in and response to emancipation efforts in one city. For the problems encountered by black veterans, see Donald R. Shaffer, *After the Glory: The Struggles of Black Civil War Veterans* (Lawrence: University Press of Kansas, 2004).

For the government's developing policies toward emancipation, see, for example, James Oakes, *Freedom National: The Destruction of Slavery in the United States, 1861–1865* (New York: W. W. Norton & Company, 2012); LaWanda Cox, *Lincoln and Black Freedom: A Study in Presidential Leadership* (Columbia: University of South Carolina Press, 1981); Louis S. Gerteis, *From Contraband to Freedman: Federal Policy toward Southern Blacks, 1861–1865* (Westport, CT: Greenwood Press, 1973); Herman Belz, *A New Birth of Freedom: The Republican Party and Freedmen's Rights, 1861–1866* (Westport, CT: Greenwood Press, 1976; New York: Fordham University Press, 2000); Allen C. Guelzo, *Lincoln's Emancipation Proclamation: The End of Slavery in America* (New York: Simon & Schuster, 2004); Michael Les Benedict, *A Compromise of Principle: Congressional Republicans and Reconstruction, 1863–1869* (New York: W. W. Norton & Company, 1974); and Eric Foner, *Reconstruction: America's Unfinished Revolution, 1863–1877* (New York: Harper and Row, Publishers, 1988). All of the works on Reconstruction era noted above touch in some way on the North's turning away from the promise held out by the war to African Americans throughout the reunited nation. On that process, see David W. Blight, *Race and Reunion: The Civil War in American Memory* (Cambridge, MA: Belknap Press of Harvard University Press, 2001); James M. McPherson, *Abolitionist Legacy*, noted above; Heather Cox Richardson, *The Death of Reconstruction: Race, Labor, and Politics in the Post-Civil War North, 1865–1901* (Cambridge, MA: Harvard University Press, 2001); and Nina Silber, *The Romance of Reunion: Northerners and the South, 1865–1900* (Chapel Hill: University of North Carolina Press, 1993).

On the constitutional effects of the war, and the ways understandings of the Constitution and the law affected the conduct of the war, see Laura F. Edwards, *A Legal History of the Civil War and Reconstruction* (New York: Cambridge University Press, 2015); Harold M. Hyman and William M. Wiecek, *Equal Justice under Law: Constitutional Development, 1835–1875* (New York: Harper & Row, 1982); Mark E. Neely Jr., *Lincoln and the Triumph of the Nation: Constitutional Conflict in the American Civil War* (Chapel Hill: University of North Carolina Press, 2011); and Timothy S. Huebner, *Liberty and Union: The Civil War Era and American Constitutionalism* (Lawrence: University Press of Kansas, 2016).

How Northern soldiers became once again members of their communities remains one of the most important understudied aspects of Civil War history. Larry M. Logue pioneered the study of Civil War veterans in his brief but suggestive survey *To Appomattox and Beyond: The Civil War Soldier in War and Peace* (Chicago: Ivan R. Dee, 1996). Paul A. Cimbala, *Veterans North and South: The Transition from Soldier to Civilian after the American Civil War* (Santa Barbara, CA: Praeger, 2015), and James Marten, *Sing Not War: The Lives of Union and Confederate Veterans in Gilded Age America* (Chapel Hill: University of North Carolina Press, 2011) provide newer analyses. Some of the above-mentioned community studies touch on the subject of the soldiers' return. Also, newer regimental histories briefly review the topic in their final chapters or epilogues; for example, see Edward A. Miller Jr., *The Black Civil War Soldiers of Illinois: The Story of the Twenty-ninth U.S. Colored Infantry* (Columbia: University of South Carolina Press, 1998). Joseph T. Glatthaar shows the significance of such work in his chapter "Life after the USCT" in *Forged in Battle: The Civil War Alliance of Black Soldiers and White Officers* (New York: The Free Press, 1990). For the political and fraternal activities of veterans, see Mary R. Dearing, *Veterans in Politics: The Story of the GAR* (Baton Rouge: Louisiana State University Press, 1952); and Stuart McConnell, *Glorious Contentment: The Grand Army of the Republic* (Chapel Hill: University of North Carolina Press, 1992). Barbara A. Gannon challenges notions of veterans, race, and reconciliation in her book *The Won Cause: Black and White Comradeship in the Grand Army of the Republic* (Chapel Hill: University of North Carolina Press, 2011). For mental health issues of returning soldiers, see Eric T. Dean Jr., *Shook Over Hell: Post-traumatic Stress, Vietnam, and the*

Civil War (Cambridge, MA: Harvard University Press, 1997). Dean's book is a groundbreaking piece of work, but new advances in brain science, head injuries, and other physical problems that produce symptoms similar to PTSD suggest it needs revising and updating.

Thomas J. Brown's *The Public Art of Civil War Commemoration: A Brief History with Documents* (Boston: Bedford/St. Martin's, 2004) provides a brief introduction to the efforts of Americans to commemorate their great national drama. An interesting look at national memory and one battlefield is Thomas A. Desjardin's *These Honored Dead: How the Story of Gettysburg Shaped American Memory* (Cambridge, MA: Da Capo Press, 2003).

INDEX

ABOUT THE AUTHORS

PAUL A. CIMBALA is professor of history at Fordham University, Rose Hill Campus, Bronx, NY. His published works include *Under the Guardianship of the Nation: The Freedmen's Bureau and the Reconstruction of Georgia, 1865–1870*; *The Freedmen's Bureau: Reconstructing the American South after the Civil War*; and *Veterans North and South: The Transition from Soldier to Civilian after the American Civil War*. With Randall M. Miller he has edited several essay collections dealing with the Civil War and Reconstruction.

RANDALL M. MILLER is the William Dirk Warren '50 Sesquicentennial Chair and professor of history at Saint Joseph's University, Philadelphia, PA. He is the author or editor of numerous books, including *Religion and the American Civil War*; *The Birth of the Grand Old Party: The Republicans' First Generation*; and *Lincoln and Leadership: Military, Political, and Religious Decision Making*. With Paul A. Cimbala he has edited several essay collections treating the Civil War and Reconstruction.